Of Khans and Kremlins

Of Khans and Kremlins

*Tatarstan and the Future of
Ethno-Federalism in Russia*

Katherine E. Graney

LEXINGTON BOOKS

A division of
ROWMAN & LITTLEFIELD PUBLISHERS, INC.
Lanham • Boulder • New York • Toronto • Plymouth, UK

LEXINGTON BOOKS

A division of Rowman & Littlefield Publishers, Inc.
A wholly owned subsidary of The Rowman & Littlefield Publishing Group, Inc.
4501 Forbes Boulevard, Suite 200
Lanham, MD 20706

Estover Road
Plymouth PL6 7PY
United Kingdom

British Library Cataloguing in Publication Information Available

Library of Congress Cataloging-in-Publication Data

Graney, Katherine E., 1970–
  Of Khans and Kremlins: Tatarstan and the future of ethno-federalism in Russia /
Katherine E. Graney.
     p. cm.
  Includes bibliographical references and index.
  1. Central-local government relations—Russia (Federation)—Tatarstan.
2. Self-determination, National—Russia (Federation)—Tatarstan. 3. Tatarstan
(Russia)—Politics and government. I. Title.
  JN6693.5.S8G73 2009
  320.447'45049—dc22

                                                              2008031567

ISBN: 978-0-7391-2635-6 (cloth: alk. paper)
ISBN: 978-0-7391-2636-3 (pbk.: alk. paper)
ISBN: 978-0-7391-3200-5 (electronic)

Printed in the United States of America

⊗ ™ The paper used in this publication meets the minimum requirements of
American National Standard for Information Sciences—Permanence of Paper
for Printed Library Materials, ANSI/NISO Z39.48-1992.

Dedication

This book is dedicated in loving memory of my aunt, Maureen F. Zambon, one of the world's great "book-women."

Contents

Acknowledgments

I would first like to acknowledge the many institutional sources of financial support that have played a part in seeing this long project come to fruition. The research for the dissertation upon which this book is in part based was funded by a grant from the International Research and Exchanges Board (IREX), administered from 1996–1997, with funds provided by the National Endowment for the Humanities and the United States Department of State, which administers the Russian, Eurasian, and East European Research Program (Title VIII). I am also grateful to the Social Sciences Research Council (SSRC), which supported this project in both its pre-dissertation and dissertation write-up phases, as did the John T. and Catherine D. MacArthur Foundation and the Global Studies Program at the University of Wisconsin. Crucial post-dissertation follow-up research was funded by Skidmore College through the form of a Faculty Development Grant in summer 2000 and by IREX through a short-term travel grant in summer 2001. The generosity of the Kennan Institute of the Woodrow Wilson Center for International Scholars in sponsoring my participation in one of their conferences in Moscow in summer 2005 provided another important research opportunity.

Happily, the intellectual and personal debts incurred during the process of researching and writing this book are far more numerous. I want to thank Dima Gorenburg, Elise Giuliano, Allen Frank, Daniel Schafer, Ned Walker, and Paul Werth for their munificent sharing of materials, opinions, and advice regarding Tatarstan at different points in this project. I have a special and large debt to Uli Schamiloglu for his long-standing help with Tatar language training, and for his help in fostering initial contacts in Kazan. My fieldwork experience and my overall understanding of this unique part of the world, as small as it is, would be much diminished without him. Crawford Young has offered detailed and useful comments on many parts and drafts of this project over the years, and many of the ideas herein have their genesis in the Cultural Pluralism Research Circle he so kindly sponsored at his home in Madison. Mark R. Beissinger, who served as my doctoral dissertation advisor at Wisconsin, has over the years offered most useful and thought-provoking comments on my work, as well as much personal encouragement and friendship. Most of all, Mark's example of producing scholarship of the highest and most exacting standards continues to be an inspiration.

In Kazan, my most heartfelt and continued thanks for the gifts of both their intellectual guidance and their friendship go to Damir Iskhakov, Gulnara Khasanova, Nadir Kinossian, Rimzil Valeev, and Guzel Valeeva-Suleymanova. Each of them has shared with me unstintingly for over a decade now their time, ideas, resources, and fellowship, and I am acutely aware of how much of this project is a product of their efforts on my behalf. I also thank Flora Ibragimova Khasanova and Elena Bondarchuk for opening their hearts and homes to me repeatedly during the course of this project, providing loving and joyful havens from which to venture forth on intellectual and other adventures in Kazan. I also want to acknowledge Jamil Zaynoullin and his family and Dora Yakovlevna Kovarskaya for their hospitality during early research trips to Kazan.

Closer to home, I am humbled and honored to have had the friendship and support of many wonderful people during the long germination of this project. From my UW days, Laura Olson has been a good friend and model scholar since day one, as has Kathleen Mulligan-Hansel, who has provided the type of intellectually and emotionally sustaining friendship that one feels lucky to come across once in a lifetime. At Skidmore, my good fortune has continued, as I have been blessed with the wise counsel and warm fellowship of my colleagues in the Government Department (and outside it). In particular, I'd like to thank my fellow Badger Chris Whann for always being available to talk shop—it has helped me more than he probably knows. Susan Walzer has been a constant and much relied upon source of good advice on all things professional and personal, and I thank her for her graceful and generous presence in my life. It is my absolute pleasure to finally be able to publicly acknowledge and thank Nancy Wheeler and the gifted, wonderful staff at the Greenberg Childcare Center at Skidmore for the expert and loving care they have shown my children these past years, which has allowed me to finish this project. I feel honored by the way they have made us part of their family.

My parents and all of my brothers and sisters have also been constant sources of moral (and material) support during the years of this project, culminating in a surprise visit to Russia one cold and dark April that sustained me through the rest of a long year of field work. As with so much else in my life, it would have been difficult, if not impossible, to have produced this book without them, especially my parents. I am profoundly grateful to them. My son, Ronan, and my daughter, Maeve Margaret, are simply gifts, and so I will simply thank them for appearing in my life and enriching it the way they do. Finally, in a true case of the last being first, my biggest overall debt is to my husband, M. Sean Loftus. I thank him for venturing with me first to Madison, then significantly further on to Kazan and Ufa, and finally on to our home in Saratoga and the wilds of parenthood, without ever (or at least rarely) losing his sense of fun or adventure. Of all the roles he has in my life—spouse, traveling companion, co-parent, friend—it is the last that he has played the longest and plays the best, which makes me a very lucky person indeed.

Permissions

The cover photo of the Kazan Kremlin is by Nadir Kinossian, and is used with his kind permission. Other photos in the book are by the author.

Chapter Four contains some material which appeared in slightly different forms in the following publications: Katherine E. Graney, "Education Reform in Tatarstan and Bashkortostan: Sovereignty projects in post Soviet Russia," *Europe-Asia Studies*, vol. 51, no. 4 (June 1999): 611–632. Available at the journal's website: www.informaworld.com; and Katherine E. Graney, "Ten years of sovereignty in Tatarstan: End of the beginning or beginning of the end?" *Problems of Post-Communism*, vol. 48, no. 5 (September/October 2001): 32–41. Copyright © 2001 by M. E. Sharpe, Inc. Reprinted with permission. All Rights Reserved. Not for reproduction.

Chapter Five contains some material which appeared first in slightly different form in: Katherine E. Graney, "Making Russia multicultural: Kazan at its millinennium and beyond," from *Problems of Post-Communism*, vol. 54, no. 6 (November/December 2007): 17–27. Copyright © 2007 by M. E. Sharpe, Inc. Reprinted with permission. All Rights Reserved. Not for reproduction.

List of Abbreviations and Sources

International News Agencies

CDPSP (Current Digest of the Post-Soviet Press)
FBIS (Foreign Broadcast Information Service Daily Report on Central Eurasia)
INTERFAX
INTERFAX-Executive

On-Line News Agencies

e-Kazan (Kazan)
Gazeta.ru (Moscow)
EWI RRR (East-West Institute Russian Regional Report, biweekly report on Russia's regions) (Formerly IEWS-RRR)
Jamestown Monitor (Jamestown Foundation Monitor, daily report on Russia and the former Soviet Union)
OMRI (Open Media Research Institute, daily report on Russia and the former Soviet Union)
Pravda.RU (Moscow)
RAS (Research and Analytical Supplement to Johnson's Russian List— For back issues go to the RAS archive at: www.cdi.org/russia/johnson/jrl-ras.cfm)

RFE/RL Newsline (Radio Free Europe/Radio Liberty Newsline, daily report)
RFE/RL Political Weekly (Radio Free Europe/ Radio Liberty weekly report)
RFE/RL Tatar-Bashkir Service Daily Report (Radio Free Europe/Radio Liberty, daily reports from Kazan and Ufa)
RFE/RL Tatar-Bashkir Service Weekly Report (Radio Free Europe/Radio Liberty, weekly reports from Kazan and Ufa)
Tatar-inform (on-line news agency of the Republic of Tatarstan)

Central Publications (Moscow)

ITAR-TASS (Russian Central News Agency)
Itogi
Izvestiya
Kommersant
Kommersant-Vlast
Komsomolskaya Pravda
Moscow Times
Literaturnaya Gazeta
Nezavisimaya Gazeta
Pravda
RIA-Novosti (Russian Information Agency)
Rossiiskaya Gazeta
Soyuz

Tatarstani Publications
(Kazan, daily newspaper, unless otherwise noted)

Altyn Urda (published in Naberezhniye Chelny)
Idel (monthly journal)
Informatsionno-Metodicheskii Byulleten' (Informatsionno-Metodicheskii Byulleten' Apparat Prezidenta Respubliki Tatarstan) (monthly journal)
Izvestiya Tatarstana
Izvestiya TOTs (Izvestiya Tatarskogo Obshchestvennogo Tsentra)
Kazanskiye Vedemosti
KRIS
Magarif (monthly journal)
Molodezh' Tatarstana
Panorama (monthly journal)
Ploshchad' Svobody (monthly journal)

Respublika Tatarstana
Segodnya Nezavisimaya Gazeta
Sovetskaya Tatariya
Tatarstan (monthly journal)
Vechernyaya Kazan'
Vremya i Dengi
Zvezda Povolzh'ya

Introduction:
Of Khans and Kremlins:
Tatarstan, Sovereignty and the
Future of Ethno-Federalism in Russia

If the state is the "master noun" of political discourse, as Clifford Geertz has argued (1980), then its chief modifier, sovereignty, must be considered the most important descriptor in our political universe. Indeed, the sovereign state is, in the words of Charles Tilly, the most coveted and intensely sought-after "prize" for various political actors in the modern era (1996). For many, particularly ethnic minority communities that feel they have ended up in the "wrong" state through historical accident or forceful imperialism, the idea of sovereignty possesses significant and enduring appeal as a vision of an ideal form of political organization. And yet as is true of other fundamentally important concepts in political science, such as power or interest, understandings of sovereignty, both in terms of what it implies theoretically and how it is exercised practically, are famously ambiguous, contradictory, and elusive. These characteristics of sovereignty—its magnetic pull for striving political communities and its conceptual and practical vagueness—combine to exert a janus-faced influence. On the one hand the aspiration to sovereignty can be a source of political instability, while the flexibility of the term makes it potentially useful as a way of resolving autonomy conflicts between existing states and the different communities that inhabit them.

Nowhere is this truth demonstrated more clearly than in the Russian Federation, a state that itself is a product of a unique process unlikely ever to be repeated again in history—the collapse of the Soviet Union through the largely peaceful usurpation of the central state's sovereignty by its own constituent units. Like the layers of an onion, first the union republics declared themselves to be "sovereign states" during 1990 and 1991, including Russia itself under the leadership of Gorbachev-challenger Boris Yeltsin. The union republics were followed in rapid succession by many of the Russian republic's own ethnic constituent units, including "national" republics such as Tatarstan and Sakha-Yakutia, as well as its nonethnic constituent units (*krais* and *oblasts*). The constituent federal units of union republics other than Russia, such as Abkhazia in Georgia, also joined this "parade of sovereignties," which ultimately led to the final dissolution of the USSR on Christmas Day 1991 (Walker 2003).

Some of the declarations of state sovereignty made during the early 1990s, namely those of the fifteen ex-union republics, have been realized as *actual* state sovereignty, in the form of Tilly's "grand prize"—unquestioned, internationally-recognized statehood, complete with UN membership as binding proof of purchase. Other former Soviet entities have seen their declarations of sovereignty evolve into violent, tragic and unresolved autonomy conflicts, particularly in the Caucasus and Moldova (Chechnya chief among them, but also including Abkhazia, Nagorna-Karabakh, and Transdneister). Still other declarations of state sovereignty made in the early 1990s, including those of most of the Russian Federation's ethnic and nonethnic constituent units have been abrogated in either theory or practice (or both), under steadily increasing pressure to do so from the Yeltsin and then the Putin administrations.

While the Chechen situation continues to bring instability and suffering to all of Russia's North Caucasus region, and while most of Russia's other constituent units have been persuaded by Moscow to allow their initial declarations of sovereignty to languish, one exceptional case, the Republic of Tatarstan in the Russian Federation, has kept the claim of state sovereignty as the guiding principle of its political, economic, and cultural development throughout the entire the post-Soviet period. The result is a multifaceted, coherent, and sustained process that I call a "sovereignty project." Contrary to the characterizations and expectations of most western observers that the sovereignty claims of Russia's constituent units were *all* largely instrumental and ephemeral in nature, Tatarstan's sovereignty project is both a significant political fact that influences Russia's contemporary development in important and often unrecognized ways, and an example rich with insights for scholars of federalism, cultural pluralism, and post-Sovietology, who nonetheless have largely ignored it. While singular aspects of Tatarstan's sovereignty project, usually the economic negotiations with the federal center in Moscow, have often surfaced as illustrative examples in the literature on Russia's post-Soviet political development, no scholar has yet treated Tatarstan's quest for sovereignty holistically, or with the breadth and depth of attention that it deserves. In this book, I attempt to remedy this situation by examining Tatarstan's remarkably enduring, surprisingly comprehensive, and politically significant sovereignty project with all the nuanced attention that it demands.

My assumption here is that examining how Tatarstan has pursued its sovereignty project—defined as the process of formulating a new vision of itself informed by both Soviet-era and contemporary international understandings of sovereign statehood and then attempting to make that vision a reality on the ground to the greatest extent possible—elicits important theoretical insights and useful applied knowledge in a number of interrelated spheres that are of crucial importance to political scientists in general and the community of post-Sovietologists in particular, with the nature and trajectory of sub-state autonomy movements and the mechanics of ethno-federalism and cultural pluralism and being chief among them. Furthermore, while it is by no means the bold experiment in democracy that its leaders often claim it is, and while it does suffer from the same depressing syndrome of pathologies—corruption, nepotism, kleptocracy—that plagues post-Soviet Russian politics more generally, in my view, Tatarstan's sovereignty project represents both the most significant and promising manifestation of the emergence of any "real" federal politics in Russia as well as Russia's best, perhaps only, chance to embody, even minimally, a liberal democratic politics of cultural pluralism in the post-Soviet period that is informed by concerns for both communal rights *as well as* individual rights. The positive roles that Tatarstan's sovereignty project plays in fostering the development of Russia as a federal state that reflects to even a minimal extent the principles of liberal multiculturalism have only become more visible and important in the wake of the devastating terrorist attacks and attendant rise in state centralization and societal xenophobic violence that have marked the Putin era.

Examining Tatarstan's sovereignty project closely and from many different angles—the federal, the international, the domestic Tatarstani, the political, the cultural, the ethno-national—as I do here, affords a unique window through which to view the evolution of federal relations in post-Soviet Russia. Many observers, noting the largely ad hoc, extra-constitutional way that Tatarstan's quest for sovereignty has evolved and the structural asymmetry that it has introduced into the Russian Federation, have argued that Tatarstan's quest for sovereignty has been unequivocally harmful for Russia's development as both a democratic and federal state (Hale 1998, 2003; Kahn

2000; Smith 1998; Triesman 1997, 1999). While sub-state sovereignty projects, of which Tatarstan's is the most prominent example, have indeed contributed in some ways to the legal confusion and paralysis that characterizes contemporary Russian federalism and exhibit, as noted above, the same pathologies as other aspects of post-Soviet politics in general, the story told in this book suggests that we would benefit from entertaining a more complicated vision of the nature of and consequences of republican sovereignty projects like Tatarstan's in Russia. Following Herrera's compelling statistical deconstruction of the argument (2005, 47), I find it counterproductive to view regional sovereignty-seeking efforts as mere instruments of self-enrichment on the part of regional elites (while not denying that they are in part that). Ultimately, I argue here, a more nuanced and more positive view of the impact of Tatarstan's and other republics' sovereignty-seeking efforts on the potential development of democracy, federalism, and liberal democratic forms of cultural pluralism in Russia is warranted.

Specifically, I aim to show here that the sovereignty project in Tatarstan has served as an imperfect but embryonic means to generate and protect the substantial political, economic, and legal powers and authorities that must be located in the constituent units of the Russian Federation if a truly functional federal system is to be established there. The very ambiguity and flexibility of the concept of sovereignty has given both Tatarstan and the federal center in Moscow the conceptual and policy freedom of movement required to hammer out the compromises that characterize the heart of any functional federal system. More importantly, the sovereignty project framework employed by Tatarstan has allowed these reforms to proceed in a peaceful and negotiated, as opposed to a violent way. The utility of the republican sovereignty framework in helping to move federalism forward in Russia by preserving and protecting sub-state unit rights and authorities while also allowing for the regions to evolve into fuller and more productive participation in the federal life of the Russian state became particularly evident during the administration of Vladimir Putin. Indeed, the alarming trends towards recentralization and unitarism that emerged during the Putin regime have led even critics of the excesses of the republican sovereignty projects to recognize that they may represent the best (and perhaps only) chance to preserve any type of real federalism in Russia in the years to come (Hahn 2004; Kahn 2002). And though it is not possible to describe Russia as either a functioning federation or a functioning democracy, the experience of other multiethnic federations which more easily carry those labels, such as Canada and Spain, suggests that keeping some aspects of the republican sovereignty projects as a more permanent structural feature of the Russian

Federation is not inconsistent with the strengthening of either democracy or federalism, and in fact may aid in both of those processes (Gagnon and Tilly 2001; Keating 1996, 2001; Knop et. al. 1995).

Furthermore, by providing an ambitious and coherent model of statehood for the republics to aspire to, the sovereignty project framework has both motivated and permitted Tatarstan to pursue and develop the types of domestic reforms and international economic and political ties that help foster the economic development of the country as a whole, not just the republic itself, and that also serve to anchor Russia more firmly as a member of the international and European communities (which in and of itself helps to foster democracy and economic development in the country). In this respect, Tatarstan's experience contributes significantly to the ongoing investigation of the changing meanings and forms of state sovereignty in the international arena in the post-Cold War world that has been led by Michael Keating (1996, 2001), Stephen Krasner (1999, 2001, 2005), Thomas Biersteker and Cynthia Weber (1996), and others (Duursma 1996; Gottlieb 1993; Hannum 1996; Jackson 1990, 1995; Osterud 1997; Sorenson 1997). These authors argue that in an increasingly globalized world, such as that Russia found itself confronted with upon the collapse of communism in 1991, those states survive and prosper which most willingly abandon outdated (and erroneous) understandings of state sovereignty as an indivisible possession of an entirely unitary state, and instead seek to transfer some of their traditional sovereign authority up to transnational networks and institutions while devolving other aspects of their traditional sovereignty down to subnational actors (the European Union and Canada are the most oft-cited examples of the benefits that can accrue from such an approach to sovereignty). Creative sovereignty-sharing arrangements, situations of "simultaneous" statehoods, and instances where state sovereignty is ambiguously divided, such as those which have evolved between the center and Tatarstan in post-Soviet Russia, are significant because they offer peaceful solutions to ethnically-motivated autonomy conflicts within states and because they are becoming ever more relevant for the increasingly interdependent world (Cerny 1993; Gow 1997; Hannum 1996; Holm and Sorenson 1995; Keohane 1995; Krasner 2001; Shehadi 1997; Sorenson 1997; Strange 1996).

Finally, and perhaps most significantly, Tatarstan's sovereignty project amounts to the most available and promising (and again, potentially the only) means to provide adequately for ethnocultural justice in multiethnic Russia in the post-Soviet period. Political theorists such as Will Kymlicka, James Tully and Charles Taylor have argued that providing for the adequate development and expression of ethnic minority group rights is a democratic imperative for multicultural states (Kymlicka 1995; Tully 1995, 2001; Taylor 1992), and indeed Tatarstan has defended its sovereignty project in part through these liberal multiculturalist arguments. Informed and shaped to a significant degree by the Soviet ethno-federal attempt to manage cultural pluralism in a manner consistent with Marxist-Leninist ideology, the contemporary Tatarstani sovereignty project should thus be understood in part as an attempt to preserve and adapt Soviet era principles and institutions for managing cultural pluralism to the new, supposedly liberal democratic, post-Soviet context in Russia. I will argue here that Tatarstan's efforts in this regard are instructive and positive, resulting both in greater awareness of and positive attention paid to issues of cultural pluralism on the part of federal officials in Moscow (as opposed to the fear-inspired centralizing impulses that otherwise dominate in post-Chechnya Russia) and in the construction of a moderate and balanced regime of both ethnic Tatar and civic Tatarstani nation-building in the republic. This is in fact one of the most significant and underappreciated aspect of Tatarstan's quest for sovereignty—absent the type of institutionalized multiculturalism provided by Tatarstan's sovereignty projects (and emulated by other republics), it is quite doubtful that Moscow would exhibit either the willingness or the ability to provide effectively for the political and cultural needs of its non-Russian citizens (nearly one-fifth of the population according to the October 2002 All-Russian Census). The guidance and leadership that Tatarstan has provided to the federal government regarding constructive relations with both Russia's Muslims and the wider Islamic world is a particularly notable example of Tatarstan's positive contributions to fostering democratic multiculturalism during a time of great religious and inter-ethnic tension in Russia.

Defining Sovereignty Projects

My use of the term "sovereignty project" to describe the efforts of Tatarstani elites to fulfill the republic's declarations of state sovereignty with discursive and empirical meaning is informed by the recent rethinking of the norms of the nation-state and state sovereignty in the wake of the end of the Cold War. These approaches criticize traditional understandings of state sovereignty which define it as an empirical quality which is either present or absent, and instead explore how the idea of state sovereignty has been understood and practiced in the international system and how these understandings and practices of state sovereignty constitute the identities and interests of political actors (Barkin and Cronin 1994; Biersteker and Weber 1996; Krasner 1999; 2001; Weber 1995; Wendt 1992). Rather than attempting to define or discern some fixed and determinant empirical criteria for state sovereignty, they see it as a practice and a process, or as "the textual and contextual prescriptions" for what those claiming statehood "must do to be recognized as sovereign" (Biersteker and Weber 1996, 12).

An important assumption of these analyses is that state sovereignty has both external and internal aspects. That is, claims to sovereign statehood must always be negotiated with and legitimated by audiences both internal and external to those making the claim to sovereignty. Both the external and internal dimensions of state sovereignty "exist only by virtue of certain intersubjective understandings and expectations" (Wendt 1992, 416–17). Sovereignty thus can be described as a "set of normative principles" that function essentially as "a script" and a "shared cognitive map" that state-seeking actors follow (Krasner 2001, 1). To be recognized as sovereign states, therefore, these actors must mount convincing performances of the attributes and practices of state sovereignty for audiences both external and internal to their claimed state.

The quality of state sovereignty being such, a sovereign state is better understood not as a discrete agent or actor but as "a work of art" (Jackson 1990, 3–4), "a play" (Tilly 1996, 304–5), "an on-going dynamic" (Migdal, Kohli and Shue 1994, 11–12), "a cultivated habit" (Lustick 1993, 34), and "a claim" (Sayer 1994, 371). When state sovereignty is understood in this way, the utility of the term "project" to describe Tatarstani efforts to attain state sovereignty becomes clearer. Indeed because political actors are "continuously engaged in differentiating between domestic and international spaces," the reproduction of state sovereignty is "an ongoing and all consuming project" (Barnett 1996, 176). In this understanding, situations of "perfect" sovereignty never exist, instead sovereignty is always partial, tenuous, and subject to negotiation. As Herrera offers in her study of economic sovereignty movements in Russia's ethnic Russian regions, sovereignty is better understood as existing to different degrees in different situations rather than as an all or nothing quality that either exists or doesn't (2005, 29).[1]

Another important aspect of state sovereignty identified by social constructivist theorists is that state sovereignty has both an institutional, material dimension and a discursive, symbolic dimension (Barnett 1996; Corrigan and Sayer 1985; Doty 1996; Migdal 1988; Jackson 1990; Young 1994). Those seeking sovereignty, like political elites in post-Soviet Tatarstan, must establish the basic institutions and practices associated with both the external and internal aspects of sovereign statehood, such as creating borders and the means of controlling and defending them (armies, citizenship norms, passports, customs duties), participating in diplomatic relations and the activity of the international community, making and enforcing laws, developing and implementing economic policy, and providing for social welfare (Beissinger 1994, 13).[2] But in addition to all this, sovereignty-seekers must also successfully represent their actions within the overarching discursive framework of the sovereign state. In other words, the production of sovereignty requires not only the acquisition of the means to actually practice it, but also that those practices be *represented* convincingly within the overarching and legitimating claim that a sovereign state exists (Beissinger 1996, 6; Doty 1996, 122; Lustick 1993, 44). The boundaries of state sovereignty thus must exist both materially and symbolically (Weber 1995).

Recognition by external audiences is the key to the construction of external state sovereignty. The external audiences onto whom political actors project sovereignty include other sovereign nation-states, international organizations and NGOs, and the international mass media. Traditionally, the elements of the "script" that political actors have followed in order to achieve external recognition as a sovereign state include such institutional practices as: obtaining membership and participating in the United Nations and other international organizations; establishing direct diplomatic, political and economic relations with other sovereign states (including the establishment of embassies, trade and political missions, the exchange of diplomats, and the ability to make and enforce multi- and bilateral treaties); and finally, demarcating, and defending the borders of the state (by establishing armies or border guards, checkpoints, customs duties, norms of citizenship and passports).[3]

There are also important symbolic and discursive dimensions of sovereign statehood that are part of the performance that those claiming to possess state sovereignty must mount convincingly if they are to receive the recognition of external audiences. In addition to establishing the institutional practices listed above, the political entity in question must successfully represent itself as a sovereign state which is a member of the international community and a subject of international law, and have those discursive claims legitimated and recognized through interaction with the international community and other sovereign states (Weber 1995). Jackson (1990) discusses the phenomena of former colonial "quasi-states" who had ready-made and already-recognized claims to sovereign statehood presented to them by the international community. However, for most sub-states seeking increased autonomy through claims to state sovereignty, the matter is not attempting to make already-recognized claims of sovereign statehood an empirical reality. Rather, their difficult task is to mount convincing performances of both the material and discursive aspects of state sovereignty in the international arena, in the hopes of gaining the all-important recognition of their statehood by other international actors. Significant here is the understanding that like other aspects of sovereignty, there is no absolute recognition of external sovereignty. Rather, it is more instructive to speak of states having relative degrees of "international personality" or presence in the international system. Thus, nominally sub-state actors such as Quebec, Catalonia and some American states have enjoyed significant success as somewhat "sovereign" actors in the international political and economic arena (Keating 2001; Keating and McGarry 2001).

Along with attempting to project state sovereignty outward and having their claims to sovereignty validated by the international community, state-seeking actors must also project internal sovereignty. Those functions which are traditionally understood as marking the presence of internal state sovereignty include: the collection and dispersion of revenue; the provision of public safety and order, including the establishment of a judicial system and providing an internal police force; making and enforcing legislation dealing with property rights and civil rights; developing an economic policy, including the provision of central banking and monetary functions, as well as setting economic development priorities; providing for public goods such as utilities, transportation, natural resources, and a postal service; and finally, providing for social welfare, including education policy and the production and dissemination of public knowledge, cultural policy, and public health.[4] The hallmark of a functioning federation, of course, is the consensual and efficacious distribution of these attributes of internal state sovereignty between different levels of government.

In addition to establishing these institutional practices of internal state sovereignty, political actors must also legitimate their rule over the domestic community of their claimed state. To accomplish this, leaders must construct a sense of "amplitude and authority" over the domestic population (Young 1994). Absent this, they will not have the legitimacy that is necessary to realize those functions that are the hallmark of internal state sovereignty. To achieve the acquiescence of citizens which assists the production of internal state sovereignty, those seeking statehood must make legitimate claims that the domestic community within their claimed state is a coherent, unique, and differentiated entity. If they can successfully differentiate the domestic community in this way, it will be in effect "turned into the foundation of the sovereign authority of the state" (Weber 1995, 5–7), thus endowing the relevant political actors with the legitimacy needed for them to act as the authoritative representative of the state both domestically and internationally.

The most effective way for political actors to pursue this type of legitimacy among their domestic state communities in the modern era is of course through the discourse of the nation (Yack 1996). Some, like Anthony Smith, go so far as to assert that in the modern world sovereign statehood is not imaginable or viable without a corresponding sense of nationhood and that "no state can be legitimate which does not claim to represent the nation" (quoted in Doty 1996, 122). In short, in the modern era, all states are nation-states and all state actors are "nationalized" (Hall 1999, 3). So inseparable are the two halves of the modern nation-state that some authors have even suggested making terminology fit reality by eliminating the hyphen and beginning to speak of "nationstates" (Barnett 1996). Because the nation-state model is the dominant institutional and cultural actor in the international arena, political actors seeking sovereign statehood must legitimate their quest by "inventing the nation" (Jewsiewicke and Mudimbe 1995, 195; Tilly 1996).

The essence of the nation-building script that political actors follow in the hopes of constructing a legitimate form of sovereign statehood is the act of situating citizens "physically, legally, socially, and emotionally" within a national community or homeland (Billig 1995, 8). This involves the creation of "collective memories and collective arguments" which allow disparate domestic elements to learn to "inhabit the same general space as other citizens" of the nation (Spinner 1994, 168). As Mark Beissinger (1995, 156) has pointed out, in addition to providing the legitimacy necessary to construct internal sovereignty, this type of nation-building also grants advantages in terms of more efficacious control over citizens and territory. The strategies and policies which political actors use to construct and mark this domestic national community are both institutional and discursive. Institutional strategies which are employed to create and mark a sense of nationhood include: promulgating official national documents such as declarations of sovereignty or independence and state constitutions; establishing the norms and practices of citizenship including standardized documentation of citizens such as passports and drivers licenses; creating centralized and universal educational systems, and naming official state languages (Lustick 1993; Corrigan and Sayer 1985).

Symbolic or discursive strategies which help to demarcate a national community by building the collective memories and arguments that bind the nation together include: the writing and rewriting of "national" and state histories through control of public knowledge in textbooks and state-sponsored institutions of knowledge production; elaborating national symbols and holidays; and creating national spaces both literally through the politics of public spaces, monuments, and museums and metaphorically in the sense of creating a "national public" by establishing common press, media, and cultural spheres (Eley and Suny 1996, 23). The methods of use of these discursive strategies of state and nation construction are familiar to students of cultural pluralism through the pioneering works of Benedict Anderson (1983) and Eric Hobsbawm and Terence Ranger (1983).

This discussion highlights the fact that political actors use the idea of the nation in instrumentalist ways to legitimate claims to state sovereignty and to help to establish and cement internal state sovereignty. In this more instrumentalist aspect, the nation is properly understood not as a concrete material entity but rather as the "name for the relationship linking the state with its subjects to distinguish them from subjects of other states" (Verdery 1996). Rather than possessing a national identity like a thing, then, a group of people instead "possess common ways of talking about nationhood," ways that produce and order the boundaries of the nation and the state (Billig 1995, 8). The sources of these collective memories and arguments that help define this "common way of talking about nationhood" may be either ethnic, that is based ascriptive identities which emphasize one or another already-existing community of origin, or on civic identities which purport to be voluntary in nature and not "a priori." Often, if not always, they are based on a mix of the two elements (Habermas 1996; Keating 1996; Verdery 1996; Yack 1996).

Yet despite the fact that the forms of "nationhood" constructed and employed for the purpose of consolidating state sovereignty may be informed by both civic and ethnic elements, pre-existing ethnic feelings of nationhood (what Anthony Smith has famously referred to as "ethnies") are also related to the understanding and production of state sovereignty in the modern era in important ways. A preexisting sense of ethnic nationhood can itself provide the impetus for political actors (such as sub-state units within established states) to formulate and press claims to state sovereignty. The powerful norms of ethno-nationalism and the right of peoples to self-determination, which posit that particular ethnic groups should have their own states, have permeated the international community in the modern era and thus inform the identities and interests of established sovereign states and sub-state actors, often motivating sub-state actors to pursue increased levels of autonomy within existing host-states (Barkin and Cronin 1994; Brass 1985; Gow 1997; Horowitz 1985, 1997; Hannum 1996; Premdas 1990; Shehadi 1997; Simpson 1996; Smith 1986a). At the very least, preexisting feelings of ethnic nationhood are one important factor in the equation which determines why sub-state units mount autonomy challenges to established states by making claims to possess state sovereignty and why these challenges vary in form and intensity (Rokkan and Unwin 1983, 136, 140; Gurr 1993, 76–78, 82).

But while ethno-nationalist norms and the right of peoples to self-determination may lead sub-state actors that possess a feeling of ethnic nationhood to seek their own sovereign states, other international norms and practices discourage ethno-nationalist state-seeking activity in the international arena (Halperin and Scheffer 1992; Hannum 1996; Horowitz 1997; Lustick 1993, 32–33). First, it is important to stress that the right to national self-determination endorsed by the international community after decolonization was a narrowly prescribed one. After the creation a limited number of new sovereign states the international community turned its energies towards consolidating and protecting the territorial integrity of all sovereign states, and rebuffed later claims to sovereignty and self-determination by various ethno-political entities (Barnett 1995; Hannum 1996; Osterud 1997). The formulation of the norm of self-determination of peoples as embodied the UN Charter was a de-ethnicized one, and the issues of minority rights and ethnic-based claims to sovereign statehood were marginalized during the Cold War (Gottlieb 1993, 27–28; Hannum 1996, 454).

Second, while the international community has legitimated some claims to sovereignty based on national self-determination in the post-Communist era (Croatia, the Baltic states), the violence in the former Yugoslavia has increased caution in the international community as regards claims to national self-determination based on ethnic claims (Gottlieb 1993, 20–22; Woodward 1995). Instead, responding to the debacle of failed states across the former colonial world and the ethnic violence in Yugoslavia, the international community has emphasized the norms of civic multiculturalism, respect for human rights and democracy, and the ability to provide good governance over claims to ethnic nationhood as the proper "criteria" for the recognition of sovereign statehood (Barnett 1995).

Further complicating the relationship between understandings of nationness and the desire for its expression through state sovereignty is that fact that many modern states are in fact "multinational" states, defined as "constitutional associations that contain two or more nations or peoples" (Tully 2001, 1), or "plurinational" states, characterized by "the coexistence within a political order of more than one national identity, with all the normative claims and implications thereof" (Keating and McGarry 2001, 26–27). Because claims to nationhood are so seamlessly tied to claims of sovereign statehood, multinational or multiethnic states are burdened with a higher risk of violent conflict, whether manifested through secessionism, forced assimilation, or even ethnic cleansing or genocide. However as constructivist theorists have identified, because sovereignty is not an absolute value that factors solely in zero-sum games, but rather a highly fungible resource that is subject to negotiation, parceling, sharing, and win-win games, conflicts over the definition of sovereignty need not automatically end in violence or stalemate. Indeed, one of the more hopeful developments in the post-Cold War international community is the type of creative sovereignty-sharing arrangements that have proliferated in Europe and elsewhere (Keating 2001; Krasner 2001). The Tatarstani sovereignty project is an important example of the potential benefits of fostering such a creative and flexible view of sovereignty and its distribution in multiethnic states, providing a peaceful framework for disentangling complex problems of statehood and nationness in Russia while also helping to facilitate (or at least possessing the potential to facilitate) the further development of federalism in Russia, the deepening of Russia's political and economic integration into the European and international communities, and the realization of greater degrees of ethnocultural justice in Russia in the post-Soviet period.

Tatarstan: An "Extreme" Sovereignty Project

This book presents a single case study that offers a "thick description" of the efforts to project sovereignty in Tatarstan since 1990 (Geertz 1973), the research for which was supported by fieldwork conducted in both Russian and in Tatar on several research trips to the republic taken since 1995. There are several persuasive reasons to focus exclusively on Tatarstan as an example of a sovereignty project. First, because Tatarstan is certainly one of, if not the, most extreme and unique cases of sovereignty-seeking in post-Soviet Russia (with only Chechnya and perhaps Bashkortostan extant as comparable cases), I am able to use a close examination of the many and varied elements of the republic's enduring and evolving quest for sovereignty (including its relations with the Russian Federation central government, attempts to construct internal and external statehood, and policies aimed at both civic and ethnic nation-building in Tatarstan), to construct a theoretically and empirically rich template of a sovereignty project. This template in turn enhances both our theoretical understanding of the nature of contemporary norms of state sovereignty, nationhood and federalism, *and* our understanding of the dynamics of contemporary Russian politics. In constructing this sovereignty project model, I aim here to provide a full, comprehensive, and theoretically well-informed account of the varied rationales, understandings, and strategies employed by, patterns of behavior displayed by, and results achieved by Tatarstan in its sustained quest for sovereignty in the post-Soviet period. My inquiry is thus shaped by the following questions: How has Tatarstan defined the parameters of the "sovereign status" it claimed in 1990, how has it pursued that goal, and how successful has it been in that pursuit? More particularly, I seek to understand to what extent Soviet-era understandings of sovereignty, international norms about sovereign statehood, understandings about the past, present and future of the ethnic Tatar nation, and political and economic, realities "on the ground" have worked together to determine Tatarstan's definition of and pursuit of "sovereignty" in the post-Soviet era. My hope is that other scholars will be inspired by my study of Tatarstan's sovereignty project to pursue some of the questions generated by my work but not explored in-depth here, including most importantly the question of why Tatarstan's sovereignty project been so much more comprehensive, sustained, and effective than those of other ethnic republics, and the possible lessons that Tatarstan's sovereignty project has to offer for the resolution of other autonomy conflicts in the post-Soviet world, in Chechnya in particular.

Tatarstan has been the undisputed leader of the process of republican sovereignty-seeking in post-Soviet Russia, and in doing so has achieved more attributes or trappings of state sovereignty than any other republic, both in terms of its domestic development as a nation and a state, and in terms of its relations with Moscow. Furthermore, Tatarstan has sought to link its sovereignty project to wider trends in the international system, attempting to embed its new "sovereign" self in a web of international tissue that includes the United Nations, the European Union, the Organization of the Islamic Conference, as well as bilateral ties with established nations and other non-state, sovereignty-seeking actors such as Quebec. Even more significantly, Tatarstan has accomplished all of this without ever expanding its claim of sovereignty into a claim for independence or secessionism (as did Chechnya), nor has violence ever been a part of the varied strategic arsenal it has employed to pursue sovereignty.

Instead, regarding its relations with Moscow and with the republic's ethnic Russian and other non-Tatar minorities, Tatarstan has practiced a finely calibrated, constantly evolving policy of pragmatic negotiation, according to which the goals of maximizing the republic's sovereignty and the ethnic Tatar nation's revival are balanced carefully against the recognition of the republic's fundamental structural limitations—its location embedded within and legal status as a member of the Russian Federation, and the multiethnic composition of its population. While the republic does not always live up to its oft-repeated claims to be advancing levels of democracy and freedom along with the cause of republican sovereignty and the construction of a "real and functioning" form of federalism in Russia, the failures of its leaders and political system in this regard are no more onerous that those of the central government itself or of the leaders of Russian *oblasts* and *krais* elsewhere in the federation. In fact, the "Tatarstan Model" of sovereignty-seeking has been so successful that it is often mentioned as a prototype for an eventual solution to the Chechen debacle as well as for other autonomy conflicts in the former communist bloc (a fact Tatarstani officials themselves point out whenever given the chance) (Sharafutdinova 2000).

Structure of the Book

Chapter 1, "The Road to Sovereignty in Tatarstan," lays the groundwork for the more detailed examination of the republic's sovereignty project that constitutes the bulk of the book by providing a brief ethnography and political history of Tatarstan. In this chapter, I pay particular attention to the ways in which both Tsarist-era and, more importantly, Soviet-era policies for managing cultural pluralism (namely ethno-federalism) helped to determine the form and timing of the republican declarations of sovereignty during the glasnost and perestroika periods (especially the "parade of sovereignties" of 1990–1991). This discussion is crucial because to better understand the present and future state of federalism and ethnic relations in the Russian Federation, and to comprehend more fully how Tatarstan's sovereignty project shapes those relations, one must have a firm grasp of the history of Russia's attempts to manage its considerable cultural diversity in the past and of how Tatarstani elites in particular interpret that legacy and are trying to shape it into a functional regime of cultural pluralism in the present.

Chapter 2, "Projecting Sovereignty in the Russian Federation Under Yeltsin: Federation-Building or Federation-Wrecking?" examines the impact that Tatarstan's sovereignty project had on the development of federal relations in Russia during the Yeltsin era. It begins with a brief discussion of the theory of federalism and a review of the critiques that have been leveled against the Russian republics and their sovereignty-seeking efforts. Then, by recounting the development of Tatarstan's sovereignty project during the Yeltsin era, including the "parade of treaties" that Tatarstan inaugurated in the mid-1990s, I put forward the case that while Tatarstan certainly pushed the Russia's nascent post-Soviet federal system to its limits during this era, it never intended to break that system, and indeed, in the process, established the only form of real, true federalism (defined as the location of actual power and authority in the periphery as well as the center) that Russia has yet had.

The next two chapters explore the other aspects of Tatarstan's sovereignty project that have proven to be beneficial for Russia's federal and overall political and economic development in the post-Soviet era. Chapter 3, entitled "Projecting Sovereignty at Home and Abroad: Internal and External Statebuilding and Its Impact on Russian Federalism," examines the institutional and symbolic attributes of statehood that Tatarstan has pursued since declaring sovereignty in 1990, including both internal, domestic, and external, international aspects of sovereignty. The evidence presented in this chapter suggests that using the sovereignty project concept as an organizational framework has provided an impetus for important domestic reforms and international initiatives (both political and economic) that are examples of "win-win" situations that benefit both the republics and the Russian Federation as a whole. The potential utility of sovereignty projects in spurring domestic political and economic development and in deepening Russia's political and economic presence in the international system makes them a strong example of the type of beneficial "post-sovereign" state development political scientists have observed in other advanced industrial countries in the post-Cold War era. This chapter also highlights the particular utility of Tatarstan's sovereignty project in helping Russia to find new and more productive ways to engage with the Islamic world in the post-Soviet era.

In chapter 4, "Projecting the Nation: Sovereignty Projects, Nation-Building and Ethnocultural Justice in Tatarstan," the focus turns to the questions of how ethno-nationalist sentiment motivates republican sovereignty projects and how the quest for sovereignty might help to meet the need for ethnocultural justice in Russia in the post-Soviet period. The ambitious programs of ethno-national revival for the titular Tatar nation that have been pursued in Tatarstan, which include linguistic, cultural, and educational components, are discussed in some detail, as are the efforts of the Tatarstani sovereignty-seeking elite to provide for the multicultural needs of the republic's non-titular citizens. In this regard, Tatarstan has made a remarkably sincere and effective effort at developing a civic sense of "Tatarstani" nationness accompanied by extensive multicultural programming for non-Tatars, which the republic holds up as a model of democratic policies of cultural pluralism for the wider Russian Federation. Indeed, Tatarstan has used its own example of successful and simultaneous ethnic and civic nation-building to argue to the federal government in Moscow that has earned the right to take the lead in ensuring that liberal models of ethnocultural justice are achieved for all non-Russian populations (though of course for Tatars especially), in Russia in the post-Soviet era.

Chapter 5, "The End of Russian Federalism? Republican Sovereignty Projects under Putin," recounts the efforts of the Putin administration to establish a "dictatorship of law" and "reestablish vertical authority" in Russia, efforts that began upon Putin's ascension in 2000 but were stepped-up considerably in the wake of the second Chechen war and attendant increase in terrorist attacks on Russian soil, particularly the horrifying events of Beslan in fall 2004. Putin's recentralization efforts have gravely threatened the imperfect but nevertheless real gains in federalism won during the Yeltsin era. This chapter demonstrates that Tatarstan has consistently pressured the Putin administration to strengthen Russia's federal structure, even when this has required shedding attributes of sovereignty the republic had gained earlier. Gradually, and to a surprising degree, Tatarstan's willingness to compromise in a "federal spirit" has been reciprocated by Moscow. Putin's initial frontal attack on any and all aspects of republican sovereignty, which refused to acknowledge that the essence of federalism *is in fact* the creative and collaborative sharing of sovereignty, has been significantly altered due to Tatarstan's refusal to relinquish its claim to sovereign status. Tatarstan's constant pressure on Moscow to allow it to retain certain aspects of sovereignty while simultaneously submitting to increased federal integration in other areas in effect has kept the embers of genuine federalism alive in Russia, and thus constitutes one of the only bright spots in an otherwise grim political landscape.

In the concluding chapter 6, "Of Khans and Kremlins: Assessing the Tatarstani Sovereignty Project and Fostering Federalism and Multicultural Justice Through Sovereignty Projects in Russia," I take final measure of the political and theoretical implications of Tatarstan's sovereignty project. Here I draw on evidence from an important ceremonial moment in Russia's recent history—the 1000th anniversary of Kazan, celebrated in August 2005 with a special meeting of Russia's State Council and a summit of the CIS both held in *Kazan's* Kremlin—as a final illustrative example of this utility. In the conclusion I also expand the argument that overall the Tatarstani sovereignty project has been a positive force for the development of both federalism and cultural pluralism in post-Soviet Russia, and that as such that it is a moral and political imperative to support those aspects of republican sovereignty projects like Tatarstan's which help to promote the better functioning and deepening of Russian federalism and which help ensure that a modicum of ethnocultural justice is provided for in Russia. Finally, I identify several steps that both the center and the republics will have to undertake for the potentially useful contributions of republican sovereignty projects to Russia's development as a democratic, multicultural federation to be highlighted, and their antidemocratic, harmful aspects to be minimized.

Notes

1. Here Hererra makes the helpful point, also made by Kahn (2000) and emerging throughout this study of Tatarstan's sovereignty project as well, that not all sub-state claims to state sovereignty are automatically "maximal" ones aimed ultimately at secessionism or Tilly's "grand prize" of independent statehood.

2. For a comprehensive and classic discussion of the "functional areas of government activity," see Riker 1964, 53.

3. Some analysts assert that in the post-Cold War era new variations on sovereign statehood that "deviate from the conventional script of sovereignty" already exist and are in fact becoming more prominent. The relevance of these works to my study of sub-state sovereignty projects in post-Soviet Russia is discussed in more detail in the conclusion of this book. See Duursma 1996; Gottlieb 1993; Hannum 1996; Jackson 1990, 1995; Keating 1996; Krasner 2001; Osterud 1997; Sorenson 1997.

4. This list is largely based on Riker's formulation (1964, 53). For other discussions of the attributes of internal state sovereignty, see Hall and Ikenberry 1989; James 1986; Smith 1986b; Young 1994.

CHAPTER ONE

The Road to
Sovereignty in Tatarstan

Mark Beissinger has argued persuasively that the August 1990 decision of
the leaders of the Tatar A.S.S.R. to declare the republic to be "sovereign"
is best understood as an integral part of the larger "mobilizational tide" of
nationalist activism which began with the inauguration of glasnost and
democratization under Mikhail Gorbachev and ended with the collapse of
the USSR (2001). During this wave of mobilization, the titular nationalities
of the Soviet ethno-federal system experienced a series of cognitive shifts
that corresponded to the progressive political liberalization of the Soviet
state, eventually helping to lead to its collapse.[1] As a result of these changes,
which occurred initially in and were spread by activists in the Baltic states,
first the non-Russian union republics of the USSR, and then, surprisingly,
ethnic Russians themselves, came to see the Soviet ethno-federal system as
illegitimate and began to demand more authentic forms of "sovereign statehood." This demand derived from four normative contexts: first, the system
of Soviet ethno-federalism itself, with its attendant unresolved questions of
whether the USSR was an empire or a state and what the sovereignty its constituent units putatively possessed really meant (Walker 2003); second, eth-
nonationalist activism among the non-Russian peoples of the USSR; third,
extant international norms about sovereign statehood, the nation-state, and
the right of peoples to self-determination, and fourth, the extreme political

utility that the ambiguity and flexibility of the concept of sovereignty con-
ferred on it as a bargaining tool.

While the powerful wave of mobilization that wrought revolutionary
changes in both the political and cognitive realms of the former Soviet
Union is the chief variable at work in explaining the decision to declare
sovereignty in Tatarstan in 1990, my longitudinal study suggests that as it
has evolved, various aspects of Tatarstan's sovereignty project also have been
shaped in significant ways by Tatarstani elites' understandings of pre-Soviet
history as well. Thus before examining the critical "mobilization tide" un-
leashed by Gorbachev, this chapter attends, however briefly, to both Tsarist
and Soviet-era policies aimed at managing cultural difference in Russia, both
in general and regarding Tatars specifically.

Introducing Tatarstan and the Volga Tatars

Contemporary Tatarstan is located in the forest-steppe zone of the Middle
Volga region of Russia, with the republic's capital city of Kazan situated
at the confluence of the Volga and Kama rivers. The republic has major
reserves of oil (roughly 7 percent of the Russian Federation total) and natural gas, and its major industries are related to the processing of these raw
materials. Tatarstan also has a substantial chemical industrial base, a strong
aviation industry, and two of the largest truck and automobile production
plants in the former Soviet Union. According to the October 2002 census
of the Russian Federation, Tatarstan had 3,780,000 residents, 51.3 percent
of whom are of the eponymous ethnic Tatar nationality. The next largest
population group is ethnic Russians, who constitute 41 percent of the whole.
Thus Tatarstan is essentially a bi-ethnic republic where Tatars constitute a
slim (and contested) majority.[2]

The writing of ethnic history and the recounting of ethnogenesis in particular is an inherently politicized enterprise. As Hobsbawm has aptly put
it, historians are to ethnonationalists as poppy growers are to heroin users—
suppliers of the raw material needed for the fix (quoted in Shnirelman
1995, 5). Furthermore, attempting to establish the historical roots of a given
population also usually involves laying claim ownership over a given territory through the medium of indigenousness—the importance of establishing
"authentic" connections to land means that anthropologists and archeologists
play vital roles alongside historians in this process. In the Soviet Union, the
inherently politicized nature of the enterprise of ethnogenesis was consciously
exacerbated and manipulated by the Soviet state. The main goal of the Soviet
"science" of ethnogenesis as it concerned the Volga Tatars was to protect

against the development of pan-Turkic sentiment by de-emphasizing the Mongol element in Tatar ethnic development (Wixman 1986; Shnirelman 1995). The influence of these Soviet-era debates continue to weigh on contemporary understandings of Volga Tatar ethnic origins, though they have been superseded by the ideological needs of the republic's sovereignty project, namely the need to establish two things which help inform and support the republic's claims to self-determination and thus sovereignty: the indigenous credentials of the ethnic Tatar nation specific to the territory of contemporary Tatarstan and the long, exalted history of Tatar statehood on that territory.

Beginning in the 1940s, Soviet-dictated accounts of Tatar ethnogenesis emphasized what has been called the "Bulgarist" interpretation of Tatar history (Shnirelman 1995, 21–22; Rorlich 1986, 8–9). This school stresses a pure line of descent for contemporary Tatars down from the Volga Bulgars, a Turkic-speaking people who arrived in the Middle Volga regions sometime between the seventh and ninth century C.E., and who eventually assimilated large numbers of the Finno-Ugric speaking indigenous residents of the Middle Volga (Iskhakov 1993b; Zakiev 1995; Shnirelman 1995). Adherents of the Bulgarist school of Tatar ethnogenesis highlight two achievements attributed to the Volga Bulgars. First is the establishment of the state of Great Bulgar or Volga Bulgaria, which arose to the south of the confluence of the Volga and Kama rivers in the tenth century and stood until its destruction by Batu Khan in 1236. The second is the adoption of Islam by the Volga Bulgar state in 922 C.E. at the hands of an emissary of the Caliph of Baghdad.[3] The utility of this theory for Soviet leaders was that it de-emphasized the Turkic and Mongol elements of Tatar history, thus simultaneously lessening tendencies towards pan-Turkism among Tatars and circumscribing the potential territorial claims of Tatars who might aspire to reconstruct Batu's empire within the USSR (as remote as that possibility might seem). The difficulty facing this theory is that contemporary Volga Tatar language and phenotypical attributes show clear and heavy influence from two other population groups, the Kypchak-speaking Turkic people who arrived in the Middle Volga sometime between the arrival of the Bulgars in the seventh century and the Mongols in the thirteenth century, and the Mongols themselves (Schamiloglu 1990; Shnirelman 1995, 29–35).

The absence of any compelling linguistic or archeological evidence to link the ancient Bulgar Turks and their language with the Kypchak Turkic language and obvious Mongol influences exhibited in contemporary Volga Tatar populations led to the gradual development of a competing theory of the group's ethnogenesis. The "modified Kypchak" thesis posits that modern Volga Tatars are the product of the interaction of these three peoples—Volga

Bulgars, Kypchak-speaking Turks, and Mongol Turks. Proponents of this theory posit that when the Mongols of the Golden Horde arrived in the Middle Volga in the 1230s, they joined the Kypchak-speaking Turks who were already in the region, with the two groups together then gradually forcing both the linguistic and political assimilation of the Volga Bulgars and the state of Great Bulgar to Mongol-Kypchak suzerainty (Alishev 1993, 219; Golden 1992, 319; Iskhakov 1993, 6; Rorlich 1986, 23; Tagirov 1993; *Tatary* 1967, 10–11; Zakiev 1995, 88). According to this theory, the state known as the Kazan Khanate (1445–1552), which arose on the ruins of both the Great Bulgar state and the remnants of the far-flung empire of the Golden Horde, is best viewed as an ethnically-mixed crucible that had a Kypchak-Mongol aristocracy but maintained elements of Volga Bulgar culture as well, and which managed, during its brief but gloried existence, to midwife the contemporary Volga Tatar people.

While the modified Kypchak thesis began to appear in writings by Tatar intellectuals as early as the late 1960s (*Tatary* 1967), this more symbiotic and inclusive understanding of Tatar ethnogenesis became dominant only after the fall of the Soviet Union, and indeed it has become the basis upon which the architects of the Tatarstani sovereignty project have operated since the late 1980s. It is clear why this theory appeals to both the political and intellectual elite invested in Tatarstan's sovereignty project more than the pure Bulgarist interpretation—not only does the pure Bulgarist theory suffer in the face of the archeological and linguistic evidence and from its association with Soviet-era ideological manipulation, but the modified Kypchak theory clearly identifies the modern-day Volga Tatars both as ancient (if only ambiguously indigenous, as the absence of Finno-Ugric elements in contemporary Tatar language remains problematic) residents of the territory of contemporary Tatarstan and makes them the direct heirs to not one, but two "great" state formations, Great Bulgar and the Kazan Khanate. Thus according to this narrative, which is enthusiastically promoted by the agents of the Tatarstani sovereignty project, contemporary Volga Tatars possess an "ancient tradition of statehood" which began in the tenth century and did not fall until the final conquest of the Kazan Khanate by Ivan Grozny in 1552. These historical self-understandings are central motivations and supports for the contemporary Tatarstani claim to self-determination and sovereignty.

Political History of the Volga Tatars and Tatarstan

The conquest of the Kazan Khanate by the Muscovite state under Ivan IV in 1552 is generally considered to be the beginning of the great imperial expansion of Russia, and it continues to figure heavily into Volga Tatar understandings of the past and present.[4] While for Russians the fall of Kazan represents the earliest triumph of a nascent imperial power (though it was seen at the time chiefly as a Christian victory over Muslim infidels), for Tatars the fall of Kazan is in many respects the equivalent of the primordial fall from grace in the western Christian tradition—the source of all lost hopes and all future woes. In turn, as the evidence presented in the rest of this book makes clear, one of the chief functions of the contemporary Tatarstani sovereignty project is to reverse this catastrophic historic loss.

For most of its existence, the Russian Empire was a classic model of a premodern imperial state, wherein most non-Russian subjects, including the Volga Tatars, expressed and experienced their communal identifications through religion and language and neither demanded nor received territorial autonomy. During the Tsarist era, at least some latitude regarding the practice of non-Orthodox religion and non-Russian culture was allowed as long as all continued to profess and practice loyalty to the Tsar (through the payment of taxes, tributes, and in some cases, the completion of military service). However pragmatic concerns alone did not govern relations with non-Russian subjects, and various ideological imperatives did shape official policy towards minorities at different points in Russian imperial history. Most significantly, as the early accounts of the sacking of Kazan demonstrate, Russia was understood first and foremost as an Orthodox Empire, the "Third Rome" whose head the Tsar served as the symbolic head of the Orthodox church, and which had a divine calling to Christianize and civilize non-Russians in the realm—an understanding which necessarily placed the Muslim Tatars in the role of "infidel" (Batunsky 1990, 1994; Pelenski 1974).

This missionary spirit was manifested at different times in different ways during the Tsarist era, ranging from coercive conversion policies to attacks on non-Orthodox places of worship and clergy to formal policies of tolerance towards non-Orthodox minorities that were which nevertheless coupled with heavy state oversight and regulation of their religious practices. For example, immediately after the fall of the Kazan Khanate in 1552, some Tatars were expelled from the center of Kazan and resettled outside its gates, while other members of the Tatar aristocracy from the Kazan Khanate were allowed to assimilate into the ranks of Russian Imperial administration and commerce in Kazan, forming a new distinct rank known as "service Tatars." This service class of Tatars gradually evolved into a powerful commercial and trading bourgeoisie, dominating both trade and industry in Kazan Guberniya in the late eighteenth and early nineteenth century. An English traveler to Kazan in the early nineteenth century noted the aptitude of Volga Tatars for merchant and trade activity, exclaiming that commerce was "almost the sole activity for Tartars [sic]" in Kazan and that a "great many" of them lived richly due to their mastery of this pursuit (Turnerelli 1854, 2: 47, 79, 82). Indeed in 1812 Tatars owned 90 percent of large industrial enterprises in Kazan (Zenkovsky 1960, 21). Later Tatar merchants from Kazan Guberniya would serve as the economic middle-men for the Russian Empire in the territory of Turkestan, leading to charges of imperialism from their Central Asian ethnic kin (Zenkovsky 1953, 1958, 1960).

The development of this powerful Tatar merchant class in Kazan Guberniya was facilitated by the policies of Catherine II, whose reign has been characterized as a "golden age" for Volga Tatars (McCarthy 1973, 313). In contrast to the reigns of Tsarinas Elizabeth and Anne, which saw the establishment of the brutal Agency for Convert Affairs in 1740, the legalization of purchase of non-Russian peasants by Orthodox clergy for the purpose of conversion in 1755, and the destruction of over 418 of the 536 mosques then standing in Russia, Catherine regarded Tatars as an educated and noble people. In addition to abolishing the hated Agency for Convert Affairs, Catherine also reversed some of the anti-Muslim rulings of earlier Tsars with her Act of Religious Tolerance of 1788, which facilitated a cultural and spiritual rebirth among Volga Tatars simultaneous with the economic development of the Tatar merchant class (Fisher 1968; McCarthy 1973; Rorlich 1986; Zenkovsky 1960, 18). The removal of official bans on printing and Muslim educational institutions in the Russian Empire allowed the economically powerful Tatar elite to begin patronizing its own printing houses, *mektebs* and *medresehs*, and university professorships at Kazan State University. Thus began the period of what Ayse-Azade Rorlich has termed "book-mania" among the Kazan Tatars, marked by the publication of an impressive number of books in Tatar and Arabic in Kazan by Tatars, both at their own publishing houses and at Kazan State University (Rorlich 1986, 69–72; Turnerelli 1854, 2: 78). As the Tatar merchant class became more successful and more integrated into mainstream Russian and European economic and social life in the wake of Catherine's reforms, an indigenous Tatar intellectual elite also began to develop.

By the nineteenth century, two ideological processes were at work in the Russian Empire that had important consequences for Volga Tatars and other non-Russians in the realm. On the one hand, as Russia's leaders became more and more invested in their membership in the exclusive club of Western European powers, they also became increasingly convinced that Russia, like other leading states at the time, had an important "civilizing mission," in this case, aimed at the myriad and manifold non-Russian peoples who inhabited

VERY SIMPLIFIED BUT WORTH DWELLING

the realm. Simultaneously, a growing sense of ethnic Russian self-awareness, which manifested itself both in Nicholas I's ideology of "Orthodoxy, Autocracy, and Nationality" and in the growing intelligentsia movement, which was quickly developing a passionate but critical sense of specifically *Russian* national history and identity, also highlighted the differences between the Russian core of the empire and its non-Russian subjects.[5] These tendencies are illustrated by the fact that by the 1860s all non-Russians, regardless of their religion, were categorized by the state as *inorodtsy* or "foreign-born," indicating that the natural, ruling core of the empire was the ethnic Russian people (Werth 2001, 130).

It was in this complicated and potentially dangerous climate of a Russian empire that was itself struggling with questions of westernization, modernization and nascent ethnic (Russian) nationalism that the fledgling Tatar intelligentsia began the process of redefining the Muslim Tatar worldview, chiefly through a movement known as *jadidism*.[6] Jadidism was an indigenous Russian variant of the broader movement among Muslims worldwide to engage modernity and to respond to the challenge of Western imperialism, and Tatar intellectuals involved in the movement had deep connections with and shared ideas with other progressive thinkers in Russia and in the wider Turkic and Islamic worlds. In particular, many Volga Tatar intellectuals were deeply involved in the reformist debates and politics of the Ottoman Empire in the late nineteenth century (Yavuz 1993). The modernist, moderate and reformist discourse of jadidism was led by Volga Tatar thinkers, and though overall they constituted a "a diverse group," they were united by the fact that "to a person, they agreed that the cultural community with which they identified most, the Islamic, was faced with economic, social, intellectual, and political challenges necessitating an urgent response" (Lazzerini 1992, 151, 160). Jadidists largely accepted that Muslim communities in the Russian Empire were in fact guilty of the stagnation, ignorance, backwardness, and fanaticism that European and Russian critics charged them with, while Europe and Russia functioned for jadidists as models of civilization and progress to be emulated by the Muslim world (Khalid 1997, 191). Jadidists argued that all aspects of Islamic society, but particularly the traditional Muslim education system, needed radical reform if Russia's Muslims ever hoped for "full participation in the world being built by modern science and capital," or to achieve a more just, tolerant, and ultimately prosperous way of life (Khalid 1997, passim; Lazzerini 1992, 162). Rather than withdrawing from modern European society out of fear and hostility, jadidists argued, Muslims in Russia should reform, adapt, modernize, and thus "join the stream of global civilization" (Batunsky 1994, 219).

Thus the most prominent Tatar ideology about cultural, ethnic, and religious difference generated during the Tsarist era was not aimed at separation from modern European, or Russian society (generally equated in jadidist thought), but rather one that sought to achieve greater success in emulating and joining that society. Similarly, while the Kazan Tatars did endure sporadic episodes of Russification and forced conversion from 1552 to the Russian Revolution (indeed, one pair of authors has argued that in the Russian Empire, "At all times, religious minorities were in effect second-class subjects of the empire") (Geraci and Khodarkovsky 2001, 7), the main and largely successful historical thrust of Russian Imperial policy towards the Tatars was to harness their economic potential and quell potential rebellious tendencies by firmly integrating them administratively and politically into the Russian state, while at the same time allowing Tatars a significant amount of cultural and religious autonomy. Under Russian Imperial rule, the Tatar community of Kazan and the Middle Volga region flourished and became the wealthiest, most well-educated and socially-advanced Muslim group in the entire Russian Empire by the beginning of the twentieth century. It is therefore perhaps not surprising that jadidism should carry an essentially conciliatory attitude towards the Tsarist state, nor that during the revolutionary years of 1905–1917 Volga Tatars limited their political demands to increased educational and cultural freedoms for Muslims within the existing administrative framework and political structure of the Russian Empire—a framework that was in fact serving most Tatars quite well by the end of the Tsarist period (Daulet 1989; Rorlich 1986, especially chapter 9; Zenkovsky 1960).

The Founding of the Tatar A.S.S.R.

The story of the incorporation of the Tatar lands into the Soviet Union through the creation of the Tatar A.S.S.R. is an extremely complex and interesting one that can only be addressed in the briefest detail here.[7] In July 1917, Volga Tatars in Kazan hosted the Second All-Muslim Conference in Kazan, attempting to foster a unified Muslim position on the acute set of questions facing all citizens of the Russian state, non-Russian and Russian alike—what actors to support and what demands to pursue amidst a volatile and revolutionary political scene. At the conference, the Volga Tatar delegation pushed for a non-territorial type of autonomy for Muslims, to be administered within existing political structures in Russia. This position is consonant with the Volga Tatar tradition of seeking accommodation within the system rather than demanding revolutionary transformation. However by November 1917, the rapid evolution in Russia's political fortunes had "substantially changed" many Tatars' views on autonomy (Rorlich 1986, 132).

A month after the October Revolution another "National" Assembly of the Muslims of Inner Russia and Siberia was held in Ufa, where many Volga Tatar activists finally joined in a long-standing Bashkir call for territorial independence for Russia's Muslims. Together these activists called for the formation of an "Idel-Ural" state that would become one of the constituent units of a new Russian Federal Republic, and formed a commission authorized to investigate the implementation of this state (Rorlich 1986, 132; Schafer 1995, 71, 84–87; Zenkovsky 1960, 168–73).[8]

The idea of an Idel-Ural state project, which was also endorsed by a small group of Volga Tatar communists led by Mir-Said Sultangaliev, was co-opted and modified by the Bolsheviks in March 1918 when the Bolshevik Commissariat for Nationalities Affairs (Narkomnats), headed by Stalin, declared the establishment of the "Tatar-Bashkir Soviet Republic" (Schafer 1995, 194–99; Zenkovsky 1960, 177). Just weeks before, the Third Congress of Soviets in Petersburg had adopted ethno-federalism as the official Bolshevik position on the border regions, a blatant attempt to win over non-Russian state-seeking nationalists to the Bolshevik cause which was eventually institutionalized and written into the first Soviet constitution in July 1918 (Beissinger 1995, 161–62; Pipes 1950, 107–13; Schafer 1995, 160; Suny 1993, 84).

While this proposed Tatar-Bashkir republic was supported by a handful of pro-Soviet Bashkirs, most Bashkir activists, including the prominent Bashkir leader Zaki Validi Togan, were against the Soviet project, fearing they would be outnumbered in the new state by both Volga Tatars and Russians (Schafer 1995, 227, 261). Plans for the Tatar-Bashkir Soviet Republic were interrupted by the full-scale outbreak of civil war in the Volga-Ural region in May 1918. Throughout the tumultuous civil war in the Middle Volga, both Tatar nationalist activists and Tatar communists such as Sultangaliev continued to push for territorial autonomy through either an enlarged Idel-Ural state or a smaller joint Tatar-Bashkir state (either of which Tatars would easily dominate demographically and politically) (Rorlich 1986, 137). However after the Bashkirs defected to the Bolshevik cause and the Bashkir A.S.S.R. was created in March 1919, Tatar activists, particularly Tatar communists, began agitating for the creation of a similar, separate "national" republic for the Volga Tatars. Throughout the spring of 1920, political and party organizations at all levels debated the issue of a Tatar republic, and eventually the Tatar Autonomous Soviet Socialist Republic (Tatar A.S.S.R.) was created by central decree on May 27, 1920.

The borders of both the Tatar A.S.S.R reflected Soviet "divide and rule" imperatives in the Middle Volga region. More specifically, the demographic composition of the Tatar A.S.S.R. and the neighboring Bashkir A.S.S.R. (created on March 20, 1919), reflected Soviet fears of Tatar domination of the Volga-Ural region (Connor 1992, 39; Wixman 1986, 457). For this reason, only one-quarter of Tatars living in Russia actually were included within the boundaries of the Tatar A.S.S.R when it was created in May 1920—besides the significant Tatar population located in neighboring Bashkortostan, there are large populations of Tatars in Moscow, St. Petersburg, Orenburg, Perm, Sverdlovsk, and Chelyabinsk oblasts as well as in the Republic of Udmurtia (Graney 1998, 154–57).

Soviet Ethno-federalism

The absolute centralization, breadth, and scale of institutionalized ethnic (nationalities) policy in the Soviet Union is unique in world history (Brubaker 1994, 26–27; Connor 1984; Martin 2001; Slezkine 1994). This is all the more surprising considering that, inspired by Marx and Engels's summons to "all working men of the world" to unite, the Bolsheviks believed that by founding the world's first socialist state in Russia, they were actually forging the first link in what they fully expected to be a chain of *internationalist* socialist states reaching across Europe and the world. And yet, the surprisingly powerful ethno-nationalist movements that the Bolsheviks encountered across the former Tsarist realm during the revolutionary era led Lenin and his People's Commissar of Nationalities, Josef Stalin, to make the idea of national self-determination for ethnic groups a fundamental organizing principle of the new Bolshevik state in Russia. In fact, as author Terry Martin has argued, the new Soviet Union was explicitly constructed as an "affirmative action empire," dedicated to accommodating and even promoting the ethno-national consciousness of its ethnic minorities through a multifaceted system. This system included the following elements: an ethno-federal political arrangement wherein some of the administrative units of the new Soviet Union were organized as "ethnic homelands" for ethnic minorities; the cultivation and promotion through affirmative action of ethnic elites to staff government, education, and industrial positions in these new homelands; the promotion (in some cases creation) of the native languages of the titular populations of the new ethno-federal units; and the creation of a whole myriad of cultural institutions such as newspapers, journals, opera, theatre, and ballet troupes, and museums to support the "national cultures" of these peoples (Gorenburg 2003; Martin 2001, 10–13).

The Soviet system of ethno-federalism has often been compared to a set of Russian nesting dolls (called a *matroishka*), as there were several layers of administration, hierarchically organized according to their respective levels of political and cultural rights. In practice, none of the administrative units had any real political autonomy, and even their rights to cultural expression were directed by the central state. Thus citizens found themselves not only residents of the new "Union of Soviet Socialist Republics," but also simultaneously inhabitants of one of fifteen "union republics," officially known as Soviet Socialist Republics, which included the Russian Republic along with the fourteen homeland republics of the peoples living near the borders of the USSR. Theoretically, according to the 1924 Soviet Constitution, the fifteen union republics were "sovereign states" that possessed the right to secede from the USSR. Despite the reality that this sovereignty was entirely fictional, the fact that the union republics possessed even this ersatz form of sovereign statehood would later have important consequences for the way in which the Soviet Union eventually collapsed (Walker 2003, 29–34).

Within the complex Soviet ethno-federal structure, citizens of the fifteen union republics might find themselves further nested within one of the "autonomous republics" (Autonomous Soviet Socialist Republics or ASSRs), homelands for peoples whose territory lay within the confines of a union republic and who enjoyed lesser levels of (theoretical) political autonomy (chiefly, the ASSRs did not possess the theoretical right to secede from the USSR, nor did they have the right to have universities with classes taught in the native non-Russian languages in their republics). Further down in the administrative hierarchy were "autonomous oblasts" and "national areas," with correspondingly lower levels of authority.

In addition to effectively creating national homelands or quasi nation-states for non-Russians within the USSR by institutionalizing and territorializing ethnic identity in the ethno-federal system, Soviet officials also fostered a strong sense of individual ethnic or national identity among its citizens not only by promoting ethnic affirmative action programs, but also by demanding that each person record their ethnicity on the internal passports that all Soviet citizens were required to carry at all times after 1932. As author Yuri Slezkine has put it: "Every Soviet citizen was born into a certain nationality, took it to day care and through high school, had it officially confirmed at the age of sixteen and then carried it to the grave through thousands of application forms, certificates, questionnaires, and reception desks" (Slezkine 1994, 450). The Soviet Union thus ended up magnifying, celebrating, and reifying the linguistic and cultural diversity that had existed in the old Tsarist empire, while also wedding it for the first time to an explicit sense of ownership over particular territorial units. As such, the "imagined community" that the Soviet people were to pledge loyalty to did not correspond to one particular ethno-national group but rather was the collective and multiethnic "Friend-ship of Peoples" that made-up and made great the Soviet Union (Martin 2001, 459). The ultimate goal of Soviet ethno-federalism was thus a unique form of "multinational unity," a never before seen "unnational" state that would ultimately take the form of a modern, socialist, "trans-ethnic" polity inhabited by a wholly new entity, the Soviet people (Blitstein 2006, 283).

Given the firm Marxist opposition to ethnic nationalism and commit-ment to internationalism, where did the Bolshevik impulse to invest so much energy and so many (scarce) resources into this complex and multifaceted system of managing multiculturalism come from? The answer lies in the way that Lenin understood the relationship between nationalist consciousness (feelings of ethnic or nationalist loyalty) and class consciousness (feelings of class solidarity) and his beliefs about the inevitable historical progression of the communist revolution. According to Lenin, nationalist feelings were a "natural" and indeed "progressive" stage that different peoples (especially more "backwards" or "primitive" peoples) had to experience and pass through on the progressive journey forward to internationalist, proletariat conscious-ness. By fostering and using ethno-nationalist feelings for their own progres-sive ends, namely modernizing the individual nations of the Soviet Union simultaneously with the country as a whole, the Bolsheviks would hasten the coming about of mature communism (Hirsch 2005). As Lenin himself put it in 1919, "We are going to help you develop your Buriat, Votiak, etc., language and culture, because in this way you will join the universal culture, revolution and communism sooner" (Slezkine 1994, 420). Accordingly, Soviet efforts to support particular national identities followed a specific formula, one that was "national in form," but strictly "socialist in content." Any expressions of na-tional identity that transgressed the narrow boundaries set by the Communist Party according to this formula were quickly and severely punished.

To help this process along in practice, the "national in form, Soviet in content" formula of Soviet ethno-federalism was accompanied by large doses of official Soviet rhetoric about the values of "internationalism" and the sanctity of the "brotherly family of people" in the USSR (Collias 1990; Connor 1992, 33). For example, the headline on the day of the celebration of the 60th anniversary of the formation of the Tatar A.S.S.R. read "In One United Fraternal Family of Peoples—Towards New Victories in the Build-ing of Communism!," while the ceremonial speeches marking this event were full of references thanking "all our brotherly nations of the USSR," but especially the "great elder brother Russian nation" for helping the Tatar A.S.S.R. flourish under socialism (*Sovetskaya Tatariya* June 18, 1990, 1; June 19, 1990, 1).

Discuss here
Yurchak

Soviet ethno-federalism was implemented chiefly through the system of *korenizatsiya*, or the cultivation of titular non-Russian political and cultural elites in ethno-federal units such as the Tatar A.S.S.R. Korenizatsiya was aimed at creating and co-opting titular non-Russian elites by offering them "genuine opportunities for participation and advancement, in exchange for loyalty and partial assimilation" (Lapidus 1984, 569, 579). Under this system, positions in state, political, party, administrative, and cultural structures were filled with members of the titular non-Russian populations of the ethno-federal units, through extensive affirmative action programs (Suny 1993, 102–06). However to guard against potential nationalist deviation by these titular non-Russian elites, "the center resolutely maintained its representatives in all republics" through a system of exchanging cadres, whereby titular non-Russian elites rotated to Moscow and representatives from Moscow also served in ethno-federal units (Connor 1992, 39). These co-opted titular elites served to effectively block the emergence of potentially dangerous ethno-nationalism in their republics by gathering representatives of the titular national intelligentsia into local ethno-federal institutions in the same way that they themselves had been co-opted into Union-level institutions (Roeder 1991, 207).

The multifaceted nationalities policy of the Soviet Union also included the creation of titular non-Russian "national" intelligentsias and the promotion of non-Russian "national" languages and cultures in the ethno-federal units.[9] This was achieved by establishing official state-sponsored cultural institutions for titular nationalities as well as educational and publishing institutions in the non-Russian languages of the titular nationalities (Brubaker 1994; Gorenburg 2003; Slezkine 1994; Wixman 1986). This extensive system of cultural and educational institutions was meant to bring all the means of producing "raw material" for the construction of ethno-national identities fully under Soviet ideological control. Both the titular non-Russian intelligentsias themselves and their creative products were subject to centralized control. For example, historical works were to convey the idea that assimilation by Russians was a beneficial experience (Black 1956; Martin 2001, 451–457; Tillett 1969), while ethnographic and archeological works were subject to ideological imperatives tied to Soviet ethno-federalism (Shnirelman 1995). Similarly, all literature (artistic, journalistic, and academic) had to reflect the benefits of Soviet modernization by following the tenets of socialist realism (Goble 1990; Luckyj 1975; Swazye 1962; Valeeva-Suleymanova 1993).

Efforts to build communism and universal culture through ethno-federalism in the Tatar A.S.S.R began in the 1920s and 1930s with the systematic destruction of the traditional social and cultural institutions that had served to construct and transmit communal identities before the Soviet period. Traditional Muslim religious and educational institutions were closed and contacts with Turkish and Central Asian Muslims were cut off. Independent Muslim publishing houses (mostly among the Volga Tatars) were closed down and replaced with Soviet-sponsored institutions, while the Arabic-based alphabets of the written Tatar and Bashkir languages were Latinized and later Cyrillicized (Shnirelman 1995, 20; Valeeva-Suleymanova 1993). Finally and most importantly, the independent-minded Muslim National Communists in the Tatar A.S.S.R. either chose to flee Soviet Russia, were deported, or were arrested and killed (like the Tatar Communist Mir-Said Sultangaliev). These leaders were quickly replaced with the first generation of Soviet-trained "national" cadres (Benningsen and Wimbush 1980; Rorlich 1986, chapter 11; Valeev 1995).

By the mid-1970s Soviet leaders were confidently proclaiming that this unique system of ethno-federalism had "completely, definitively and irrevocable resolved" the nationalities question in the Soviet Union (Connor 1992, 43).[10] And yet in the early 1990s, it was the "triumph of the nations," as Helen Carrere d'Encausse (1993) put it, which effectively felled the USSR when Gorbachev's experimental "revolution from above" of glasnost and perestroika was effectively "hijacked from below" by massive waves of ethno-nationalist protest by non-Russians and Russians alike (Suny 1993, 132). The mechanism that triggered this process was the aforementioned parade of sovereignties, which began with Estonia's declaration of sovereign statehood on November 16, 1988. Together with the collapse of the Communist Party and other administrative hierarchies in the USSR, the parade of sovereignties eventually led to the peaceful dissolution of the Soviet Union on December 25, 1991.

The Road to Sovereignty: Glasnost and the "Triumph of the Nations" in the USSR

There is general consensus that when Gorbachev initiated his policies of glasnost and perestroika in 1985 he had no expectation that his actions would trigger the types of widespread ethno-nationalist protests which ensued in the late 1980s in the Soviet Union (Beissinger 1996, 105–06; Dunlop 1993, 3, 9). Like many Western Sovietologists and even Soviet dissidents, Gorbachev believed the official Soviet line on the nationalities question in the USSR—that it had been solved. Despite Gorbachev's lack of premonition, the policies of glasnost and perestroika opened up wide political spaces in the Soviet Union into which ethno-nationalist protest by the non-Russian titular nationalities of the Soviet Union expanded. These sentiments were expressed chiefly as the desire for renewed and more authentic forms of "sovereign statehood" to replace those empty forms that existed under the Soviet ethno-federal system, which was judged to be both illegitimate and obsolete. The declaration of state sovereignty issued by the Tatar A.S.S.R. in August 1990 is a direct product of this "mobilizational cycle," which began in the Baltic republics of the USSR (Beissinger 1996; 2001).

While there was some early protest activism around ecological issues in the Baltic states, the first major popular protests in the region occurred in summer 1987 on the anniversary of the signing of the Molotov-Ribbentrop pact. In a span of months the focus in the Baltics switched from ecological issues to political issues. The commemorative actions of the summer of 1987 quickly evolved into mass protests demanding increased economic autonomy within the Soviet Union. Citizens in the Baltic republics also began celebrating the traditional independence days of the inter-war Baltic states for the first time in fifty years (Gerner and Hedlund 1993; Lieven 1994). By spring 1988 the sentiments generated by popular remembrances of lost Baltic independence had been channeled into direct political action in the form of mass-based political organizations known as popular fronts. The first to form was the Estonian Popular Front in April 1988, with both the Latvian Popular Front and the Lithuanian equivalent, called Sajudis, holding their inaugural congresses in October 1988.

Official incorporation of popular nationalist attitudes in the Baltics did not take long. The trend began in Estonia on November 16, 1988, when the Supreme Council of the Estonian S.S.R. declared Estonia to be a "sovereign state." Despite strong popular support and activism around the idea of declaring sovereignty, local officials in Lithuania and Latvia were more tentative, and delayed their own declarations of sovereign statehood until May and July 1989, respectively. During this period, the meaning of the claim to "sovereign statehood" was still ambiguous, possibly by design (Beissinger 1996, 117; Lieven 1994, 224; Walker 2003). Indeed, throughout the glasnost era, discussion of sovereignty would be among the "most charged and most divisive," with the usage of the term on the part of the union and later autonomous republics being "replete with misunderstandings, confusions, vagueness and self-deception" (Kahn 2002, 90–93). Could the new sovereign status claimed by the Balts still be accommodated within some renewed Soviet Union, or did it carry with it the connotation of full independence and thus presage the eventual dissolution of the USSR? Despite, or perhaps more accurately because of the leeway provided by the ambiguous nature of these claims to sovereign statehood, during 1989 and early 1990 political elites in the Baltic republics made moves to give their newly-declared sovereignty shape by passing legislation that established official state languages, authorized local control of economic resources and industry, and created new and controversial citizenship policies (Lieven 1994, 229; Muiznieks 1995, 14; Walker 2003).

In March 1990, Lithuania became the first republic in the Soviet Union to "upgrade" its declaration of state sovereignty to an unambiguous declaration of independence, despite the fact that the United States and other powers had warned Lithuania not to expect international recognition of a claim to independence (Lieven 1994, 233–35). This hesitance on the part of the U.S. to endorse the Lithuanian declaration of independence illustrates that international actors perceive a qualitative normative difference between a claim to state sovereignty and a claim to independence. The fact that Lithuania chose to issue a separate declaration of independence on top of their declaration of sovereign statehood also illustrates the subtle but important differences between these two claims. The leaders of the other Baltic republics also demonstrated that they understood the important difference between making a claim to independence as opposed to state sovereignty. Instead of issuing unequivocal declarations of independence after Lithuania had done so, both republics issued statements saying they were in a period of "transition to independence" and appealing to the international community and the UN for guidance and help during this process (Lieven 1994, 242–43).

Threatened by these moves, Gorbachev responded by first instituting an economic blockade in the Baltics and later resorting to force to stop Baltic sovereignty projects (in January 1991). However this hard-line strategy backfired, and in spring 1991 the already generally high levels of popular support for independence in the Baltics coalesced to a boiling point (Muiznieks 1995, 15). In 1991, all three Baltic republics held wildly successful referenda on independence, after which they began to withdraw from Soviet political and economic institutions, creating their own budgets and stopping transfers to the all-Union budget (White 1992, 163–82). These events helped to precipitate the failed August 1991 coup against Gorbachev, in the wake of which the independence of all three Baltic states was immediately recognized by international audiences and the remaining members of the USSR. Thus in less than four years, the Baltic states generated sovereignty projects which evolved from tentative probes based largely on the rhetorical formulations of sovereignty contained in Soviet ethno-federal documents to "maximal" efforts whose full-blown claims to sovereign statehood were based on international normative understandings of that term and were eventually recognized and legitimated as such by the international community. For the independence-minded Baltic states, the "profound ambiguity" and extreme elasticity of the term "sovereignty" would be wielded skillfully, and the "extreme political efficacy" of employing the term in the struggle to remake the political structures of the state would be demonstrated loudly and clearly to the other residents of the Soviet Union (Walker 2003, 1, 6–7).

Sovereignty Projects in Russia's Republics

The Baltic activists who inaugurated sovereignty projects also actively sought to generate popular fronts and sovereignty projects among the other non-Russian nationalities of the Soviet Union. Indeed Baltic activists saw themselves as "locomotives" of change in the Soviet Union—as their own sovereignty projects progressed, they "exported" their ever-more revolutionary ideas and protest to titular non-Russian nationalities in other Soviet ethno-federal units, offering legal and political advice and help with formulating and publishing documents and journals (Muiznieks 1995, 5, 10–11). While the Caucasian republics of Azerbaijan and Georgia were the first to declare sovereign statehood after the Balts had (in September and November 1989, respectively), the Baltic influence was particularly felt in Moldova, Ukraine, and Belorussia, which declared themselves to be sovereign states in June and July 1990 (Muiznieks 1995, 12).

Activists within the Russian Federation, both Russian and non-Russian, also were inspired by the ideas and resources transferred from the Baltics. Because Gorbachev was a "true believer" in the USSR (Dunlop 1993, 3), a Russian sovereignty project was inconceivable to him. However as popular fronts and other more nationalist organizations like Pamyat' grew in Russia, Boris Yeltsin, Gorbachev's main rival for power during glasnost, began to realize that he could capitalize on the increasing pro-Russia, pro-sovereignty, and anti-center feelings in Russia to strengthen his hand versus Gorbachev (Dunlop 1993, 22–24, 54–55). After becoming a deputy in March 1990 and then Chairman of the Russian Supreme Soviet in May 1990, Yeltsin began openly advocating for Russian sovereignty, trying to court both Russians and non-Russians alike in the R.S.F.S.R. and using the appeal of sovereignty as a weapon in his struggle for power with Gorbachev. Despite the fact that Yeltsin himself did not appear to be "the slightest bit interested in the precise legal definition of sovereignty" (Walker 2003, 80), immediately after his election in May 1990, he proclaimed, "Russia must and will acquire real sovereignty! Russia will be independent in everything!" (Dunlop 1993, 26). With such a ringing endorsement from their new Chairman, the Russian Supreme Soviet obediently declared Russia to be a sovereign state on June 12, 1990.

After declaring Russian sovereignty, Yeltsin set about consolidating his own power by reaching out to non-Russian titular minorities in both the union republics of the USSR and in the autonomous republics of Russia with a message of "radical decentralization" aimed at weakening Gorbachev and the Soviet center (Dunlop 1993, 26; Kahn 2002, 103–10).[11] Most importantly, in August 1990 in Kazan he encouraged the sovereign ambitions of the republic's leadership by telling the crowd to "take as much sovereignty as you can swallow" and to "take all the power you yourselves can ingest" (Dunlop 1993, 26). The "solely short-term allegiance" that Yeltsin sought from the republics by endorsing this brand of "feel-good sovereignty" was readily delivered; the Supreme Soviet of the Tatar A.S.S.R. was the first to take up Yeltsin's challenge to begin seeking sovereignty, declaring the republic to be sovereign state in August 1990. Ultimately, fourteen of the sixteen Russian A.S.S.R.s would declare themselves to be sovereign within six months of Russia's own June 1990 declaration (Kahn 2002, 103, 120).

Embarking on Sovereignty Projects: Activism in the Tatar A.S.S.R. 1987–1990

According to Tatar sociologist and political activist Damir Iskhakov, the roots of Tatar political activism during glasnost were visible even in the 1960s and 1970s, when Tatar academics attempted to get permission to write an ethnohistory of the Tatar people, petitioned the Soviet government for more Tatar-language schools, and even appealed to the Soviet government during the deliberations over the 1977 Soviet Constitution to have the Tatar A.S.S.R. upgraded to a full-fledged union republic (Iskhakov 1993b, 25–27; 1996, 10–13). While the request was not granted, the Tatar A.S.S.R. did enjoy "more control over its own affairs and more influence over central policy" than any other A.S.S.R. during the Soviet era, in particular enjoying a well-endowed Institute of Tatar Language and Literature as part of the Tatar A.S.S.R. branch of the Soviet Academy of Sciences (Gorenburg 2003, 33–36). Thus perhaps unsurprisingly, during the earliest days of glasnost, a nationalist movement took shape in Tatarstan, in the form of heated "discussions about the culture, language, and spiritual problems of Tatars, and also questions about the history and ethnography of the Tatar people" (Gubadullin 1995, 32).

In June 1988, a group of academics from Kazan State University and the Kazan branch of the Russian Academy of Science met during the Communist Party congress with the goal of turning nationalist talk into a more organized political movement in Tatarstan. This meeting, held under pressure from students who felt that the Communist Party could no longer "defend the national interests of Tatars," declared its intention to establish a group called the "Tatar Public Center" (T.P.C.) (*Tatar Public Centre* 1990, 155). On October 15, 1988, the day which Tatars traditionally commemorate as the fall of the Kazan Khanate and capture of the Kazan Kremlin by Ivan Grozny in 1552, 800–900 people gathered at the Kazan Kremlin to help finalize the new T.P.C.'s platform. One leader of the T.P.C. has referred to this day as the day when "the Tatar nationalist movement began to breathe again" (Grigorenko 1997, 11).

At first Tatar Communist Party Obkom officials were skeptical of the T.P.C., but as glasnost and democratization became more institutionalized in other parts of the Soviet Union, Tatar party officials relented and gave permission for the T.P.C. to hold its founding congress in Kazan in February 1989. The congress was attended by Tatar Obkom officials, but the *apparat* in Tatarstan remained cautious and did not allow the T.P.C. to register formally as a social organization until after the May 1989 Writer's Union conference in Tatarstan demanded that the T.P.C. be officially recognized. During this time the T.P.C. developed contacts with activists in the Baltic popular fronts, who helped to publish the proceedings from its inaugural conference in February 1989 when it proved difficult to get them published in the Tatar A.S.S.R. (*Tatar Public Centre* 1990, 155).

The T.P.C. platform was heavily informed by the Baltic popular fronts and their conception of self-determination and sovereignty. It argued that the hierarchical structure of Soviet ethno-federalism was illegal because it prevented the Tatars and other "nations" in the USSR from fully exercising their right to self-determination as provided for by the Helsinki Accords of 1975 and the Vienna Conventions of 1989 (article 2).[12] As such, the T.P.C. demanded that the Tatar A.S.S.R. should acquire "equal rights in the family of nations" by claiming the status of "a sovereign, union state" within the USSR. Relatedly, they argued that the hierarchical ethno-federal system of the Soviet Union must be equalized, and Tatarstan, like all other republics, henceforth should be considered a "sovereign state" (article 2.2, 2.3). Furthermore, in this newly-equalized Soviet Union, the central government would exercise only those powers which would be freely delegated to it by the constituent sovereign states of the union (article 2.3). The T.P.C.'s platform also called for Tatar to be declared an official state language in a newly sovereign Tatar republic (article 5), for the republic to maximize its economic sovereignty (article 6), for the social position of Tatars in the Tatar A.S.S.R. to be increased (article 8), for Tatar national education to be reformed and expanded (article 9), and for science and culture to be reformed and developed in the new Tatar republic (article 10).

After being officially registered in July 1989, the T.P.C. began to campaign for "upgrading" the Tatar A.S.S.R.'s status from an autonomous republic within Russia to that of a union republic. By August 1989, it had gathered 100,000 signatures in support of this goal (Gubadullin 1995, 42). The T.P.C. and other nationalist movements in Tatarstan such as the more radical "*Ittifak*" ("Unity") organization gained more and more popularity throughout 1989 and 1990, drawing large crowds to public meetings, holding poetry and other cultural gatherings, and eventually claiming as much as 12.2 percent of the population within their collective membership by late 1990 (Iskhakov 1996, 14–15).

As mass organizations and pro-sovereignty sentiment grew in the Tatar A.S.S.R., political and economic hierarchies between Moscow and the peripheries were also breaking down rapidly (Solnick 1996). Regional political elites could no longer count on Moscow to provide for their political legitimacy or economic livelihoods, therefore they began to court the emerging popular political forces in their own republics to promote their own power base in a time of rapid political change (Beissinger 1992; Roeder 1991). In essence, as glasnost and democratization progressed, and the Baltic sovereignty projects began to cast doubt on the future viability of the Soviet center, regional political elites began to try to co-opt the pro-sovereignty agenda which had spread from the Baltic states to Russia and its regions. Thus in the Tatar A.S.S.R. in February 1990 then First Secretary of the Tatar Obkom Communist Party Mintimer Shaimiyev publicly endorsed the T.P.C. for the first time (*Sovetskaya Tatariya* February 23, 1990, 1). By June 1990, the seventieth anniversary of the formation of the Tatar A.S.S.R., Shaimiyev was openly calling for the "increased right of the autonomous republics to direct their own economic and cultural development themselves," while asserting that the Tatar republic "remained an inalienable part of the united organism of the USSR" (*Sovetskaya Tatariya* June 17, 1990, 1).

While the activism of the T.P.C helped to push Shaimiyev to start seeking increased autonomy for the Tatar A.S.S.R., it was not until after the Russian Republic itself declared sovereignty in June 1990 that Shaimiyev and the Tatar Obkom elite began to consider seriously the possibility of formulating a unilateral Tatarstani claim to the status of sovereign statehood and union republic status. As one T.P.C. member recalled about the events of summer 1990 in Tatarstan, "What was there to fear if Russia herself had already declared sovereignty? The precedent was already there" (Grigorenko 1997, 11). At this point, for the leadership of the A.S.S.Rs, declaring sovereignty "appeared to pose little risk but offered the possibility of increased regional control and political legitimacy" (Kahn 2002, 107). Thus, during the Tatar A.S.S.R. Supreme Soviet session in August 1990, the T.P.C. and other organizations held daily mass demonstrations aimed at pressuring the Supreme Soviet to adopt the draft declaration of sovereignty which had been widely circulated in the republic in early August, and finally, on August 30, 1990 the Supreme Soviet of the Tatar A.S.S.R. adopted the "Declaration of Sovereignty of the Tatar S.S.R."

Understanding Sovereignty Projects in the Late Soviet Union

Why did claims to sovereign statehood become the central demand motivating popular protest in the Soviet Union during the collapse of communism? The author who has addressed this issue most frequently and directly, Mark R. Beissinger, argues that state-seeking behavior became the dominant mode of mobilized protest in the former Soviet Union because first political activists and eventually the mass public in the F.S.U. came to view the Soviet Union not as a legitimate ethno-federal state but rather as an illegitimate multi-ethnic empire (1993, 95; 1995, 162; 1996, 113–14; 2001 passim). In essence, the boundaries of Soviet ethno-federalism, which had been accepted as legitimate forms of statehood for seventy years of Soviet rule, came to be seen as "prisons" for the "captive" nations within the Soviet empire. Those who once had contented themselves with the ersatz, indeed "Orwellian" form of sovereignty under the Soviet Union, wherein sovereignty, usually connotating autonomy, instead meant total subjugation and unification, began instead to demand a more true and full experience of the word (Kahn 2002, 70–72). Beissinger's innovative work has detailed the intricate dynamics by which this "cognitive shift" and "massive reimagining of political communities" occurred. Several other authors have argued that, ironically, the "revolt of the nations" in the Soviet Union was in fact a direct consequence of the Soviet ethno-federal system that was meant to contain the ethno-nationalist aspirations and sentiments of non-Russians in the Soviet Union (Brubaker 1994; 1996; Slezkine 1994; Suny 1993; Vujacic and Zaslavsky 1991). Brubaker has formulated this argument most succinctly, asserting that the multifaceted and comprehensive Soviet ethno-federal system actually served to "institutionalize territorial nationhood" among the titular nationalities in the Soviet Union, creating "internal quasi-nation-states" which "provided a ready-made template for claims to sovereignty" (1994, 17, 41–42).

While this explanation of state or sovereignty-seeking behavior in the former Soviet Union is useful, it remains incomplete. Even if we accept that Soviet ethno-federal institutions fostered a territorially-based sense of nationhood among the non-Russians of the Soviet Union, focusing on the role of Soviet institutions can't explain fully how these actors came to believe that the forms of nationhood and statehood provided for under the auspices of Soviet ethno-federalism were inadequate and inauthentic and thus needed to be replaced with more real and authentic ones. There are at least two other models that activists in the Soviet Union were comparing their experience of nationhood and statehood under Soviet ethno-federalism against and finding it lacking; first, interpreted historical experiences of past nation-statehood specific to each non-Russian ethnic group generated by ethnic intellectuals and entrepreneurs; and second, the normative discourses about sovereign statehood, the nation and the right of peoples to self-determination which came to permeate the international community in the post-World War II era.

Some Western observers (d'Encausse 1993), but especially nationalist activists and intellectuals from the former Soviet Union themselves, often argue the "sleeping beauty" theory of nationalism when explaining state-seeking behavior in the former Soviet Union. According to this idea, the principle normative source of the nationalist state-seeking behavior which arose during glasnost was the "ancient," "long-buried," "dormant," and "re-pressed" ethno-nationalist consciousness of the group in question which was "reawakened" during glasnost. According to this interpretation, the national communities that began seeking new sovereign states during glasnost were not themselves constructed during the Soviet period by the system of ethno-federalism, but rather were preexisting nations that had been buried by the Soviet state, only to reemerge once the repressive and totalitarian political edifice of that state began to crack. Those who argue in this vein point to the importance of historical memories of earlier, pre-Soviet, independent statehoods in keeping the flame of national consciousness alive during seventy years of Soviet rule, until it could be fully rekindled and expressed during the period of Soviet decline. Yet this theory also fails to explain why "frozen" national communities in the Soviet Union would, upon their thawing during glasnost, come to view sovereign statehood as the ultimate attainment that would mark the salvation of the nation from its seventy-year Soviet prison and the fulfillment of long-buried national potential.

Implicit in both of these useful yet incomplete explanations for the sovereignty and state-seeking behavior during glasnost is the assumption that communities which conceive of themselves as nations, whether constructed by Soviet ethno-federalism or preexisting entities frozen by the repression of the Soviet state, will automatically seek statehood (more precisely, sovereign statehood), as the way to fulfill their longings and potential as a collective national entity. Walker (2003), Beissinger, and others demonstrate that the forms of "national self-determination" and "sovereignty" that Soviet ethno-federalism provided for non-Russians came to be viewed during the glasnost era as inadequate and inauthentic, thus presupposing that some other, more valid understanding of how national self-determinationist yearnings should be realized through sovereign statehood came to replace old Soviet models. The influence of pervasive international normative understandings about the relationship between nations, their self-determination, and sovereign statehood in the modern era in this process must be made more explicit. Essentially, this is the belief that sovereign statehood is the pinnacle of social and political organization in the international system, the logical aspiration for nations seeking to fulfill their "right to self-determination"; in other words, all nations should seek states, and all states are in actuality or should be ideally, nation-states (Hall 1999; McNeely 1995; Smith 1986b; Tilly 1996). It is this pervasive understanding of the relationship between sovereignty, statehood, and nationness that helped to inform the belief of Soviet actors that the sovereignty they "enjoyed" under Soviet ethno-federalism needed to be replaced by a more real and authentic form.

The pervasiveness of international normative understandings about sovereignty and nation-states was cultivated by the Baltic diaspora and transmitted first through the networks of Baltic activists who rekindled the desire for a "more authentic" form of Baltic statehood modeled on contemporary international norms of statehood and then passed that model on to other actors in the former Soviet Union. For activists in the Soviet Union during glasnost international normative expectations about nations deserving sovereign states (which are largely the product of the international norm of the right of peoples to self-determination), and international normative prescriptions about how those sovereign nation-states should act (that sovereign nation-states should enjoy budgetary and legislative independence, engage in diplomacy, and participate in the life of the international community), came to *supplant* the more constrained and limited (in effect, empty) parameters of the models offered to national communities under Soviet ethno-federalism.

This shift was an evolutionary process and it was not immediately clear that the early sovereignty-seeking demands of the Baltic states and other union republics could not be accommodated by reforming the Soviet ethno-federal system (Beissinger 1993, 1996; Walker 2003). By spring 1990, however, the Baltic states' expectations had evolved to a "maximal" point where they sought full and unambiguous independence from the Soviet Union and international recognition of that independence. Shortly after the August 1991 coup, the rest of the Union republics also "maximized" their sovereignty projects and sought full and unambiguous independence from the Soviet Union, resulting in the dissolution of that state and the creation of the C.I.S. in December 1991. The Tatar A.S.S.R. was a full participant in this cognitive shift and subsequent mobilizational wave, which led its leaders to make claims to sovereign statehood in 1990. However, as subsequent chapters demonstrate, the republic's sovereignty project has never become "maximal" in the sense that it has ever made a formal declaration of independence or secession from Russia. Indeed, the crucially important aspect of Tatarstan's attempts to fill its claims of state sovereignty with legal and empirical meaning over the next decade and a half is that, due to the ambiguous and fungible nature of sovereignty and the intersubjective, negotiated and always partial nature of constructing sovereignty in practice, Tatarstan has effectively (if not intentionally) crafted a framework for the negotiated, consensual, and meaningful division of the empirical and symbolic attributes associated with nation-statehood between the center and the periphery (which is the essence of federalism, especially in a multiethnic context). And it has done so *without* pushing Moscow to the point of violence, as was done in Chechnya. The later chapters of this volume chronicle the development of this pattern, and discuss the impact of these evolutions on Russian federalism, Russian statehood, and Russian multiculturalism. Before turning to that discussion, however, a careful look at Tatarstan's declaration of sovereignty itself is warranted.

Analyzing Claims to Sovereignty: Tatarstan's 1990 Declaration of Sovereignty

The August 1990 Tatarstani Declaration of Sovereignty is a brief document composed of only six articles, which closely follows the Russian declaration issued two months earlier.[13] It asserts that because the Tatar A.S.S.R.'s existing status as a mere autonomous republic "no longer serves to promote the interests and political, economic, social, and spiritual development of the multinational people of Tatarstan," the republic unilaterally declares its "state sovereignty" and makes itself a "democratic legal state" whose *own* constitution and laws henceforth have legal precedence on its territory (emphasis mine) (preamble, articles 1 and 6). The declaration also claimed the status of a union republic (S.S.R.) for Tatarstan, asserted that Tatarstan would participate in the formation of a new USSR Treaty, and that the republic would begin preparing to sign a bilateral treaty with the R.S.F.S.R. (articles 4 and 5).

Like the leaders of the Baltic republics and Russia before them, the Tatarstani elites who crafted the August 1990 Declaration of Sovereignty willfully employed the ambiguity inherent in the concept of sovereignty to their advantage (Kahn 2002; Walker 2003). On the one hand, Tatarstan claims to possess state sovereignty, indicates that its actions are motivated by the right of all peoples to self-determination, signals its intention to sign treaties with both the Russian republic and the other sovereign states of a renewed USSR, and claims full legislative independence on its territory. All of these provisions imply an understanding of state sovereignty informed previous Soviet norms of sovereignty and yet extended by an understanding of contemporary international norms about state sovereignty and diplomatic practice. For example, nowhere in the document does Tatarstan specify its exact legal relationship to either the Soviet Union or the Russian Federation beyond stating its intention to conclude treaties with these two parties (a sharp break from the Soviet past). Yet despite these indications of the aspiration to a more authentic form of sovereign statehood informed by international norms about sovereignty, the declaration is oddly bereft of any real details about how this sovereignty is to be exercised. There are no provisions in the declaration for border control and defense, currency and customs regimes, or any other of the institutional practices of sovereignty as they exist in the international community.

On the other hand, Tatarstan's Declaration of Sovereignty changed the name of the republic to the "Tatar Soviet Socialist Republic," dropping the autonomous qualifier and in essence claiming union republic status within the USSR. This indicates that at this point in 1990, the form of "sovereign statehood" Tatarstan's elites envisioned for the republic was a form of political organization which could be contained within and was largely based on the parameters set by the existing system of Soviet ethno-federalism. As will be shown in the next chapter, however, when the framework of Soviet ethno-federalism disintegrated, Tatarstani elites' understandings of the parameters of their republic's claimed sovereign statehood evolved and indeed expanded, becoming more and more closely modeled on international practices of sovereign statehood.

The August 1990 Tatarstani Declaration of Sovereignty also contained what would become an enduring tension about the nature of the national community in whose name the republic's quest to project state sovereignty was being undertaken. The preamble states that the declaration of sovereignty was being issued out of a feeling of responsibility for "the fate of the multinational people of the republic" but also in order to "realize the inalienable right of the Tatar nation and all the peoples of the republic to self-determination." The declaration goes on to guarantee equal rights for citizens regardless of nationality and guarantees the preservation and development of the national languages of other national minorities in Tatarstan, but names only Tatar and Russia as official state languages in Tatarstan (article 3). Thus while the eponymous Tatar nation's "inalienable" right to self-determination is cited as a source of the republic's sovereignty and the Tatar language is given official state status, these ethno-nationalist identification are qualified by a policy of official civic multiculturalism which is conveyed by the document's many references to the multiethnic population of the republic. Indeed in his speech congratulating the population of Tatarstan on the adoption of the declaration of sovereignty, President Shaimiyev emphasized the civic and multiethnic nature of the republic's claimed sovereignty *over all other aspects* of the declaration (*Sovetskaya Tatariya* August 30, 1990). That both Russian and Tatar were named as official languages in the declaration (as opposed to Tatar alone, as some ethnic Tatar nationalist activists had wanted), and that respect for other national languages in the republic was given lip service in the document as well further indicates the intention of Tatarstani sovereignty seekers to promote civic, multicultural understandings of nationhood alongside ethnic Tatar claims from the very beginning of the sovereignty project.

Given the political climate in Russia in 1990, it was relatively costless politically (and potentially quite lucrative economically) for Tatarstan to issue its declarations of state sovereignty (Kahn 2002, 107). The truly difficult, and truly interesting, task lay ahead—trying to fill those paper declarations with real empirical and symbolic meaning. The next decade and a half would be a continuous struggle with the Yeltsin and Putin administrations about what the republic's newly claimed sovereignty actually meant in terms of its status and powers at home in Tatarstan, in the new Russian Federation, and in the international arena.

Notes

1. See also Herrera (2005) for a highly pertinent and very interesting discussion of the cognitive revolution in economic thinking and its relation to regional sovereignty claims that occurred during the late 1980s and early 1990s in Russia.

2. The 2002 census of the Russian Federation was highly politicized in Tatarstan—there was a great deal of controversy about a Russian Federal proposition to classify ethnic Tatars into many subcategories to "dilute" their numbers, while as early as 1995 it was deemed very important by some Tatar intellectuals that Tatars remain a plurality or even a majority in Tatarstan according to any new census. See Iskhakov (1995) for an early discussion of the politics of the census in Tatarstan. On the politicization of censuses in general see Arel and Kertzer (2002); for the Russian case in particular see Arel (2002) and Sokolovsky (2002).

3. In the year 921 the head of the Great Bulgar state, Almas, sent a request to the Caliph of Baghdad for instruction in Islam. In reply, the caliph sent his ambassador Ibn-Fadlan, whose chronicles of his journey supply much of our information about Great Bulgar. In 984 the Bulgar state signed a trade agreement with the princes of Kiev and Rus, which lasted until Batu's invasion of 1236. For further discussion, see Golden (1982, 257) and Rorlich (1986, 12).

4. On relations between Moscow and Kazan see Pelenski (1974) and Ostrowski (1998). See chapter 4 of this book for further discussion of the role that the fall of Kazan in 1552 plays in contemporary Tatar understandings of statehood, nationhood, and sovereignty-seeking.

5. This distinction is represented in the Russian language through the use of two different adjectives: "Russkii," which signifies all things having to do with the ethnic Russian people, and "Rossisskii," which signifies all things having to do with the Russian Empire, implying the multiethnic nature of its subjects.

6. The term jadidism comes from the term for the "new method" of teaching Arabic that these Muslim reformers favored, usul-al-jadid.

7. The most comprehensive work in English on this period in the Volga-Ural region is the excellent study by historian Daniel Shafer (1995). Also see Zaki Validi Togan's memoirs (1997). On the revolutionary period among the Volga Tatars, Rorlich (1986) has an excellent chapter on Muslim national communism, but the definitive work is by Bennigsen and Wimbush (1980).

8. The Tatar language name for the Volga River is "Idel." As conceived of by these Tatar and Bashkir activists, an Idel-Ural state would extend broadly in the Middle Volga and Ural Mountain region, and would encompass other ethnic groups within the Middle Volga region, such as the Chuvash, Udmurt and Mari people. Such an expanded Idel-Ural state is thus in contrast to a more limited Tatar-Bashkir state which would be limited to the territories of the just those two ethnic groups within the Volga-Ural region. I am indebted to Uli Schamiloglu for pointing out this important distinction. For more on the idea of an Idel-Ural state, see the recent reprint of Gayaz Ishaki's early twentieth-century classic *Idel-Ural* (Kazan: Tatarskoye Knizhnoye Isdatel'stvo, 1993), which contains an interesting afterward by Tatarstani Presidential Advisor Rafael Khakimov. It should be noted that many Bashkir activists rejected outright the idea of an Idel-Ural state, fearing it would be dominated by the wealthier, more numerous Volga Tatars.

9. I put "national" in quotes here because the idea of a "national" community is one that is problematized in this study, while under Soviet ethno-federalism the cultural and educational institutions of titular populations in ethno-federal units were unproblematically referred to as national.

10. For example, in 1984, Gail Lapidus noted that while there was the theoretical possibility that national cadres would use the ethno-federal system to "promote cultural or political nationalism in its various manifestations," she concluded that the widespread majority of national cadres and intellectuals were "devoted to working within the system" (1984, 576). Similarly, in 1987, Alexander Motyl concluded that the extreme control of "social space" by the Communist Party and the KGB disallowed the possibility that non-Russian native cadres would rebel against the Soviet system in any substantive way. Even after glasnost, many Western Sovietologists continued to believe that the Soviet ethno-federal system possesses a basic legitimacy and that it was not in imminent danger of collapsing from within (Beissinger 1993, 93). Many western Sovietologists also believed that the Soviet state had succeeded to a large degree in its quest to co-opt its non-Russian populations through ethno-federalism.

11. Dunlop (1993, 61) argues that like Gorbachev, Yeltsin was naive in his views of inter-ethnic relations in the Soviet Union and didn't understand that encouraging sovereignty projects and radical decentralization would lead to the break-up of the Soviet Union. Yeltsin's later attempts to limit the sovereignty projects of the Russian republics, half-hearted and ineffectual as they were, suggest that Dunlop is correct.

12. All citations in this section are drawn from the Tatar Public Center's program, reprinted in the journal *Central Asian Studies* in 1990. See *Tatar Public Centre* (1990).

13. All references to the Tatarstani Declaration of Sovereignty are from the reprint of the document in *Suverennyi Tatarstan: Sovereign Tatarstan*, (Moscow: Plenipotentiary Representation of Tatarstan, 1997), 7–8.

CHAPTER TWO

Projecting Sovereignty in the Russian Federation: Federation-Building or Federation-Wrecking?

Tatarstan's sovereignty project has helped to fundamentally transform the shape of the Russian Federation in the post-Soviet period. In the opinion of many observers, however, this influence has been almost uniformly negative. The Russian republics' sovereignty projects, and Tatarstan's in particular, have been charged with: introducing an "astounding" degree of institutional asymmetry that poses a "serious concern" for the long-term stability of the Russian Federation (Kahn 2002, 48); with pushing Russia closer to a confederal state governed by the doctrine of nullification rather than a true federal spirit through their insistence on "treaty-based federalism" (Kahn 2002, 40); and, perhaps most damagingly, with providing a "breeding ground for ethnonationalism and authoritarianism" in the republics (Hale 1998; King 2000; Opalski 2001, 301–03; Smith 1998). In short, sovereignty seeking regions such as Tatarstan stand accused of "threaten[ing] the whole transition to democracy in Russia" (Kahn 2002, 4).

A close examination of the trajectory of relations between Tatarstan and the federal center in Moscow since the collapse of communism suggests that while some of this criticism in warranted, in fact the overall and potential future impact of Tatarstan's sovereignty project on the evolution of federal relations in Russia is much more nuanced and positive than most analysts have allowed. It also demonstrates that some of the more deleterious effects

of Tatarstan's sovereignty project on federalism in Russia have been enabled
or promoted by the federal center itself, particularly under the administration of Boris Yeltsin. This suggests that blame for the failure of federalism to
develop more robustly in Russia must be shared between the center and the
regions. Furthermore, as I will discuss in chapter 5, the most recent "federal
reforms" proposed by the Putin administration have cast doubt on the proposal that it is sovereignty-seeking regions who pose the greatest threat to
Russia's federal integrity; in the climate of extreme recentralization fostered
by the Putin administration, the republican sovereignty projects, subjected
to certain limitations and regulations, many of which have already been
adopted by Tatarstan's leaders, represent the best of hope of preserving the
faintest hint of true federal spirit and structure in Russia.

Theories of Federalism and the
Problem of Sovereignty Projects

Theoretically speaking, there is no reason to assume a priori that Tatarstan's
sovereignty project would represent a dangerous or even "fatal" threat to the
development of a functioning form of federalism in Russia in the post-Soviet
period. Indeed, as even a critic of the sovereignty projects like Jeffrey Kahn
notes, federalism as a system "requires a complex understanding of sovereignty—never absolute, always partial and parceled among multiple levels of
government" (Kahn 2002, 98). This is even more true in multiethnic states,
where federalism is considered appropriate because it "assumes the worth
and validity of diversity" (Gagnon and Gibbs 1999, 75), and also provides
the framework for the "institutionalization of both the plurality and asymmetry of allegiances in compatible ways" (Karmis and Gagnon 2001). Federal
frameworks can accommodate even severely divided societies that are made
up of one or more self-proclaimed nations, such as Canada and Spain, and in
such cases, even extreme federal asymmetry, such as that potentially engendered by Russia's republican sovereignty projects, "can in fact be a condition
for governmental success" (Agranoff 1999, 11–12).

However for federalism to serve as a successful way of accommodating
ethnonational diversity, as the leaders of Tatarstan's sovereignty project
envision it to be, the scales of regional sovereignty or asymmetry must be balanced by an analogous commitment on the part of the regions to "a political
project that ensures at least a minimal federal unity" (Karmis and Gagnon
2001, 172). That is, those who seek recognition for their difference and
aspirations for autonomy in some form of institutionalized asymmetry, like

Tatarstan, must also demonstrate a fundamental respect for and commitment to the "fabric of wholeness" that envelops the entire federal entity they reside in (Agranoff 1999, 14).

It is on exactly this count that Tatarstan's sovereignty project has been found wanting by the observers quoted above, accused of not allowing that a federal system must be considered as something more than just the sum of its parts and of not displaying any, let alone sufficient, commitment to the federal project in Russia (Kahn 2002, 11–12, 170). Yet when the full course of relations between Moscow and Tatarstan in the post-Soviet period is considered, we see that the perpetrators of the Tatarstani sovereignty project have in fact demonstrated a consistent and increasing commitment to "federal unity" in Russia, while simultaneously pushing Moscow to accept the fact that the "real and substantive decision-making powers" that the republics have achieved through their sovereignty projects in fact represent the "actual essence" of federalism and not a plot to destroy Russia's state integrity (Konitzer-Smirnov 2003, 49).

Furthermore, given the direction that President Vladimir Putin pushed political reforms in Russia, the strategy pursued by Tatarstan during the Yeltsin years—striving for the maximal projection of state sovereignty in the Russian Federal arena and then backing off when met with resistance from center—now appears to be a wise one. Having learned from historical experience and thus perhaps anticipating that the heavy hand of unitarism and centralization would eventually come back down on them, the leaders of the republican sovereignty project in Tatarstan took Yeltsin at his word in 1990 and sought to "swallow as much sovereignty" as they could for as long as they could, without raising the ire of Moscow. Yet now, in the face of federal pressure, they are willing to sacrifice some attributes of their sovereignty in the name of finding a workable and optimum balance of powers between the center and periphery in Russia. Indeed the chief goal and chief utility of the republican sovereignty projects during the Putin era appears to be to act as the potentially final bulwark against the return of unitary, vertical, government in Russia. To that end, framing the push and pull between center and periphery in the form of republican sovereignty projects has proven quite useful over the past decade and half and will remain so in the future. The claim to a form of republican sovereignty that is protected but not absolute, meaningfully shared and negotiated rather than jealously horded and wielded as a weapon by either side, provides a highly effective discursive and institutional logic for the future development of federalism in Russia, particularly given its multinational character.

The Yeltsin Era: Apogee of Tatarstan's Sovereignty Project

The federal system that emerged during Boris Yeltsin's nearly decade-long presidency is emblematic of that entire era, being variously described as "more unplanned and more asymmetrical than nearly any other federation" (Smith 1998, 3), and as an "entirely ad hoc" system (Hahn 2004) that represented "the anarchy of the political marketplace rather than the consideration of a coherent nationalities policy" (Smith 1998, 3). In fact, some authors question whether the system Yeltsin bequeathed to Russia should be considered a federation at all, asserting that "behind the thin veneer of federal structures, a mass of conceptual and legal contradictions reduce[d] federal rules into a sink of malfeasance, noncompliance and brinkmanship" (Kahn 2000, 4). Some observers are more sanguine about the development of Russian federalism under Yeltsin, arguing that the push and pull between the center in the Moscow and the periphery during this period (led by Tatarstan), ultimately resulted in the establishment of "actual" federalism in Russia, defined as the presence of subnational governments with real and substantive decision-making power and sovereignty, for the first time in over a millennium (Kontizer-Smirnov 2003, 49; Moses 2003). Others take a positive view even of the controversial "parade of treaties," again led by Tatarstan, that resulted in 47 of Russia's 88 subjects signing separate bilateral agreements with the Yeltsin administration, claiming that this process represented "a reasonably acceptable start" to federation-building in Russia, despite the fact that the process was not fully democratic nor its results ever fully institutionalized (Hahn 2004).

A careful review of the way in which Tatarstan attempted to fulfill its claims to sovereignty in the Russian federal arena during the Yeltsin administration reveals that while the republic certainly engaged in an effort to maximize both its symbolic and institutional powers within the federal framework during this era, and certainly worked to push the limits of federalism in Russia to a further horizon than they had ever been before, at no point in this process did the leaders of Tatarstan's sovereignty project ever make any type of claim to any form of statehood *independent of or outside of* the Russian federal framework. Yes, Tatarstani elites assertively used claims to sovereignty to shape the federal framework to their advantage, but also assiduously and consistently reaffirmed to audiences in Moscow and at home that the republic was fundamentally and integrally a part of the Russian federal framework. Thus I argue that Tatarstan's actions during the Yeltsin era represent an example of federation building in action—the disputatious but necessary, contentious but negotiated, parceling out of the attributes of sovereignty between center and periphery that is the very heart of federal systems. In this regard, the Yeltsin period is of fundamental importance, resulting in the achievement of a much more genuine federal system than ever existed under the Soviet federation, and perhaps representing the freest and most egalitarian negotiation of political authorities between center and periphery in Russia at any point ever, with the possible exception of the 1905 and 1917 revolutions.

Negotiating Sovereignty and Federalism Through the Federal Treaty and 1993 Constitution

During the chaotic period when the USSR was dissolving, Tatarstani elites pursued a pragmatic and flexible strategy aimed at acquiring the attributes of state sovereignty. While never openly declaring independence as the union republics had done, they nonetheless continued to demand the same political rights as the union republics and to mimic the actions of the union republics, such as inviting themselves to participate in the C.I.S. and seeking allies among the former union republics in the sovereignty-seeking process. As the union republics themselves took on more and more of the attributes of sovereign statehood and began to loosen themselves from the confines of the Soviet ethno-federal system, Tatarstani elites sought to do the same in the name of their own newly-declared state sovereignty.

That the legacy of Soviet ethno-federalism continued to define Tatarstan's understanding of the limits and possibilities of its own declared state sovereignty is also evident from the fact that the republic never unambiguously announced its independence from or intent to secede from Russia. This careful strategy of seeking the maximal possible levels of empirical sovereignty without making explicit claims to maximal juridical sovereignty (which could be politically harmful) is the hallmark of Tatarstan's sovereignty project, sometimes referred to as the "Tatarstan Model" (Bukharaev 1999; Tagirov 1997). However, after the final collapse of the USSR at the end of 1991, the type of sovereign statehood Tatarstani elites began to imagine as possible and thus pursued through the Tatarstan Model became less constricted by old Soviet norms and became directly modeled on international understandings and practices of sovereign statehood.

After the disappearance of the USSR, the demand for the conclusion of a new bilateral, "treaty-type agreement" between Tatarstan and Russia became the centerpiece of Tatarstan's pursuit of sovereignty. In March 1992, in an effort to consolidate domestic support for their ongoing efforts, Tatarstani officials held a republic-wide referendum aimed at gaining support for Tatarstan's claim to be "a sovereign state and subject of international law" and for the demand that Russia restructure its relations with the new sovereign state of Tatarstan on the basis of a treaty-type agreement. The referendum asked voters if they agreed that, as a sovereign state, Tatarstan should be considered "a subject of international law whose relations with the Russian Federation and other republics and states should be now formed on the basis of bilateral agreements" (Verkhovnogo 1992b, 13). In explaining the referendum to the citizens of Tatarstan, the Supreme Soviet of Tatarstan introduced what would become an important discursive element of Tatarstan's sovereignty project in the Russian Federation in the post-Soviet period—the assertion that while Tatarstan's sovereign statehood demanded a new "interstate" bilateral treaty with Russia, such a treaty would not indicate the secession of Tatarstan from the Russian Federation or the fracturing of the territorial integrity of the Russian Federation in any way:

> The question on the referendum doesn't address the exit or non-exit of Tatarstan from the composition of the Russian Federation, or the "freeing of Tatarstan" from Russia. The goal of the referendum is to determine if the change of Tatarstan from an autonomous republic to a sovereign state which remains united with the Russian Federation in a common economic and geopolitical space but, which based on commonly-recognized principles of equality and self-determination of peoples, seeks to build its relations with Russia and other states and republics in a new way, on the basis of bilateral agreements and the delegation of some authorities to the Russian Federation on this basis, answers to the will of the people of Tatarstan. (Presidium 1992, 14)

This quotation illustrates the essence of the Tatarstan Model of sovereignty-seeking. Tatarstan asserts its sovereign statehood and inherent equality with Russia and other states (hence the demand for bilateral, treaty-based relations), but denies that this necessitates a rupture of Russia's geopolitical or economic unity. This then is the central thrust of Tatarstan's sovereignty project; the attempt to maximize Tatarstan's juridical and empirical state sovereignty in both its external and internal aspects without provoking the Russian Federation into possible negative political, economic, or military retaliation by making overt claims to geopolitical or territorial secession or independence.

Tatarstan's Supreme Soviet's assurances to the contrary notwithstanding, Russian federal officials, including Constitutional Court Chairman Valery Zorkin and President Boris Yeltsin, did indeed interpret the proposed March 1992 referendum in Tatarstan and the demand for treaty-based relations with Russia as a threat to the constitutional and territorial integrity of the Russian Federation (CDPSP 1992, #11, 21–22). Russian president Boris Yeltsin went so far as to directly address the population of Tatarstan on the eve of the referendum, warning them that the leadership of Tatarstan was pursuing a course which "presupposes that Tatarstan is not part of Russia" and that passing the referendum could have "grave consequences for the future of Russia as a state" (*CDPSP* 1992, #11, 21–22).

Eventually, the referendum passed with 61.4 percent of the 81.6 percent of those Tatarstani citizens who participated voting for it, prompting President Shaimiyev to assert that the referendum had truly "codified Tatarstan's status as a sovereign state" (*CDPSP* 1992, #12, 6). He continued on to say that in light of this new reality, Tatarstan could not sign the Russian Federal Treaty as scheduled on March 31, 1992, "for fear that [Tatarstan] might lose its sovereign status." Rather he argued that Tatarstan's next move should be the conclusion of an "equitable" treaty with Russia, in which certain powers such as defense, security, and border protection would be "delegated by Tatarstan to the Russian Federation" (*CDPSP* 1992 #12, 6). It is important to emphasize the use of language by Tatarstani officials in these exchanges. By insisting that any future agreement with Russia be an equal one between two equal parties and that in such an agreement Tatarstan would delegate certain powers to the Russian Federation, political elites in Tatarstan attempted to assert the symbolic agency and independence of the republic as a sovereign state. This allowed them to represent the concrete limitations of Tatarstan's sovereignty-seeking project in the Russian Federation (i.e., the fundamental location of Tatarstan in the Russian Federation and the impracticality of Tatarstan controlling its own borders or defense) in a way that nonetheless legitimated and strengthened the overall thrust of the republic's claims to sovereignty.

After declining to sign the Russian Federal Treaty in April 1992, Tatarstani elites continued to call for the conclusion of a bilateral treaty-type agreement with Russia and maintained on-going negotiations with the Russian Federal government toward this end. They also made preparations to draft and adopt an independent constitution for Tatarstan. In fall 1992, as the Tatarstani Supreme Soviet neared its vote on a draft republican constitution, Russian Federation officials arrived in Tatarstan in order to make sure that the Tatarstani Constitution "conformed" to the Russian Federation's constitution. These officials observed that if the republic were to adopt the new Tatarstani constitution in the form being proposed, it would amount to "the legal codification of Tatarstan's detachment as a state from the Russian Federation, no matter what Tatarstan's leaders might say" (*CDPSP* 1992, #43, 16). In the first instance of what became a pattern of staking out a maximal position and then backing off and agreeing to compromises demanded by the center, Tatarstan's leadership agreed to some changes that Moscow requested, and the new constitution was adopted by the republic's Supreme Soviet on November 6, 1992.

The new Tatarstani Constitution contained many interesting formulations aimed at legally establishing both the external and internal aspects of the republic's state sovereignty while not rupturing the political unity of Russian space. While it unambiguously states that the republic is a sovereign state (articles 1 and 61), and a subject of international law (article 61), it also acknowledged that Tatarstan is "associated" with the Russian Federation on the basis of a treaty of mutually-delegated authorities and powers (article 61). The claim to be "associated" with the Russian Federation by virtue of a treaty is one of two times Russia is mentioned in the Tatarstani Constitution, the other being article 19, which asserts that while Tatarstan has its own citizenship norms, residents of the republic also simultaneously possess citizenship in the Russian Federation.

In the wake of the signing of the constitution, Mintimer Shaimiyev took pains to publicly insist that Tatarstan "was not destroying and did not plan on destroying the territorial integrity of Russia," pointing out that the new constitution merely codified the long-standing Tatarstani call for a new federation based on "treaty-based relations" with Russia (*Rossiiskaya Gazeta* December 19, 1992, 1). Shaimiyev went on to assert that this type of treaty-based "federal union" of sovereign states, wherein the member units would "delegate some powers to the center" would serve as a much stronger state structure for post-Soviet Russia than the one currently being held together tenuously by the Russian Federation Treaty of March 1992.

In the months following the adoption of the November 1992 Tatarstani Constitution, Tatarstani elites continued negotiations with Russian Federation officials about the possibility of a bilateral treaty, and also participated in the process of drafting a new Russian constitution. The Shaimiyev administration in Kazan insisted that any draft of a new constitution must contain a special provision acknowledging Tatarstan's declared sovereign status within a renewed Russian federation. As Shaimiyev put it, "without such a special provision for Tatarstan, no real federation can exist in Russia, but only the continuation of a unitary state" (*Tatarstan* 1993, #10, 25). Several aspects of the 1993 draft constitution lent credence to the republic's fear that without special recognition of its new sovereign status, the document would likely serve up a wolf-like unitary state in sheep-like federal clothing. For example, while article 1.1 of the text refers to Russia as a "democratic, federal, rule of law state," article 1.4 boldly states that "the sovereignty of the Russian Federation shall apply to its entire territory" and that the federal constitution and federal laws "shall have supremacy throughout the entire territory of the Russian Federation." Tatarstan and other regions were also disappointed that the 1993 draft constitution did not refer explicitly to or include the text of the 1992 Federal Treaty, that it privileged individual rights over minority group rights, that it did not explicitly recognize republican sovereignty, and that in general it "allowed the federal center to control the well of power, with the republics permitted only to take for themselves what little remained outside the limits of federal jurisdiction" (Kahn 2000, 137–38).

The only concessions to the regions in the 1993 draft constitution were article 5.2, which allowed republics to have their own constitutions and legislation, and article 11.3, which stated that the delimitation of powers and authorities between the federal center and the regions (the heart of any federal system) would be determined by "the present Constitution, Federal and other Treaties on the delimitation of scopes of authorities and powers." These provisions were not sufficient to support the type of "bottom-up" federalism the regions envisioned, however, and combined with the generally unreceptive attitude of the Russian federal leadership to recognizing a special constitutional status for Tatarstan, prompted the republic to symbolically signal its displeasure with the shape the federation was taking.[1] This tendency is illustrated by Tatarstan's "unofficial boycott" of the April 1993 referendum on Yeltsin and the future of the Russian Federation, when Tatarstani officials allowed voting booths to open, but openly discouraged citizens to participate. Ultimately, only 23 percent of eligible voters participated, making the results of the referendum invalid in Tatarstan (McAuley 1997, 75).

Later in 1993, as Yeltsin prepared to offer the new draft federal constitution to the citizenry in another nation-wide referendum to be held simultaneously with the December 1993 elections to the Russian Federation Duma, Tatarstani officials continued to insist that any new Russian Federation must be based on the principles of "bottom-up delegation of powers" and "treaty-based relations." The chair of Tatarstan's Supreme Soviet, Farid Mukhametshin, argued that while Tatarstan wanted to work within a Russian federal framework, the republic also wanted its sovereign status within that federation clearly marked by the signing of a bilateral treaty with Russia (*Izvestiya Tatarstan* September 8, 1993, 2). President Shaimiyev's closest political advisor, Rafael Khakimov, offered that Tatarstan should push for some type of creative federal relationship with Russia, perhaps like the "freely-associated status" Puerto Rico enjoyed within the United States (*Sovetskaya Tatariya* November 27, 1993, 4).

In November 1993, the Tatarstani Supreme Soviet issued a resolution that was highly critical of the new Russian Federation draft constitution, and while there was not an official boycott of the December 1993 Russian Federal Assembly elections and constitutional referendum in Tatarstan, there was an informal boycott urged by both the republican leadership and nationalist opposition in Tatarstan, which led to only a 14 percent participation rate and the results being nullified in the republic (McAuley 1997, 78). While this marked a low-point in federal relations with Moscow, it is important to point out that Tatarstan did not try to disrupt the elections in the republic nor did they use the opportunity to assert the illegality of the new Russian constitution or to declare independence or secession from Russia. In this sense, the contentious moment of December 1993 in Russia is somewhat analogous to the vote on the repatriation of the Canadian constitution in 1982, which also failed in Quebec. The 1982 Canadian vote, while serving to reinforce the striving for sovereignty among the Quebecois, also did not lead to the destruction of the federation but rather to a revival of creative attempts at federation-building in Canada (though both the Meech Lake and Charlottetown Accords would later prove unsuccessful)(Karmis and Gagnon 2001; Knop et. al 1995).

The February 1994 Treaty and Agreements Between Russia and Tatarstan

Dismayed by Tatarstan's continued antagonism towards federation-building efforts in Russia, and hoping to entice the republic to participate in the Russian Federal Assembly make-up elections scheduled for March 13, 1994, Russian federal officials, led by the personal efforts of Boris Yeltsin, finally reached a compromise with the Tatarstani delegation on a bilateral, treaty-type agreement in February 1994. Officially titled the "Treaty on the Delimitation of Jurisdictional Subjects and Mutual Delegation of Authorities Between the State Bodies of Power of the Russian Federation and the State Bodies of Power of the Republic of Tatarstan," the February 1994 document was the realization of Tatarstan's long-standing demands for recognition of its unique status in the Russian Federation. Like the 1990 Tatarstan Declaration of Sovereignty and 1992 Tatarstani Constitution, the language of the February 1994 treaty is quite vague in places, and quite contradictory in others, allowing much room for interpretation and negotiation on the part of both parties. However in essence the agreement divides political and administrative authority for the various institutional practices of sovereign statehood between Russia and Tatarstan into three main categories—those reserved solely for Tatarstan, those that Tatarstan and Russia are "jointly" authorized to pursue, and those reserved solely for the Russian Federation.

The preamble of the February 1994 treaty proclaims that Tatarstan is "a state united with the Russian Federation according to the Constitution of the Russian Federation, the Constitution of the Republic of Tatarstan, and this Treaty, [a state] which also participates in international and foreign economic relations."[2] Article 1 of the treaty goes on to state that the delineation of sovereign authorities in the agreement is "governed by both the Constitution of the Russian Federation and the Constitution of the Republic of Tatarstan." The imprecision and seemingly deliberate vagueness of these formulae is intriguing. Tatarstan is declared a state (although not a "sovereign" state), which is "united" with the Russian Federation, but united only by virtue of said treaty, and united in such a way that both its own constitution and the Russian federal constitution are recognized as authoritative sources of state sovereignty. Recall that in the 1993 Russian Constitution, the 1992 Federal Treaty and "other" treaties are also cited as authoritative sources for the division of sovereignty between the center and periphery in Russia. Thus the February 1994 Treaty muddied the legal waters surrounding the division of powers and authorities between Moscow and Kazan almost to the point of absurdity, with at least five documents (Tatarstan's 1990 Declaration of Sovereignty, the 1992 Federal Treaty, the 1992 Tatarstani Constitution, the 1993 Russian Federal Constitution, and the 1994 Treaty) serving as legal reference points for the structure of the federal relationship between Tatarstan and Moscow.

The 1994 Moscow-Kazan treaty in particular is fraught with contradictions. The attempt to divide state powers and authorities into three discreet baskets is not entirely successful—many of the elements that fall under the joint competency of Russia and Tatarstan in Article 3 of the February 1994 treaty also appear to be listed as belonging solely to the authority of Tatarstan or of Russia elsewhere in the document. For example, determination of pricing policy, the mobilization and management of the military industrial complex, and management of power, transport, communication, and information systems are listed in both Article 3 as being jointly administered by the two parties and in Article 4 as being only Russia's responsibility. Likewise, according to Article 2, Tatarstan is supposed to be solely responsible for all questions of jurisprudence on its territory, while Article 4 gives the Russian Federation sole responsibility for "the judicial system" (it is also not clear if this responsibility is for the specifically federal judicial system or not). The treaty is also silent about how those institutional practices and policy arenas which are to be jointly administered by between the two parties will work in practice.

Further complicating the already hazy legal divisions of sovereign authority between Tatarstan and Russia are the several supplementary agreements signed between the two parties before and at the same time as the February 1994 treaty.[3] Some of these agreements do provide more detailed provisions for the joint or coordinated exercise of sovereignty by Russia and Tatarstan in certain policy areas than does the February 1994 treaty. One of the most significant of these agreements is the February 1994 agreement on bank and monetary policy wherein Tatarstan's national bank is described as "a fundamental and constituent part of the Central Bank of the Russian Federation" and the governments of Tatarstan and Russia pledge to work together to determine yearly levels of central credit resources to be given to Tatarstan's national bank by the Central Bank of Russia. Another important supplementary agreement is the February 1994 one addressing defense policy. According to this document, all questions "addressing the provision and defense of the Republic of Tatarstan" are transferred to the Russian Federation. Yet according to the same text, questions of the mobilization and use of the armed forces of the Russian Federation in Tatarstan lie within the *joint* authority of Russia and Tatarstan while the presence of Russian troops in Tatarstan is said to take place only with the consent of the government of Tatarstan.

These supplementary agreements between Tatarstan and Russia further demonstrate the Tatarstani government's desire for symbolic sovereignty, including the insistence on regulating these relations through bilateral agreements, the provision for a separate Tatarstani national bank, and the at least symbolic recognition of Tatarstan's sovereignty in the sphere of defense provision. However they also demonstrate Tatarstan's willingness to acknowledge sole Russian competency in certain arenas. This is particularly evident in the realm of economic policy, where the Tatarstani government has pledged to stay within the Russian Federal banking system and customs regime. A side agreement signed with Russia in February 1994 did give Tatarstan a more favorable tax regime than other members of the federation, including a single-channel system where Tatarstan has the right to collect all taxes on its territory and then send a portion to the Federal budget, but the republic has never made demands for an independent currency or customs regime.[4]

Yeltsin's decision to sign a treaty-type agreement with Tatarstan (which set off a "parade of treaties" in which eventually 47 of Russia's 88 federal subjects would conclude some form of treaty with Moscow), was criticized for the "secretive and executive-driven" nature of the negotiations that led to it, and for the ultimately negative impact it had on federation building by virtue of "eroding conceptions of federal civic identity, a unified legal space, and fiscal burden-sharing" in Russia (Kahn 2000, 185–87). And yet, particularly in retrospect, it is possible to view the initial Tatarstan-Moscow treaty and those that followed as a more positive step towards federation building, in the sense that these agreements helped to articulate, defend and protect the substantive gains in sovereignty that the regions in Russia must possess for any truly functioning federal system to exist there. Furthermore, while the "parade of treaties" in Russia was certainly more ad hoc and undemocratic than the analogous process in post-Franco Spain (Stepan 2000), it nonetheless was characterized by "some elements of consensual agreement and negotiation" and therefore represented "a reasonably acceptable" step-forward in federation-building for Russia (Hahn 2004).

From the Parade of Treaties to "Legal Chaos": Projecting Sovereignty during Yeltsin's Second Term, 1996–1999

There is reason to believe that Yeltsin viewed the 1994 agreement with Tatarstan (and the other 46 agreements that his administration signed with other regions during the rest of his administration) as merely another means of buying regional loyalty until his second term in office was assured, much as his original endorsement of regional sovereignty had been a tool to win their support in his battle with Gorbachev, and also that he expected the republics to become more pliant and receptive to federal overtures in the wake of the signing of the treaties (Kahn 2002). For soon after the signing of the February 1994 treaty with Tatarstan, Yeltsin expressed his desire that Tatarstan's president and parliament would voluntarily take unilateral moves aimed at bringing the republic's constitution and legislation in line with the analogous Russian Federation documents (*Informatsionno-Metodicheskii Byulleten'* 1996, #8, 4–8; *RFE/RL Newsline* October 31, 1997; June 11, 1998; *RFE/RL Tatar-Bashkir Service Daily Report* June 9, 1998). Furthermore, in spring 1996, at Yeltsin's urging the Russian Federation Duma produced a draft of a "Law on Federal Relations in the Russian Federation" which would require that all treaties signed between Moscow and the regions be amended to bring them into strict "harmony" with the Russian Federation Constitution within a three-month period—though the law ultimately would not be passed and signed until July 1999 (*Tatarstan* 1996, #10, 13).

During the remainder of the Yeltsin regime, the Duma, the Constitutional Court, and Yeltsin himself continued to press for the "harmonization" of republican constitutions and legislation with Federal law. Yet during this same period, in the name of what it saw as its constitutionally-protected right to continue its sovereignty project *within* the framework of the Russian Federation, Tatarstan reacted with silence or defiance to the various court rulings, laws and presidential decrees demanding that it change its laws and bring them into harmony with their federal counterparts. Because during the Yeltsin regime the Russian Federal government was far too divided and weak to implement these multiple rulings in favor of "harmonization," this disobedience by Tatarstan went largely unpunished and other regions followed suit (Stoner-Weiss 1999). The result was that by 1999, over one-third of the 16,000 regional laws that the Justice Department of the Russian Federation had reviewed since 1995 were deemed to be "in contradiction" with federal legislation (*RFE/RL Newsline* January 20, 1998).

Tatarstani elites offered several different rationales for why they chose to continue their sovereignty projects in the face of Yeltsin's calls for voluntary "harmonization" of the republic's legislation with Russia's. The first was that according to the February 1994 treaty with Russia, the republic had the full legal right to exercise sole jurisdiction over all matters of internal political organization and development in the republic (*Jamestown Monitor* March 25, 1996; *KRIS* June 24, 1997, 1–2; *RFE/RL Tatar-Bashkir Service Daily Report* March 24, 1999). According to this reasoning, Kazan's "defiance" was actually the protection and fostering of the kernels of real federalism—substantive governing powers in the regions, as legally transferred to Kazan from Moscow by treaty. The second was that because the Russian Duma proved to be such an ineffective legislative actor during the 1990s, effectively shirking its part of the federal bargain, as it were, Tatarstan in fact had a legal and moral imperative to develop its own independent legislation in policy areas where the Duma had failed to act (*RFE/RL Newsline* July 24, 1998).[5] Thus during the 1990s the Tatarstani parliament adopted pioneering legislation in economic reform, crime prevention and alternative military service, legislation that has in some cases was then used by the Russian government as a model for its own federal legislation and programs (*Literaturnaya Gazeta* March 30, 1994; *RFE/RL Tatar-Bashkir Service Daily Report* April 23, 1998, September 30, 1998; *RFE/RL Newsline* July 24, 1998).

Similarly, Tatarstani President Mintimer Shaimiyev argued that because both Russia's 1993 and Tatarstan's 1992 constitutions are cited as the legal sources underpinning the February 1994 treaty with Moscow, that treaty recognizes the inherent legality of Tatarstan's constitution and the basic equality of the Tatarstani and Russian constitutions. Because of the mutual recognition of the two constitutions, Shaimiyev insisted that any future "harmonization" will have to occur in a process of *mutual and bilateral change*, wherein the Russian Federation must be willing to change its own legal documents in the name of furthering, federalism and not simply to expect that it can demand or dictate unilateral changes in the Tatarstani constitution or republican legislation (*INTERFAX-Executive* June 29, 1994; *Informatsionno-Metodicheskii Byulleten'* 1996, 8: 4–8; *RFE/RL Newsline* June 9, 1998; January 28, 1999; *IEWS RRR* October 15, 1998).[6]

Working from this assumption that harmonization, and indeed federalism itself, must be a bilateral process, President Shaimiyev remarked that "the Russian Federation Constitution is far from a finished document" and urged President Yeltsin to consider changes in the Russian Constitution which would help to systematize and institutionalize the treaty-type agreements the federal center has signed with the regions in Russia (*Respublika Tatarstan* August 30, 1996, 1).

Dual(ing) Citizenship: One Passport or Two?

Citizenship is one of the main hallmarks of both internal and external state sovereignty, as it marks the boundaries of the political community for both the domestic audience and the international community. Thus the negotiation of citizenship questions between Russia and Tatarstan is one of the more crucial aspects of their post-Soviet relationship. While the Russian Federation constitution does not contain a provision for separate republican citizenship, the February 1994 treaty between Tatarstan and Russia did address this issue, if not clearly.

According to article 2 of the February 1994 treaty, Tatarstan has the authority to provide its own republican citizenship, while article 3 of the treaty states that Tatarstan and Russia together must "settle the common and contradictory questions of citizenship." During the Yeltsin years, this process at times seemed more contradictory than common, with Tatarstan pushing to develop its own separate citizenship norms to the point of passing a separate citizenship law, refusing to issue Russian Federation passports, and making plans to issuing its own Tatarstani passports. And yet, ultimately, the resolution of the citizenship and internal passport issue, which would come early in the Putin administration, must be seen as a strong example of creative federation building and the type of win-win situations that have been fostered in Russia through the framework of republican sovereignty-seeking.

The November 1992 Tatarstani constitution contained a clause for a separate republican citizenship, because, as President Shaimiyev explained, "citizenship is perhaps the most important attribute of statehood" (*Sovetskaya Tatariya* November 7, 1992, 1). However despite this clause, and despite the fact that the February 1994 treaty with Russia theoretically gave Tatarstan the right to develop its own citizenship, no draft of a Tatarstani citizenship law was seriously considered by the State Council of Tatarstan until fall 1997, the time at which the Russian Federation began to reform its own norms of citizenship, including the design of its internal passports. When a proposal to abandon the traditional designation of ethnicity in Russian Federation internal passports was introduced in the Duma, non-Russian minorities viewed the move as a chauvinistic ethnic-Russian attempt to marginalize non-Russians and the ethno-national republics within Russia. Tatars, along with the neighboring Bashkirs, protested this "provocation" more vociferously than any other non-Russian groups in Russia (*RFE/RL Newsline* October 21, 1997; *Jamestown Monitor* October 21, 1997).

Citing the legal authority of the 1992 Federation Treaty and the 1994 Treaty with Russia, Tatarstani President Shaimiyev ordered the Ministry of the Interior of Tatarstan to stop issuing Russian Federation internal passports and demanded that the Federal government return the ethnicity designation to Russia's internal passports. He also requested that Russian officials add another provision to the passports which would give meaningful recognition to "Tatarstan's statehood" and the fact that Tatarstani citizens in fact held "dual citizenship" in Tatarstan and the Russian Federation (*Jamestown Monitor* October 21, 1997; November 5, 1997; *RFE/RL Newsline* November 6, 1997; November 14, 1997). Unsurprisingly, Russia refused to assent to this request, inspiring Tatarstani officials to accelerate their own efforts to draft and pass a Tatarstani citizenship law. Citing the fact that he was "bound to uphold the Constitution of Tatarstan," which called for a separate Tatarstani citizenship, and spurred on by a group of Tatarstani deputies who urged the quick adoption of a Tatarstani citizenship law as "a real step toward the birth of Tatarstan's statehood," a draft law on citizenship was introduced in Tatarstan at the end of 1997. The first draft of this law contained a provision which would have allowed citizens of Tatarstan to voluntarily renounce their citizenship in the Russian Federation, a provision which was eventually removed at the urging of President Shaimiyev and some of the legal advisors to the Tatarstani parliament, who found the provision "too radical" (*Jamestown Monitor* February 11, 1998; *RFE/RL Newsline* February 26, 1998).

The final draft of the Tatarstani citizenship law, which was officially adopted in a second reading on November 2, 1998, provided automatic dual citizenship in Tatarstan and the Russian Federation for citizens of Tatarstan. It also contained two controversial provisions, one calling for separate Tatarstani passports and the other allowing anyone whose grandparents had been born in Tatarstan to apply for citizenship in Tatarstan (*RFE/RL Newsline* April 16, 1998; *Vechernyaya Kazan'* November 3, 1998).

The decision by the Tatarstani parliament to issue its own passports was provocative to the Russian federal center for obvious reasons. Separate Tatarstani passports would be a direct challenge to the Russian federal government's centralized control over the population of the country (internal passports are used for several important functions in Russia, including the allocation of housing). While the provision allowing anyone whose grand-parents were born in Tatarstan to apply for citizenship did not limit this right to only ethnic Tatars, the clause was obviously intended mainly for ethnic Tatars who might view Tatarstan as a homeland and apply for citizenship out of feelings of ethnic solidarity.[7]

Russian federal officials reacted strongly to Tatarstan's attempts at providing for their own separate citizenship. In February 1998 the Russian Presidential Representative to the Federation Council, Anatolii Sliva warned Tatarstan that the introduction of separate republican citizenship was "inadmissible" despite the February 1994 treaty, because "the Russian Federation is already itself a subject of international law," indicating that Tatarstan's pretensions to introduce its own citizenship were an unacceptable challenge to Russia's state sovereignty in this area (*RFE/RL Newsline* February 26, 1998).

In response to Moscow's hostility, and in a classic example of the republic's strategy of pushing the maximal limits of sovereignty within the Russian federal framework and then pulling back to compromise with the federal center when pressure was applied, the government of Tatarstan never actually began the process of issuing its own passports, despite its stated intentions to do so. Instead, from 1997 on, Tatarstan held almost constant negotiations with Moscow on the issue of how the republic's desire for some form of republican citizenship could be reconciled within federal citizenship norms. While the Yeltsin administration was never able to overcome this impasse, despite continued negotiations, in December 2000, a year after Putin had been appointed as acting president by Yeltsin, it was announced that a compromise on the citizenship and passport dilemma had finally been worked out. In what would be one of the only concessions to the regions during the Putin era (see chapter 5), it was revealed that Putin had agreed to the proposed Tatarstani (and Bashkortostani) solution—the federal passports issued in these two republics would include an additional four pages printed in the respective national languages of the republics and bearing the state symbols of the republics, indicating that the holder was also a citizen of the given republic as well as a Russian citizen. A final demand of the republics, which held up the issue of the passports for several months before Moscow finally assented to it, was that the special insert be sewn into the passports as "an integral part" of the document and not be "merely an inlay" to the documents, as Moscow had originally proposed (*RFE/RL Tatar-Bashkir Service Daily Report* March 19, 2001).

This final demand is an apt metaphor for the type of federal relationship Tatarstan was seeking to build in Russia under the rubric of its sovereignty project—realizing that the demand for total separation (their own passports) stretched the federal framework too far, the republic nonetheless demanded that the federal government too make some meaningful concessions to Tatarstan's sovereignty and recognize it as "an integral," *but distinct*, part of the federation, not just an "inlay" whose sovereign status could be easily ignored or legislated away (as the Putin administration would try its hardest to do).

Sharing the Money: Budget Relations between Tatarstan and Moscow under Yeltsin

As with the division of political authorities like citizenship norms, Tatarstani elites used the sovereignty project framework to attempt to maximize their economic powers and advantages vis-à-vis the center during the renegotiation of Russia's federal structure under Yeltsin, and again, they were remarkably successful at crafting new relations that struck a balance between regional autonomy and the recognition of their location in a federal milieu. As was referred to earlier, the special agreement governing budgetary issues between Moscow and Kazan signed at same time as the main February 1994 treaty provided for a "single-track" tax system whereby Tatarstan would collect all taxes on its territory and then transfer a portion of them to the Russian federal budget "for the realization of those tasks Tatarstan has delegated to the Russian Federation"—similar to the tax regime that the Basque Territory and Catalonia enjoy in Spain (Agranoff 1999b).

After the signing of the 1994 agreements, Tatarstani officials were bold in asserting their sovereignty control over those aspects of budgetary policy they felt had been legally transferred to them, and were not afraid to call Moscow on its perceived failures to live up to their end of the federal bargain in budget matters. But during the second half of the Yeltsin administration, Tatarstan was also willing to recognize that there were (and are) limits to its sovereign budget ambitions, owing to its fundamental situation as a member of the Russian Federation.

In one example of the Tatarstani sovereignty project in action in the budgetary realm, Kazan argued in early 1994 that the export duties Russian Federation officials collect on Tatarstani oil (which Tatarstani officials must pay if they want to continue to use federal pipelines), amount to "extra" transfers into the federal budget that are not accounted for in the budget treaty, thus giving Tatarstan the right to unilaterally decrease its "transfers" to the federal center when it felt the need to (*FBIS* January 24, 1994, 35). Furthermore, in 1995 and 1998, Tatarstani officials threatened to stop all payments from Tatarstan to the Russian Federation budget, citing as rationale the nonpayment of wages by Moscow to workers in federal defense industries in Tatarstan. Because Russia was not fulfilling its part of the interstate treaty on budget relations (i.e., taking responsibility for those authorities Tatarstan had transferred to it, including partial responsibility for the functioning of the military-industrial complex in Tatarstan), Tatarstani officials argued that Russia was in violation of the budget treaty between the two polities and had in effect reneged on its half of the evolving federal bargain. As such, Shaimiyev argued, Tatarstan had the right to unilaterally nullify the treaty and bring the entire budget and tax regime of the republic "under the exclusive authority of Tatarstan" (*Izvestiya Tatarstana* July 12, 1995, 1; *RFE/RL Tatar-Bashkir Service Daily Report* September 10, 1998; November 2, 1998).

In early 1999, Shaimiyev claimed that the federal center had violated the existing principle of mutual negotiations and treaty-based relations between Tatarstan and Russia by adopting a Russian Federation budget that had been developed "without the needs of Tatarstan being considered" (*RFE/RL Newsline* February 2, 1999). In response, Shaimiyev again threatened to unilaterally decrease or end payments to the Russian federal budget. While negotiations over the renewal of the five-year February 1994 budget agreement between Tatarstan and Russia were strained by Tatarstan's refusal to allow any significant changes in the budget and tax arrangements between it and Moscow, eventually in March 1999 the agreement was renewed for another five years (*RFE/RL Tatar-Bashkir Service Daily Report* March 4, 1999; March 19, 1999; *RFE/RL Newsline* March 23, 1999).

Despite Tatarstan's attempts to exercise state sovereignty in the realm of budget relations, the fact that the republic remains heavily integrated into the Russian Federation economy as a whole means that their efforts at projecting sovereignty in this realm have clear limits. Tatarstani leaders readily admitted that the republic remained dependent on the center for "easy credits" in the agricultural sphere (*FBIS* May 6, 1994, 31), and Russian wage and other payments to federal defense industries in Tatarstan (*FBIS* June 6, 1994, 20). Yet, as was illustrated above, Tatarstani officials have also tried to use the fact of the deep interpenetration of the Tatarstani and Russian federal economies as a weapon in their battle to exercise more state sovereignty in the budgetary sphere, such as when they threatened to stop or decrease Tatarstan's payments to Russia because of Russia's nonpayment of wages and debts to federally-owned defense industries in Tatarstan. The overall weakness of the Russian state and the Russian economy has only facilitated the sovereignty-seeking behavior of Tatarstan in the sphere of economic relations with Russia, sometimes by default. For example, in January 1999 the Tatarstani government took over control of the seven largest defense industries in Tatarstan, claiming that "no one in Moscow had shown the least interest in them"—a situation that would change radically upon Putin's ascension to the Russian presidency (*RFE/RL Newsline* January 21, 1999).

Assessing Shared Sovereignty and Federalism in Yeltsin's Russia

If Russian President Boris Yeltsin signed the 1994 treaty with Tatarstan and the other regions in the hopes that these documents would remain, like so much other post-Soviet legislation, either ignored or inert, this wager proved wrong, particularly regarding the case of Tatarstan. Instead, Tatarstani elites have demonstrated a strong commitment to realizing as much sovereign authority as possible within the bounds of the February 1994 treaty and the limitations engendered by the republic's continued geopolitical and legal location within the Russian Federation. Tatarstani attempts to "act like a state" regarding its federal relations with Moscow during the Yeltsin era were consistently flexible and informed by changes in the perceived political opportunity structure, and took pains not to threaten overt ruptures of the Russian federal structure, but also show a continual desire to "maximize" the republic's symbolic and institutional attributes of sovereignty whenever possible. Despite the fact that after 1994 it displayed increased skepticism and even open hostility towards the system of "treaty-based federalism" which it itself had helped to create, the Yeltsin administration proved largely unable to block or effectively counter the republics' exercise of their newly-won sovereign rights within the Russian Federation, as the 1999 decision to renew the budget agreement with Tatarstan (and the failure to stop the 1998 presidential elections in Bashkortostan) demonstrate. Thus by the end of the Yeltsin administration, the Russian Federal system was a decidedly asymmetrical one, with the ethnic republics enjoying greater rights and authorities, by virtue of their own constitutions and the treaties with Russia, than most of the nonethnically designated oblasts and krais, even those that had signed treaties with Moscow (Kahn 2002 185–87).

The resultant federal system has been criticized for its ad hoc nature and its incoherence; however it is important to reiterate that asymmetry in federal systems is not an inherently negative quality, and that in multiethnic societies like Russia, asymmetrical federal structures can have normative as well as practical utility, a point that will be elaborated on in chapter 4 (Agranoff 1999; Gagnon 2001). Therefore, it is possible to see the Yeltsin years not as a missed opportunity for rationally-planned federal development in Russia, but rather as positive evidence of the type of dynamic negotiation resulting in substantive governing powers at the sub-state level that characterizes "actual" federation (Hahn 2004; Konitzer-Smirnov 2003).

Furthermore, this close look at negotiations between the center and the regions during the Yeltsin era does not, in my opinion, support the assertion that the regions were "entirely uncommitted" to the federal project in Russia, nor that they were engaged only in "crude localism" during this period or refused to acknowledge that "sovereignty was in any way divisible or diminishable by a new Russian Federation" (Kahn 2002, 30–31, 149, 170). Rather, as the treaty, citizenship, and budget issues discussed in this chapter illustrate, Tatarstan has been willing to compromise with Moscow to find mutually acceptable solutions to thorny federal problems. Indeed, as chapter 5 demonstrates, it is the federal government in Moscow under the Putin administration that has taken a hard-line position against the sharing of any meaningful attributes of state sovereignty with the regions, thus jeopardizing the future of any truly federal political system in Russia. In this regard, the strong attempts by Tatarstan to fill its declaration of state sovereignty with meaningful legal, symbolic, and actual attributes during the Yeltsin years seems less a strategy aimed at *preventing* the development of federalism in Russia than a prescient attempt to build as firm a foundation as possible for *actual* regional self-government, a hallmark of federalism that none of the various central governments in Russia had ever allowed historically, while the opportunity presented itself.

The story of how Tatarstan's sovereignty projects have served to protect the cause of the federalism in Russia in the face of increased central pressure towards unitarism under Putin is picked up in chapter 5. The next two chapters help prepare the groundwork for that discussion by elucidating the other ways in which Tatarstan's sovereignty-seeking efforts have helped or demonstrate potential to help to foster important aspects of political development in Russia—by stimulating economic and political developments at the republican level that have enriched the country as a whole (chapter 3), and by furthering the cause of ethnocultural justice in Russia (chapter 4).

Notes

1. Early drafts of the Russian Federation constitution did contain provisions for the "state sovereignty" of the Russian republics, along with clauses allowing for separate republican citizenships. However these clauses were not included in the final draft of the Constitution, nor was Tatarstan's demand for its special status to be written into the Russian Constitution honored. For a discussion of Tatarstan and Russia's negotiations over the 1993 Russian Constitution, see Teague (1994).

2. All references to the February 1994 Treaty between Tatarstan and Russia are from the reprint of the document in *Suverenni Tatarstan:Sovereign Tatarstan*, (Moscow: Plenipotentiary Representation of Tatarstan in Moscow, 1997), 33–46.

3. These include an agreement on economic cooperation signed in December 1991, an agreement on the division of state property signed in June 1993, agreements on oil production and transport, environmental protection, higher education, the provision of a unified customs regime, and the conversion of the military-industrial complex also signed in June 1993, as well as agreements on crime prevention, foreign economic policy, bank and monetary policy, budget relations, and an agreement on defense cooperation signed at the same time as the February 1994 treaty. For the text of these agreements, see *Suverennyi Tatarstan:Sovereign Tatarstan*, (Moscow: Plenipotentiary Representation of Tatarstan, 1997), 143–81.

4. Specifically, the February 1994 agreement on tax and budget relations allowed Tatarstan to keep 50 percent of the VAT tax which is set yearly by Tatarstan and Russia (other regions can only keep 25 percent of the VAT), 1 percent of the income tax, 13 percent of the profit tax, and all excise taxes on alcohol, oil, and gas. For the text of the agreement, see *Suverennyi Tatarstan:Sovereign Tatarstan*, (Moscow: Plenipotentiary Representation of Tatarstan, 1997), 175–76.

5. Thus during the 1990s the Tatarstani parliament adopted pioneering legislation in economic reform, crime prevention, and alternative military service, legislation that has in some cases then been used by the Russian government as a model for its own federal legislation and programs (*Literaturnaya Gazeta* March 30, 1994; *RFE/RL Tatar-Bashkir Service* April 23, 1998, September 30, 1998; *RFE/RL Newsline* July 24, 1998).

6. There are several discrepancies between the Tatarstani and Russian Federal Constitutions, as there are between most of the republican constitutions and the federal document. See Kahn (2002) and Stoner-Weiss (1999) for a general discussion of this trend in post-Soviet Russia.

7. Indeed the "grandfather" clause in the new Tatarstani citizenship law was applauded by diaspora Tatars participating in a Tatar-email list which the author is also a member of. Many participants indicated their desire to take advantage of this law.

CHAPTER THREE

Projecting Sovereignty
at Home and Abroad:
State-Building in Tatarstan and
Its Impact on Russian Federalism

The previous chapter examined how Tatarstan pursued its sovereign status regarding the development of federal relations between the Russian Federal center and Kazan during the Yeltsin era; the present chapter expands this investigation by examining how Tatarstan has attempted to shape and project its newly-claimed sovereignty to two other audiences during the post-Soviet era—its domestic population at home in Tatarstan and the international community. As was noted in the introduction, state sovereignty has both internal and external aspects, each of which in turn is composed of both symbolic and institutional elements. In the course of its efforts to truly "become sovereign," Tatarstan has endeavored, to differing degrees, to realize attributes in all of these spheres. And while they are aimed at different audiences, the sovereignty-seeking policies that Tatarstan has directed towards its own domestic population and the international community have been crucially important at shaping federal relations with Moscow as well. In fact, it is in the context of examining Tatarstan's domestic and international state-building efforts that we begin to see more clearly how the republic's sovereignty project has served not chiefly as a means of rupturing Russia's federal space, but rather as the vehicle for enriching and strengthening federalism in Russia. It has done so by fostering the realization of the significant and meaningful political, economic, and legal powers and authorities that must be located in the member units of the Russian Federation for a real federal system to take hold there. Specifically, this chapter examines Tatarstan's domestic politics of state symbols, urban renewal, social welfare and education, as well as Tatarstan's post-Soviet forays into international relations.

In addition to providing the kernel for the development of a real form of federalism in Russia, the Tatarstani efforts to project sovereignty discussed in this chapter have also helped to strengthen Russia's position in the international community in the post-Cold war era. Among the most powerful observations to come from the reexamination of the concept of state sovereignty that has been taking place among international relations theorists recently is that the "complex, multiple webs of divided and dispersed" opportunities for actors to exercise political and economic authority that characterize the post-Cold War international system favor an analogous movement within existing states to find new and creative methods to divide and share the attributes of sovereignty between central state, sub-state, and non-state actors in ways that prove mutually enriching for all involved (Keating 2001, 28). In other words, in the context of an increasingly globalized international environment, those states that foster the creative sharing of sovereignty, giving over some traditional attributes of state sovereignty to transnational institutions while allowing sub-state or non-state actors in their midst to exercise other aspects of sovereignty traditionally reserved for the central state will prosper more than those that rigidly hold on to old conceptions of the grasping, unitary state (Cerny 1993; Habermas 1996, 2001; Holm and Sorenson 1995; Keating 2001; Keohane 1995; Mann 1993; Sorenson 1997). Even members of the central government in Moscow are beginning to recognize this truth—no less a figure than Putin's Deputy Head of Presidential Administration Vladislav Surkov argued in a United Russia policy speech in February 2005 that in the context of globalization, Russia must begin to understand the protection of its sovereignty in terms of "increasing its competitiveness in the world environment" (Surkov 2005).

Federal states are in some aspects better positioned than nonfederal states to take advantage of the new opportunities presented in the post-Cold War world. Because federalism is already premised (theoretically) on the assumption that sovereign authority can and must be shared within a federal framework, federations potentially should have an easier time crafting and their citizens an easier time adapting to the "multiple and nested" political, economic and social identities that will afford them success in a globalized world (Keating 2001, 19–20). In multiethnic federations like Canada and Spain, the desire for self-determination among constituent national communities like Quebec or Catalonia can actually help spur this process on, as these member units strengthen the federation's overall position in the global economy and community by fostering their own bilateral and multilateral contacts internationally. Allowing or even encouraging political and economic experimentation and innovation on the part of sub-national communities (including international activities) that is encompassed within a broad and flexible federal framework is one of the best ways that states can enhance their political effectiveness and economic prosperity in the post-Cold War world. At least one author has suggested that allowing this type of regional autonomy (under the guise of what he calls "managed pluralism") will be an important part of Russia's continued political and economic development both domestically and in terms of its further integration with the global economy and the international community (Balzer 2003).

The evidence presented in this chapter supports this conclusion. While Tatarstan itself has certainly acted on its own initiative in its quest to project attributes of sovereignty at home and abroad, Tatarstani elites have also demonstrated a growing understanding of the need to and in fact the desirability of working together with the Russian federal government in Moscow to make those initiatives more successful. In other words, the independent initiatives inspired by Tatarstan's quest for sovereignty, as manifested in its domestic and international pursuits, have actually strengthened the process of federation-building not only by locating significant policy-making powers in the regions for the first time in Russia's history, but by allowing the two sides to actually see the benefits of federalism in practice, as they come to terms with the reality that they need one another to effectively realize their respective goals in the post-Soviet world.

More specifically, in the post-communist era, Moscow needs the republics to take on more of the responsibilities the central state no longer can or will provide for and, at least partially, is beginning to realize that the claim to sovereignty and aspiration to statehood on the part of the republics makes them both more able and willing to undertake these tasks. Moscow has also seen over the past decade and a half how republican foreign policy moves and international aspirations (again, this applies to Tatarstan in particular) can help raise Russia's political and economic presence in the international community, particularly as regards ties to Europe and Islamic world. For their part, the architects of the Tatarstani sovereignty project, through a process of trial and error, have come to see that they absolutely need the federal government's administrative and financial support to ensure the success of many of the ventures they have adopted in the name of sovereignty. Programs and legislation initiated by the republics often need to be funded in part by the federal government, and particularly in the international sphere, the republics have found that both their political and economic overtures are often rebuffed unless foreign partners are ensured that the venture has Moscow's blessing and oversight. Ultimately, then, allowing the regions to continue to pursue some domestic and international initiatives in the name of projecting their sovereignty while Moscow continues to strengthen the federal framework that oversees and facilitates, rather than strangles and smothers, those regional initiatives, seems both wise and possible.

However, if protecting and encouraging republican initiative in some legislative, state-building and international arenas will prove beneficial for the further growth of federalism in Russia, those more negative developments that have arisen in the republics in the name of sovereignty, specifically the tendency towards ethnocracy and rising authoritarianism, must simultaneously be curbed (Hale 1998). Though the presence of some ethnocratic features and the trend of growing authoritarianism in the republics is a disturbing one, and one that is not absent in Tatarstan, stripping the regions of any autonomy, particularly when the alternative is a return to centralized control by a central government in Moscow that is dominated by a narrow class of oligarchs and *siloviki* and that seems to be squarely on the same path of creeping authoritarianism, does not seem to be the best way to foster either democracy or federalism in Russia. Instead, pressing for democratic reforms in both the center and the regions while allowing the regions to continue to exercise those sovereign powers that are appropriate for them and which increase the general welfare of the Russian Federation seems a more desirable alternative.

Having taken the first steps towards realizing the republic's declared sovereign status by promulgating a new Tatarstani constitution in 1992, elites in Tatarstan then turned towards the task of bringing that document to life through both institutional and symbolic means. Sovereignty-seekers in Tatarstan erected a comprehensive set of new republican executive, legislative, and judicial institutions to replace their Soviet-era counterparts, including independent republican presidencies, plus an attendant Cabinet of Ministers and full array of ministries to administer executive decisions, and set before those institutions to the challenging task of crafting new symbolic, political, and economic policies designed to help the republic conform both to its new ideal of sovereignty and to the new realities of post-Communist Russia.[1]

The consistent message of the leaders of Tatarstan's sovereignty project is that these symbolic, political, and economic state-building measures are legal (according to the 1993 Russian Constitution and 1994 treaties with Moscow), necessary for federalism (in the sense that federalism requires that sub-state units possess meaningful policy-making authority), and essential for the further political and economic development of Russia (in the sense that the federal government in Moscow has itself largely abdicated responsibility for governing the country). For their domestic audience, republican elites tied sovereignty to federalism, and in the name of both promised their citizens that they would enjoy greater economic freedom and prosperity, political stability and democracy, and international prestige than they ever had when the central government in Moscow ran the entire show itself. Simultaneously, the republican elite sought to reassure its citizenry that while sovereignty meant better economic and living conditions in Tatarstan than elsewhere in Russia, it did not mean separation from or acrimonious relations with Russia. Instead, they argued that Tatarstan's sovereignty project was meant to serve as the beacon of federal progress, leading Moscow (however reluctantly) down the path towards a stronger, more prosperous "bottom-up" form of federalism.

Acting Like a State by Looking Like a State: Symbolic Strategies of Domestic Sovereignty Projection in Tatarstan

While the new Tatarstani executive, legislative, and judicial institutions and the political and economic policies they have promulgated are the most concrete embodiment of domestic sovereignty in the post-Soviet period, republican elites in Tatarstan have also attended assiduously to the symbolic aspect of Tatarstan's quest to become more like a sovereign state in its own domestic arena. Official state symbols such as flags, heralds and hymn, and official state ceremonies like state holidays are meaningful because they have become the conventional and universal markers of statehood and thus are important parts of the script for the performance of statehood and nationness in the modern era (Billig 1995, 85–86; Tilly 1996). The content of these official state symbols is significant not only because they carry messages about the state itself, but also because they contain particular understandings about the nation or nations in whose name the state claims to exist. Because they are potential rallying points for patriotic feeling, these symbols and ceremonies are important resources in the attempt to construct sovereign states and the national communities that inhabit them.

Soon after declaring the republic of Tatarstan a sovereign state, the Supreme Soviet of Tatarstan took up the issue of a new state flag, seal, and hymn for the republic. Republican leaders in Tatarstan insisted that the old Tatar A.S.S.R. symbols "did not sincerely reflect the status of the republic as a sovereign state" (*Sovetskaya Tatariya* November 18, 1990, 2). The Tatar

A.S.S.R. flag, which was essentially the Russian Republic's flag with Tatar language inscription, was pointed out as being particularly unsatisfactory in light of Tatarstan's new sovereign status.

The debate over the forms of the new state symbols illustrates both the government's desire to embody concretely the sovereign statehood of Tatarstan and the attempt to reconcile civic and ethnic elements in the Tatarstani national community that was to inhabit that new state. The Tatarstani government declared that the new symbols should reflect the principles of the Declaration of Sovereignty of Tatarstan, including the provision which asserted "equal rights for all peoples of the republic regardless of nationality." Yet at the same time, the symbols were to also reflect the fact that "the people who gave the republic its name" (that is, ethnic Tatars), had a "one thousand year tradition of their own statehood"—a tradition that was now resurrected with the establishment of the new republic of Tatarstan (*Sovetskaya Tatariya* November 18, 1990, 2).

In an attempt to represent this delicate balance of civic and ethnic heritages through the language of symbols, Tatarstani deputies debated such issues as whether or not the new flag should have the traditional Islamic crescent moon on it (*Vechernyaya Kazan* September 28, 1996, 1). Reflecting a fear that such a blatant Islamic symbol would prove too divisive a symbol to represent the fledging "Tatarstani" national community, the flag that the Tatarstani Soviet adopted in September 1991 did not carry the crescent, although it did carry a green stripe at the top. President Shaimiyev later attempted to downplay the Islamic connotations of this aspect of the flag, pointing out that Ireland and Italy also both had green stripes in their flags as well (*Komsomol'skaya Pravda* January 16, 1992).

The state seal of Tatarstan adopted by the Supreme Soviet did, however, carry an image explicitly associated with the history of the ethnic Tatar nation—a white leopard with wings (called the *ak bars*—"white leopard" in Tatar). This is the symbol of the ancient Bulgar state, which ethnic Tatars consider their first state formation. The choice of such a symbol was explained as "a show of respect to the traditional symbols of statehood of *our* people" (emphasis mine—note implication of the Tatar people as "our" people), although the authors expressed a hope that "it would appeal to people of all nationalities," and, more importantly, would sufficiently and proudly represent the new state of Tatarstan "in international society" (*Sovetskaya Tatariya* February 15, 1992, 3).

Thus the official symbols that Tatarstan adopted to represent itself show some sensitivity to the multiethnic nature of the republic (no Islamic crescent moon), but also openly reflect the past of the ethnic Tatar nation and

Figure 3.1. The Tatarstani flag flies solo over the Tatar State Council building on Freedom Square in central Kazan.

directly link the statehood of modern-day Tatarstan with that of the ancient Tatar state of Great Bulgar. The adoption of these hybrid civic-ethnic symbols seems not to have caused any type of negative reaction from the public of Tatarstan, either in 1991 or after. The government of Tatarstan has filled the physical space of the republic with these new state symbols—they are ubiquitous on official publications, near public transportation stops, on public billboards in parks (especially those extolling the friendship between the peoples of the republic), and especially in and on government buildings and vehicles (especially police cars). Thus it seems the leadership of the republic is pursuing a policy of quietly attempting to make the hybrid civic-ethnic state symbols of Tatarstan seem everyday, natural, normal, and "banal" (Billig 1995). By making these symbols so ubiquitous, the republican leadership is attempting to situate citizens physically in a national community that is definitely distinct from other national communities (i.e., the Russian Federation), and attempting to make the presence of Tatar-identified imagery (the white leopard, the green stripe) seem equally banal and normal.[2]

Yet while Tatarstani elites have invested considerable time and effort into the creation and propagation of these domestic symbols of sovereignty, they have been treated for the most part as a meaningful *supplement* to Russian federal symbols and holidays, *not* as a replacement of their federal analogues.

In this regard, Tatarstan's domestic symbology should properly be seen as evidence in support of the aforementioned assertion that federations, particularly multiethnic ones, can and do tolerate (and perhaps require) that citizens cultivate and support multiple levels of political identity and loyalty, as is the situation in other states like Canada and the United States, where constituent federal units also have their own state symbols and holidays (Gagnon and Tully 2001; Keating 2001).

For example, Tatarstan's September 2003 Law on State Holidays declares that all Russian Federal holidays must be celebrated in the republic *along with* Tatarstan's own new holidays: Republic Day (August 30, the day sovereignty was declared in 1990), Constitution Day (November 6, the day Tatarstan's constitution was adopted in 1992), and Native Language Day (celebrated on April 26). Likewise, most official buildings, documents, and other institutions in Tatarstan (including police cars) routinely display the republican and federal insignias *together*, as is called for in the Russian federal law on state symbols. The exception to this rule of "dual display" is the Tatarstani State Council building on Freedom Square in central Kazan, which flies only the republican basis atop its highest peak, though at the front entrance of and inside the parliament building the republican and federal flags and symbols are displayed together. In 2005, a few months after the Russian Federation had finally, officially registered Tatarstan's state symbols of Tatarstan in the Russian State Heraldic Register,[3] federal and republican prosecutors formally requested that Tatarstan begin to fly the Russian flag along with the Tatarstani flag on this most symbolic and prominent of public perches in the republics (*RFE/RL Tatar-Bashkir Service Daily Report* May 25, 2005). Tatarstani State Council speaker Mukhametshin urged Tatarstan's parliament to "take the prosecutors' request into account" and explained that while ongoing reconstruction work made it difficult to place another flagpole atop the building at the present moment, the republic would "continue looking for technical ways to solve this request" (*RFE/RL Tatar-Bashkir Service Daily Report* May 25, 2005 and May 27, 2005), which is certainly an innovative way to avoid taking responsibility for this continued act of mild symbolic insubordination by Tatarstan! (see Photo One)

In an even more large-scale attempt to "act like a state" through domestic sovereignty projection, Tatarstani elites have also endeavored to transform the republic's capital city, Kazan, into a metropolis—one that reflects Tatarstan's new and upgraded "sovereign" status. President Mintimer Shaimiyev in particular, has demonstrated a clear understanding that in his mind, a successful, capable, respected modern state must also necessarily *look like* it possesses the sovereignty it claims—in other words, it must have a capital

Figure 3.2.   The blending of Tatarstani and western commercial symbolism at McDonalds in central Kazan conveys a message of prosperity and modernity.

city that reflects its status (Liebowitz and Simon 2000, 2002; Monclus 2000). Just as European states like Belgium lined up in the nineteenth century to upgrade their capital cities in the image of Paris, seeking a city that would "represent the dignity worthy of a respectable nation" (Wagenaar 2000, 4), Tatarstani elites have invested substantial resources in urban planning, development, and reconstruction projects for Kazan that are intended to transform the physical landscape of the capital city to reflect the modernity and economic efficacy of the new sovereign Tatarstani state. While this intention is easy enough to deduce from the Shaimiyev administration's policies in Kazan, Rafael Khakimov, President Shaimiyev's closest advisor, clearly articulated this position in a 2005 interview with the Kazan newspaper *Zvezda Povolzhe(Volga Star)*. Khakimov stated that while Kazan did not have pretensions to be "the third Rome," in his opinion the city did "fulfill a number of the conditions and functions of a capital city like Rome." He also offered that he admired Barcelona, which although "just being the capital of the province of Catalonia," also "is famous throughout the whole world," suggesting that Kazan aspired to the same status (*Zvezda Povolzhe* August 4–10, 2005, 1–2).

The most prominent of the efforts to transform Kazan into a capital-type city are: an ambitious, controversial, and expensive "Program for Slum

Clearance and Modernization of Slum Areas (1995–2004)" (which has cost the republic over $685 million), which has transformed large swaths of the center city; the construction of a new Metro system for Kazan (the first in the city's history); a large-scale reconstruction of Kazan's main commercial street into a "European-style" pedestrian boulevard complete with decorative fountains and sculptures, mosaic squares, and new commercial enterprises like McDonald's; and a series of grandiose, "showcase" building projects in the city center aimed at "raising the cultural level of the city to a world-level" (Kinossian 2005, 2).

The decade-long slum clearance and renewal project in Tatarstan was initiated by the Tatarstani President Mintimer Shaimiyev in 1995, and is so closely associated with him that it is often known simply as "the President's housing project" (Kazan's Metro project is also largely a product of Shaimiyev's private bargaining with Russian president Vladimir Putin).[4] Unlike myriad other proposed projects of the post-Soviet era, the ambitious goal of eliminating unsightly, decrepit and unsafe housing in Kazan's city center and providing its former tenets, who number over 30,000, with new housing in the outer areas of the city, has actually been realized in the republic—in large part due to President Shaimiyev's willingness to use some of Tatarstan's significant oil export revenues to effect these drastic changes. The slum liquidation program, which Kazan Mayor Kamil Ishakov rather hyperbolically calls "unique in the whole world" and "a gift to Kazanites" (*Kommersant*, Special Supplement "*Kazan'—1000*," August 26, 2005 15, 18), in some cases meant "the knocking-down of entire city blocks" (Kinossian 2005, 45). Ultimately, vast districts of Kazan's city center were cleared of substandard housing and replaced with attractive and expensive "urban dachas" for the republic's political and economic elite or with modern commercial high-rise buildings.

The unusual speed and efficiency with which these transformations occurred is seen by one author as solid evidence of the great symbolic importance President Shaimiyev himself places on Kazan as the "calling card" of the new and successful sovereign state of Tatarstan, and also as testament to the heavy-handed tactics the government was willing to use to realize its vision of Kazan as an enhanced capital city—residents of the housing projects targeted by the plan were not consulted about the scheduling of the demolitions nor were they given input as to where they'd be relocated. As Kinossian states, the program "removed from the city center not only slums, but 'social pollutants' too, in order to make it look more attractive—this aspect fits very well to Shaimiyev's general line of converting Kazan to a capital of a "sovereign state" (Kinossian 2005, 45). That much of the republic's population has met the "bulldozer method" of reconstruction and restoration with "equanimity" and views the beautification of Kazan positively does not entirely excuse the undemocratic nature of the undertaking (*Kommersant*, Special Supplement "*Kazan'—1000*," August 26, 2005 13, 19).

The ambitious and successful attempt to replace Kazan's "slum housing" with housing more befitting the capital city of a "sovereign state" has attracted admiring attention from Moscow as well. In August 2003, Russian Federation Construction Committee Chairman Nikolai Koshmain awarded President Shaimiyev the "Creator of the Year" award, praising Tatarstan for its role as the "absolute leader" in the replacement of substandard housing in Russia and urging all Russian Federation housing officials to travel to Tatarstan to learn from its example (*RFE/RL Tatar-Bashkir Service Daily Report* August 11, 2003).

The other parts of this project—the construction of the Kazan Metro system (behind schedule and scandal-plagued, as might be expected), the reconstruction of Kazan's central Bauman Street, and the numerous showcase projects undertaken since 1990, are all efforts clearly intended to help upgrade Kazan's public spaces to a level more consonant with the enhanced level of statehood the Shaimiyev government aspires to. Bauman Street's new façade includes widened, European-style expanses, expensive fountains, sculptures, and mini-piazzas, all of which are lit at night not only by new (and retro-Victorian) streetlamps, but also by the significant increase in blazing neon shop-signs and storefronts that have accompanied Bauman's transformation. This "flashification" of Kazan's Bauman Street is reminiscent of a trend observed by Julia Holdsworth in Donetsk, Ukraine, where she sees a similar process of commercialization, signified by billboards and neonscapes, as attempting to "associate the possibility of economic success and lavish consumption with the state and nation of Ukraine" (Holdsworth 2004, 8). It is hard to imagine a better description of what state officials hope Kazan residents will feel about Tatarstan when they stroll down the new Bauman Street in the evening. In one case, this identification is made even more explicit—Kazan's McDonald's franchise has the flag of Tatarstan inscribed on its façade, the indicating that the republic under Shaimiyev itself embodies the modernity, sophistication, ease, customer service, pleasure and plenty that are symbolized by the Golden Arches worldwide (see figure 3.2.).

Tatarstan's government has also sponsored a number of "showcase projects" in Kazan that aim to be the type of grandiose, architecture-as-event buildings meant to redefine a city and elevate its status simply by their presence. The most famous of these in recent European history is Frank Gehry's Guggenheim Bilbao, and while of course the Kazan equivalents are not on the same scale, they have been erected with similar intentions. These showcase projects include a gleaming five-story glass pyramid housing various restaurants and boutiques, located next to Kazan's first five-star hotel in the city center (known simply as "The Pyramid," it is "the only building of its kind in Russia" as its promotional materials proudly announce); a new concert hall and refurbished opera house on the city's central square (formerly Lenin Square, now Freedom Square); a grandiose new hippodrome where a $3 million race was held in Putin's honor in August 2005; a state of the art basketball arena constructed on the site of the city's former oddball, 1960's-era, flying-saucer shaped circus hall; and the elaborate reconstruction of the buildings in Kazan's Kremlin complex (to be discussed at length later). All these expensive, modern, quasi-civic projects appear to be products equally of Shaimiyev's vision of what a "capital" city of a modern state must have in order to be taken seriously and of his own personal preferences and business interests (his son's company built the pyramid structure and Shaimiyev personally owns several race horses—about which more below). Indeed, when questioned about the huge price tag for the new Kazan hippodrome, Shaimiyev replied that, "It was necessary to spend such sums because we had to have a world-class structure where Kazan could host competitions of a world-class level" (*Izvestiya* August 26–28, 2005, 2).

Acting Like a State by Providing Like a State: Social Policy, Education Policy and Domestic Sovereignty in Tatarstan

While "looking like a state" in terms of heraldry and the level of development of one's capital city are important parts of the script of sovereign statehood in the modern era, states which fail to deliver more concrete public goods to their citizens will soon find that these symbolic strategies alone do not suffice to create the type of domestic legitimacy they crave. The architects of Tatarstan's sovereignty project demonstrate a clear understanding of this basic principle, and have devoted considerable resources to the pursuit of "sovereign" economic reform and social welfare strategies in the republic in the post-Soviet period, strategies which they claim have resulted in a higher standard of living for Tatarstanis than that of their compatriots living in other Russian provinces, and thus stand as evidence of the essential rightness of the republic's sovereignty project as a whole.

Tatarstan's independent economic reform and social welfare policies have evolved through several incarnations since the declaration of sovereignty, but the basic elements have remained more or less the same throughout. These include: the rejection of the Russian version of extreme "shock therapy" in favor of a less radical, more state-controlled process of market reform and privatization; a commitment to a more comprehensive and generous array of social welfare benefits than is found in the Russian Federation as a whole; and a more aggressive courting of world market share and foreign investment capital than is found in the Russian Federation in general.

In his official speech celebrating the decision to declare sovereignty in Tatarstan in August 1990, Mintimer Shaimiyev indicated that engineering market economic reforms while simultaneously increasing the social welfare and standard of living of the Tatarstani population would be one of the main priorities of the new sovereign state of Tatarstan (*Sovetskaya Tatariya* August 30, 1990, 1). Still, the government did not offer a coherent program of economic reform and social welfare provision until an important speech by Shaimiyev to the Supreme Soviet of Tatarstan in February 1992, when Tatarstan's strategy of a so-called "soft entry" into the market was first elucidated (*Sovetskaya Tatariya* February 5, 1992, 1).

The main goals of Tatarstan's soft entry strategy were to ease the pain of economic transition for citizens of Tatarstan by avoiding shock therapy, pursuing a slower rate of reform and maintaining adequate social protections throughout the process of transition. In practice, this meant maintaining price controls on basic foodstuffs and fuel as well as subsidies to consumers for housing and transport, only partially implementing the Russian federal government's privatization scheme while also developing and implementing a more conservative Tatarstani privatization regime,[5] and giving priority to the agro-industrial sector of the Tatarstani economy by supporting it with extensive government subsidies and credit (*Sovetskaya Tatariya* September 30, 1992, 1; August 1, 1993, 1; October 19, 1993, 1).

Six months after introducing the soft entry strategy Shaimiyev compared the results of Tatarstan's course favorable with those of Russia, boasting that while Russia had undertaken "radical reforms" which had decreased the standard of living of the Russian citizenry and "pilfered" resources from them, the unique Tatarstani strategy had led to a lower growth in consumer prices, and a continued commitment to the social welfare of the population and the most underprivileged elements of society (*Sovetskaya Tatariya* September 30, 1992, 1).

The Tatarstani government maintained its commitment to the soft entry strategy through spring 1994. In March 1994 the republic's Cabinet of Ministers and the Council of Trade Unions of Tatarstan joined together to create a "well-oiled system of social protection" for the country's population, while the government further vowed to continue to control prices on energy, food, medicine and transportation (*Izvestiya Tatarstana* March 18, 1994, 1). However by this time the flaws of the soft entry strategy were becoming evident, as even Tatarstan's economic ministers admitted. For example in April 1994, Ravil Muratov, who would later emerge as the dominant economic policy maker in Tatarstan, declared that while Tatarstan had learned from Russia's mistakes and thus avoided them, the republic was now facing mistakes generated from its own strategy. In particular, he complained that the extensive social programs and subsidies which the Tatarstani government had committed to were over-burdening the Tatarstani economy so that no significant reforms were taking place in the republic (*Segodnya* April 19, 1994, 2).

In response to these criticisms, and the deepening all-Russia crisis in production which was effecting Tatarstan along with the rest of the country, Shaimiyev asked the Tatarstani parliament to grant him special powers to regulate the economy in an effort to stimulate production, which they agreed to in June 1994 (*Izvestiya Tatarstana* June 10, 1994, 1). Shaimiyev and his advisors used these increased powers to issue pro-reform decrees on increasing tax discipline in Tatarstan, on liberalizing some prices in Tatarstan, and on establishing more favorable conditions for foreign investment in Tatarstan (*Republika Tatarstan* June 15, 1994, 1; *INTERFAX* July 19, 1994; September 20, 1994; *Nezavisimaya Gazeta* April 26, 1995, 2).

Despite the new pro-reform bent of the Tatarstani government, which was cemented in January 1995 when Shaimiyev named "convinced marketeers" Farid Mukhametshin and Ravil Muratov as the new Prime Minister and his first deputy, respectively, the commitment of the Tatarstani government to providing expansive (and expensive) social welfare provisions for the population of Tatarstan continued (*Komsomolskaya Pravda* January 17, 1995, 3). For example one of Muratov's first acts was to raise the minimum wage in Tatarstan, and to present a "radical, maybe even revolutionary" program of social reform in Tatarstan based on maintaining the incomes of citizens at a level 1.5 times the subsistence level as determined by the Tatarstani government (*Izvestiya Tatarstana* January 24, 1995, 35; *Respublika Tatarstan* January 25, 1995, 1). Muratov stressed that such an innovative and comprehensive social welfare program "had no such precedent in the Russian Federation" and would "effectively maintain the higher standard of living that citizens of Tatarstan enjoy" (*Respublika Tatarstan* January 25, 1995, 1).

Other republican officials also forwarded this argument. Indeed, on numerous occasions Shaimiyev asserted that "people live better here in Tatarstan, and this is mainly a result of Tatarstan's sovereignty" and that Tatarstan's decision to reject shock therapy had resulted in a minimum wage that was two times that of Russia and an unemployment rate that was one-half of Russia's (*ITAR-TASS* May 30, 1995; *Respublika Tatarstan* August

30, 1995, 1; *Segodnya* August 25, 1995, 3). Tatarstan's new Prime Minister Mukhametshin noted that despite price liberalization, basic foodstuffs in Tatarstan in 1995 still cost ¼ less than they did in Russia, a fact that was true in late 2002 as well (*Respublika Tatarstan* June 22, 1995, 1–2; *RFE/RL Tatar-Bashkir Service Daily Report* October 8, 2002).

The success of Tatarstan's strategy of pursuing gradual economic reform and integration into the world economy while maintaining a high level of social welfare provision for the population of Tatarstan inspired the republic to undertake more independent economic initiatives. In December 1997 Tatarstan passed a law allowing land to be bought and sold in the republic, arguing that Russian Federation legislation on the topic was "weak" and that Tatarstan had decided to "take the matter into its own hands according to its own national interests" (*RFE/RL Newsline* December 9, 1997; February 15, 1998; February 22, 1998). In February 1998, the Tatarstan government declared that it was establishing its own Bank for Reconstruction and Development to work with Western and Asian banks to help speedup defense industry conversion in Tatarstan. Again the Tatarstani government stressed that this was "Tatarstan's own problem" and as such it would search for the economic solutions to this problem on its own (*IEWS RRR* February 5, 1998).

The continued success of Tatarstan's "sovereign" economic policy was thrown into question by the August 1998 ruble crash and ensuing economic crisis in Russia, an event that forced the republic to acknowledge the great degree to which its economic fortunes were tied to those of the federation as a whole. In response to the events of August 1998, the Tatarstani government introduced its own "anti-crisis program," which included banning the shipping of butter, flour and other basic foodstuffs produced in Tatarstan outside of the republic, the decision to pay defaulted Russian Federation pensions and wages with food from Tatarstan, and the introduction of emergency protection measures for children and mothers (*RFE/RL Tatar-Bashkir Service Daily Report* September 29, 1998; October 2, 1998; October 10, 1998). These social protectionist measures in Tatarstan drew the ire of Russian Federal officials who claimed they "contradicted the principle of a unified market" (*IEWS RRR* September 1, 1998). Yet Tatarstani officials claimed they had no choice but to provide for their citizens during the economic crisis, given that the federal government seemed unable or unwilling to do so itself (*RFE/RL Tatar-Bashkir Service Daily Report* September 22, 1998). The continued willingness (and ability) of the republican leadership to subsidize basic foodstuffs for the population at least partially in the name of increasing support for the sovereignty project is evidenced by the fact that in early 2008, the cost of a "minimum food basket" was lower in Tatarstan than anywhere else in the country (*Tatar-inform* January 10, 2008).

Similarly, the Tatarstani government used the Putin administration's controversial decision to monetize in-kind social benefits, introduced in January 2005, as an opportunity to reinforce the positive benefits that sovereignty has brought to its citizens. While Tatarstan agreed to introduce the new reforms, and was one of only a handful of regions to do so fully and on-schedule, thus allowing the republic to play the role of good federal subject, Kazan also supplemented the new cash payments with additional outlays drawn from the republican budget, thus allowing republican leaders to again portray Tatarstan itself as a more generous, stable, and efficacious state than the Russian Federation itself.[6] Tatarstan's aggressive courting of the international community, discussed in more detail below, has also paid off in terms of helping the republican government to continue to be able to provide so lavishly for its poorest citizens—in October 2005 the government announced that the World Bank would be giving the republic over $1.3 million to help families living below the poverty line in Kazan (*RFE/RL Tatar-Bashkir Service Daily Report* October 11, 2005).

For political elites in Tatarstan, pursuing independent economic and social welfare reform policies and representing Tatarstan as an efficacious and capable state which is more able to provide materially for the present and future of their citizens than the Russian Federation has been an integral and effective part of the attempt to build internal sovereignty over the past decade. It is clear why these types of economic policies would be popular in the republic. Indeed, republican elites in Tatarstan have been remarkably open about the aims of their "sovereign" economic strategy. When asked about this matter in an April 1997 interview, Presidential advisor Rafael Khakimov replied that:

> We understood, that if the economy were to go bad, then the Russian-speaking portion of Tatarstani society would go sour on sovereignty. Tatars will always support sovereignty because it fulfills their national longings. But there is no ethnic argument for sovereignty for Russians. The neutrality of Russians in Tatarstan illustrates that they support sovereignty—they show their support passively. Our economic strategy and high standard of living have played a role in this. Russians have shown that they are for the economic course of the republic, that they are for Shaimiyev. (*Vremya i Dengi* April 8, 1997, 11)

The special attention that the republic has paid to cushioning the blows of economic reforms has paid off handsomely both in concrete terms and in terms of support for local government. Republican officials took heart from (and heavily publicized) UN data released in 2005 indicating that Tatarstanis enjoyed the third-highest standard of living in Russia, ranked only behind Moscow and Tyumen Oblast (*RFE/RL Tatar-Bashkir Service Daily Report* April 18, 2005). And while in general, citizens in Russia voice more faith in regional governments than the federal government to provide for their economic and social well-being (De Bardeleben 2003), this trend is particularly evident in Tatarstan. In just one recent example, 76 percent of citizens surveyed said they trusted Tatarstan's leadership, and 65 percent felt that the economic situation was "good and calm," while the corresponding numbers regarding the Russian federal government were at less than 35 percent (*RFE/RL Tatar-Bashkir Service Daily Report* April 11, 2003).

Thus it is possible to criticize the republic's economic policies for pandering to local interests and "obstructing" the development of a coherent national economic policy for Russia, as some have done. On the other hand, it is also possible to see the economic developments in the republics as support for the argument that the great advantage of federalism is that it allows the member units to act as laboratories for economic reform and also allows economic strategies to be tailored more closely to local realities, resulting in a more salubrious overall economic situation. Furthermore, given that the federal government in Moscow has consistently sought to transfer more and more of the burden for social welfare to the republics (by the end of the 1990s, regional governments were responsible for over 70 percent of social programs in Russia, including almost everything except prisoner and veteran affairs), the early experience that Tatarstan has developed in providing these services will allow the republic to serve as a model for other federation members in Russia in this arena (Konitzer-Smirnov 2003, 51).

Education Policy as Domestic Sovereignty Projection

Institutions of public knowledge production and dissemination are another important set of resources that Tatarstan's elites have attempted to use to strengthen their internal state-building efforts. Because a centralized education system is where important collective goals of social reproduction are articulated (such as a sense of statehood or national identity), political elites seek to control these institutions and use them in the pursuit of increased legitimacy (Appiah 1994). Towards this goal, over the past decade elites in Kazan have attempted to wrest control of the means of the production and dissemination of public knowledge away from the Russian federal center in Moscow in three ways. First, they have "republicanized" the former branches of the Soviet and Russian Academy of Sciences (R.A.N.) located in Tatarstan. Second, they have attempted to transfer the production of textbooks used at all levels of the educational process away from Moscow to the republic. Finally, they have introduced a significant republican-initiated component into the general education system in Tatarstan that is aimed at strengthening feelings of civic pride and patriotism towards the republic.

Under the Soviet system of ethno-federalism, republican level educational institutions, including republican filials of the Russian Academy of Science (RAN), were subject to strict centralization to both the Communist Party and the Soviet state. Academics working in the republican branches of the RAN were subject to Communist Party control over their choice of subject matter and their final projects (Black 1956; Shteppa 1962). In accordance with the policy of "national in form, socialist in content," the curriculum of the general education systems of the Russian national republics was determined in Moscow and was identical to that of all other educational institutions in the Soviet Union (Connor 1984; Bilinsky 1968; Slezkine 1994).

The claim of state sovereignty has been used as the pretext for the process of republicanizing the former Russian Academy of Science filial in Tatarstan in the post-Soviet period. In fact the main impetus behind the decision to take over the former RAN in Tatarstan and make an independent Tatarstan Academy of Science (ANRT) out of it was the desire to realize the republic's new sovereign status as fully, completely, and successfully as possible in the post-Soviet period. Shortly after the founding of the ANRT one commentator described it as "one of the most visible attributes of sovereignty" for Tatarstan (*Sovetskaya Tatariya* January 21, 1992, 2), while the first president of the ANRT explained the reasoning behind its creation in the following way:

> Tatarstan's intellectual resources and standing were that of an independent state, not just a union republic! Without the sovereign right to decide our own scientific problems, we can't decide the socio-economic, political, and cultural problems of state sovereignty and political-economic independence in the Republic of Tatarstan (*Sovetskaya Tatariya* February 13, 1993, 3).

Political elites in Tatarstan argued that the republic needed to obtain control of the scientific resources that were necessary to "solve the problems of state sovereignty" and that the creation of the ANRT was the most proper way to go about this. This indicates that elites in the republic harbor a long-term view of and commitment to the process of state-building. Indeed, the research agenda of the new ANRT is geared towards those hard sciences which are relevant for the future economic and political development of the republic—oil and chemical industries (*Sovetskaya Tatariya* February 13, 1993, 3).

The newly-republicanized academy of science also proved crucial for relocating the production of cultural and historical knowledge away from Moscow and to Tatarstan. Those parts of the new ANRT that produce historical and cultural knowledge are important actors in the attempt to distinguish the domestic and internal discursive space of the "sovereign" republic of Tatarstan from that of the Russian Federation. Moreover, the intellectual elites who inhabit these new institutions reveal themselves to be active and loyal participants in the Tatarstani sovereignty project, and are committed to the idea that the republic alone has the exclusive right to represent its own history and public image in the post-Soviet period.

A new Institute of History of the ANRT was formed in Kazan 1996 when several members of the ANRT asserted the need for a conception of Tatar history that was up to "international standards." The lack of such an "independent" account of Tatar history was said to be "severely limiting the new sovereign state of Tatarstan" (*KRIS* May 17, 1996, 1). At a series of debates which were held in 1996–1997 to discuss the Institute of History, members of the new collective asserted the need to produce textbooks with a "Tatarstani" interpretation of history to rectify the years of Soviet and Russian falsification of Tatar history (*Kak nam* 1996; *Tatarskaya* 1997; Seminar 1997). Some spoke of the need to "decolonize our history" and to "take it back from Russian control, while others criticized the portrayal of Tatars and Tatarstan in Moscow-produced texts used in classes about the history of Russia, and questioned the need to continue the teaching of courses in Russian history in a "sovereign Tatarstan" (*Kak nam* 1996; *Tatarskaya* 1997; Seminar 1997). In order to combat discriminatory portrayals of Tatars in textbooks, a new publishing house under the auspices of the Ministry of Education of Tatarstan called "Magarif" (the Tatar word for education or enlightenment) was created.[7] Together with the ANRT, Magarif has been charged with the task of creating all-new, indigenously produced textbooks for Tatarstan's educational system at all levels (in both Tatar and Russian language editions) (Zaripov 1997). The Magarif publishing house is now on its third-generation of textbooks, each one better adapted to its target audience, as one member of the Tatarstani Ministry of Education proudly told the author in the summer of 2005 (Gibatitdinov 2005).

Language asserting the presence of statehood and sovereignty has also been used to legitimate other education policy changes in Tatarstan since 1990. The most important of these is the introduction of a significant republican-designed and republican-mandated curriculum component for all schools and

institutions of higher learning in Tatarstan. The degree to which the imperative of state-building is shaping reform of the education system in the republic
is illustrated by a quote from Tatarstan's Minister of Education:

> As historical experience shows, to build a sovereign state and defend its inde-
> pendence is possible only for those peoples who have their own system of edu-
> cation. Therefore it is no coincidence that such established states as the U.S.,
> Germany, France, and England direct a substantial portion of their resources
> to the funding of education. The Republic of Tatarstan has also made the de-
> velopment of the educational system in Tatarstan a priority, as is embodied in
> the Law on Education of Tatarstan (Gaifullin 1996, 45).

The use of analogy in this quote is very powerful. The statement forcefully asserts that Tatarstan is in the process of building a sovereign state, and
legitimates that project by linking Tatarstan and its efforts at education reform with other "established states" like the U.S. and the European powers.
Thus it indicates that the aspirations of Tatarstan's sovereignty-seeking are
in fact international, and are not confined within the discursive or material
space of the Russian Federation. On the ground, new republican-mandated
curricular elements were introduced during the academic year 1991–1992
in Tatarstan. These new requirements include classes in the ecology and geography of Tatarstan, but more importantly include courses on the history,
culture and literature of the republic. The amount of time devoted to classes
about, "The History and Culture of Tatars and Tatarstan" averages about
three-and-a-half hours a week, and has remained consistent throughout the
post-Soviet period (MORT 1991b; Zaripov 2005). Tatarstan's republican
component of education has an additional aspect of major importance—the
mandatory study of the Tatar language and literature at an average of three-
and-a-half hours a week for all students in Tatarstan, regardless of nationality, starting from grade one (MORT 1991b). This policy, discussed in more
detail in chapter 4, was introduced in 1992 when the Tatarstani parliament
adopted the Law on Languages of the Peoples of Tatarstan, which named
both Tatar and Russian as official state languages. The teaching of Tatar
to non-Tatar students was expanded after June 1994, when an ambitious
government program for the fulfillment of the law on language was passed
(*Zakon* 1996).

The implementation of these new policies has been pursued vigorously
in Tatarstan. A new department has been opened at Kazan State University
to produce teachers who will teach Tatar to Russian-speaking children in
Tatarstan (*Izvestiya Tatarstana* September 24, 1993, 3). An even more extraordinary development is a new bureaucratic office, the Assistant Directors

for National Education, which was established by the Ministry of Education of Tatarstan in October 1994. These officials, one of whom is now present in every Russian-speaking school and mixed Russian-Tatar school in Tatarstan, are charged with overseeing and facilitating the implementation of the new Tatar language and literature classes and the classes on the culture, literature, and history of Tatarstan (MORT 1994).

Acting Like a State Abroad: Projecting Sovereignty in the International Arena

Dividing up the powers and authorities associated with the internal or domestic aspect of state sovereignty is the very essence of federalism, but sharing the international spotlight by allowing sub-state units to engage in some degree of foreign economic and political activity is generally a less common and much more contentious process for federations (Adelcoa and Keating 1999; Hocking 1993a, 1993b; Michelmann and Soldatos 1990). This is despite the fact that fostering autonomous regional foreign policy action within the framework of federalism (which may require loosening or changing that framework) can bring both economic and political benefits to the federation as a whole. In the case at hand, we see ample evidence to support the contention that in the context of an increasingly complex global economic and political environment, republican international economic and political initiatives that have been mounted in the name of sovereignty projects have accrued exactly the types of advantages for Russia that similar efforts have produced in countries like Britain, Canada, and Spain (Keating 2001). More specifically, Tatarstan's desire to project sovereignty outward to the international community to the greatest extent possible, which has led it to vigorously pursue foreign economic investment and a higher international profile for the republic, has not only contributed to Russia's economic development, but has been essential in deepening Russia's engagement with international multilateral institutions such as the European Union, the United Nations, and especially the Islamic world, including the Organization of the Islamic Conference. It also has provided a model for other regions and republics, such as Bashkortostan, to emulate, thus further amplifying the positive impact of its actions.

Part of the reason sharing sovereignty in the international arena is so difficult for states is that states jealously guard both their international reputation and of course their international security. Indeed those powers most often reserved solely for federal governments include the provision of national defense. Thus the overzealous pursuit of "international personality" by sub-state units, especially when it is informed by aspirations to sovereignty that include pretensions of statehood and nationness, could potentially be quite damaging to federations. However here again, what we see in the case of Tatarstan is that that the worst-case scenario anticipated by opponents of republican sovereignty projects has not occurred. Instead, negotiations between the center and the periphery regarding sovereignty sharing in the international arena have proceeded much like they have in other spheres—Tatarstan has pushed the center to adopt truly federal policies that allow some meaningful economic and political autonomy for the regions in the global arena but has also accepted that the federal government in Moscow has the right to impose some limits to the regions' sovereign aspirations in this sphere. As a result, a potentially divisive and confrontational situation is one that, upon closer examination, has turned out to be a win-win one that strengthens the Russian Federation as a whole, both economically and politically, while also allowing Tatarstani elites to exercise some of the imperatives of statehood in the international arena.

Tatarstan Takes on the World

From the beginning, Tatarstan's sovereignty project has included a strong international dimension. The March 1992 referendum on sovereignty in the republic, which was discussed in chapter 2, asked voters to support the bold assertion that Tatarstan was "a sovereign state and a subject of international law" (Presidium 1992). By forwarding a claim to sovereignty that embodied both statehood and international legal subjecthood, Tatarstan's political elites made it clear they aspired to something beyond the mere achievement of new levels of political and economic autonomy *within* the Russian Federation. And yet these claims are also ambiguously presented—the claim to "international subjecthood" is a vague and imprecise formulation. Tatarstan's claim to have the right to some form of sovereignty in the international arena thus seems to have been crafted with the intent to cast as wide a net as possible, while also not alienating the Russian Federation or the international community with inflammatory secessionist demands.

After the March 1992 referendum passed in the republic, the government of Tatarstan issued a decree which appealed to "states and international organizations" with the proposition that they begin to build relations with the republic "according to her new status" as a sovereign state and subject of international law (Verkhovnogo 1992a). Such an appeal demonstrates an understanding on the part of the Tatarstani leadership that direct ties to the international community would provide powerful legitimation of Tatarstan's claims to sovereignty in the face of probable Russian opposition to those claims. Later in 1992, articles 61 and 62 of the Tatarstani Constitution reaffirmed the republic's status as a sovereign state and subject of international law and enumerated Tatarstan's specific rights and responsibilities in the international sphere. These included the right to enter into relations with other states, to exchange diplomats and other representatives with other states, and to participate in the activity of international organizations. Article 62 also sought to link the republic more closely with the international community by asserting that international law has precedence on the territory of Tatarstan. The February 1994 treaty with Russia, while not explicitly referring to Tatarstan as a sovereign state, did recognize Tatarstan's claimed status as "an international actor." Specifically, article 11 of the treaty with Russia gives Tatarstan the right to:

> . . . participate in international relations, establish relations with foreign states and conclude treaties which do not contradict the Constitution or international obligation of the Russian Federation, the Constitution of the Republic of Tatarstan, or the present agreement, and to participate in the activity of international organizations.

Furthermore, articles 12 and 13 of the February 1994 agreement give Tatarstan the right to create their own national bank, and to "conduct foreign economic activity independently."[8]

Besides these efforts to legally codify their right to a sovereign international presence, Tatarstani political elites have also attempted to increase the republic's political and economic participation in the international arena in order to strengthen its claims to some type of membership in the international community. In the political realm, Tatarstan has initiated contacts with several international organizations, including the United Nations, the European Union, the League of Arab States, and the Organization of the Islamic Conference. Tatarstan's leadership has sought enthusiastically to broaden its ties with these international organizations, and has made clear that it views participation in them as a key way to realize its claims to sovereignty in the international community.

In November 1994 the Assistant Secretary General of the UN, Joseph Verner Reed, paid an official visit to Kazan to announce the opening of a UN information and resource center in Tatarstan called the "Association for Cooperation with the UN" Reed praised Tatarstan's attempts to resolve autonomy conflicts in the Russian Federation and expressed his hope that cooperation between the UN and Tatarstan would continue to grow. President Shaimiyev used the occasion to inform Reed that Tatarstan had "laid the political legal-bases for sovereign statehood," and noted the important role of the international community in helping Tatarstan to "evolve as a democratic state" in the post-Soviet period (*Izvestiya Tatarstan* November 29, 1994, 1). Several UNESCO conferences have been held in Kazan, and UNESCO held a series of "Tatarstan Days" at its headquarters in Paris in June 2001. In 2003 UNESCO's World Heritage Cities organization established a new "Euroasian" regional department headquarters in Kazan, and has announced that in 2007 Kazan would host the organization's ninth international symposium (*RFE/RL Tatar-Bashkir Service Daily Report* November 14, 2005). In a sign of his growing personal reputation in UN circles, Tatarstani President Shaimiyev was invited to address the UN General Assembly at a special session on the "Dialogue of Civilizations" in August 2001 (*RFE/RL Tatar-Bashkir Service Daily Report* August 7, 2001).

Since 1990, Tatarstan has also expanded its involvement with European political structures. Tatarstani elites have interpreted their participation in the regional institutions of the EU as evidence of the republic's declared statehood and have used their new EU contacts to strengthen their hand in negotiations with Moscow over certain contentious political issues. In October 1996 Tatarstan and the European Union sponsored an international conference on the budgetary and tax problems of federal systems in Europe and the former Soviet Union (*Molodezh' Tatarstana* October 11, 1996, 1). The next month in Moscow Tatarstan's Vice-President Vasily Likhachev chaired a meeting of the Congress of Local and Regional Organs of Power in Europe, aimed at increasing ties between Russia's regions and Europe, in order "to allow Russia's regions to make a real contribution to the architecture of Europe and the EU in the 21st century" (*Respublika Tatarstan* November 23 and 26, 1996, 1). In 1997 Tatarstan hosted a related conference sponsored by the EU entitled "Democracy at the Local Level," and was accepted into formal membership in the Assembly of the European Regions (*Vremya i Dengi* March 18, 1997, 1; *Respublika Tatarstan* June 17, 1997, 1).

Significantly, in May 1998 Likhachev was named the Russian Federation's permanent representative to the European Union in Strasbourg. This appointment reflected both the important role that Tatarstan has begun to play in European politics in the post-Soviet period and the seriousness with which Russia regards Tatarstan's international sovereign ambitions. However appointing Likhachev to this important post was also a strategic attempt by Yeltsin to co-opt Tatarstan's quest for membership in the international community and to contain the republic's efforts towards this end within both Russian Federal and European *regional* frameworks. By giving Tatarstan's Vice-President such a prestigious post, Yeltsin was able to simultaneously help limit Tatarstan's international ambitions to the European realm, while also increasing Russia's overall integration into European political and economic institutions. Upon taking the job, Likhachev commented that while he was Russia's representative to the EU, one of the most important parts of his job would be to represent the interests of Tatarstan there. (*RFE/RL Newsline* May 6, 1998). Tatarstan's former Vice-President and current State Council Chairman Farid Mukhametshin has also been heavily involved in European politics throughout the post-Soviet era, serving as the chairman of the Committee on Culture and Education of the Council of Europe's Congress of Local Regional Authorities in 2005 and encouraging that body to increase its cooperation both with Russia's regions and the European Union (*RFE/RL Tatar-Bashkir Service Daily Report* October 3, 2005 and November 29, 2005). Perhaps most revealing of Tatarstan's growing European reputation and profile, the republic played host in May 2007 to the annual meeting of European Bank for Reconstruction and Development (EBRD) shareholders, the first time the meeting was held in Russia since 1994; significantly, this honor is one that was negotiated jointly by Russian and Tatarstani officials with the EBRD (*RFE/RL Tatar-Bashkir Service Daily Report* September 8, 2005; *RFE/RL Newsline* May 21, 2007).

In its efforts to project external sovereignty, Tatarstan's leadership has also attempted to develop direct bilateral ties with foreign countries. In the early years of the sovereignty project (1990–1993), Tatarstan established official political and economic contacts with all of the C.I.S. states, much of the former Soviet bloc and Europe (especially Hungary, the Czech Republic, and Germany and France), as well as with Turkey, Canada, and the U.S.[9] On many of these visits, the Tatarstani President Mintimer Shaimiyev signed general agreements pledging to increase "trade-economic, scientific-technical and cultural" trade cooperation between Tatarstan and the various other polities—by 2001 Tatarstan had signed 27 such bilateral agreements.[10] During these years Tatarstan also hosted foreign economic and business delegations from the U.S. and various European countries including Sweden, Hungary, and Germany. Eventually these contacts led to the opening of "official representations" from Tatarstan in thirteen countries, including Cuba, France, Turkey, the United States, and Vietnam, while both Iran and Turkey have established Consulate General offices and cultural centers in Kazan.[11]

Tatarstan has not limited itself to building political bridges in the international community, also seeking out new economic relationships for the republic in the global arena. President Mintimer Shaimiyev represented Tatarstan at the January 1995 Davos World Economic Forum, emphasizing in his news conferences that Tatarstan had been invited to the forum "as an autonomous actor" (*Izvestiya Tatarstan* January 31, 1995, 1). Later in 1995, claiming that "whether Russia or the C.I.S. likes it or not Tatarstan is located in international economic space," the government of Tatarstan hired an American consulting firm to do a comprehensive survey of the republic's economy and to devise a program for its long-term economic development and integration into the world economy (*Izvestiya Tatarstan* March 16, 1995, 3–5; *Vremya i Dengi* March 28, 1996, 3 and July 9, 1996, 3–4.). The company's recommendations, which included using the republic's hefty oil revenues to propel the country out of its reliance on raw material exports and toward a more investment and innovation-driven economy, became the basis for a new "Program for Social and Economic Progress" in Tatarstan.[12]

In a further effort to increase its contacts with the international economy, Tatarstan has adopted some of the most liberal and generous legislation governing foreign investment anywhere in Russia.[13] The vigorous pursuit of a new international economic presence has paid off handsomely for Tatarstan—the republic has consistently been one of the top ten regions in Russia in terms of foreign investment, and in both 2001 and 2002 Tatarstan had the highest percentage of companies appearing on the "Russia's best exporters" list of any region in Russia.[14] In the post-Soviet period as a whole, foreign trade turnover grew by a factor of six, totaling $6.3 billion in 2004 (*RFE/RL Tatar-Bashkir Service Daily Report* July 8, 2005). Furthermore, in May 2002 the republic was singled out by Russian Federal officials as one of only six Russian regions considered ready for membership in the WTO (*RFE/RL Newsline* May 14, 2002), a prestigious and enviable status reiterated in 2005 by Moody's Investors Service when it gave Tatarstan the highest credit rating given to any region within the Russian state (*RFE/RL Tatar-Bashkir Service Daily Report* September 28, 2005). TATNEFT, the republic's main oil concern in which the republic owns a 40 percent share, continues to be the focus of much international investment interest, with joint projects being established with South Korea's LG International Corp. in 2004 and the Iranian Oil and Gas Ministry in 2005.

Tatarstan has made particular efforts to reach out to the Islamic world, both economically and politically, claiming that its "Euro-Muslim" heritage makes it the perfect actor to rebuild and strengthen ties between Russia and the worldwide umma (with all of its attendant economic and political opportunities) in the post-Soviet era (Graney 2006). Besides twice receiving official delegations from Iran and Turkey and visiting those countries as the personal guest of their presidents, signing several business and other agreements with these and other Islamic states such as Sudan, Iraq, and Libya, Shaimiyev has offered himself as a mediator for both the Chechen and Afghan crises. Tatarstan recently made history when it cosponsored an international conference on "One Thousand Years of Islamic Civilization in the Volga Region" together with the Organization of the Islamic Conference (OIC), the first such joint venture between the OIC and a Russian republic. At the conference, which was held in Kazan in June 2001, the OIC deputy director announced that Tatarstan would be invited to begin the process of joining the OIC as an observer member, while in August 2004 the OIC's newly-elected secretary general, Ekmeleddin Isanoglu announced that at long last, "Tatarstan has attained its representative to the OIC" (*RFE/RL Tatar-Bashkir Service Daily Report* August 12, 2004). Kazan has pursued its goal of being Russia's "intermediary" to the Islamic world even more vigorously since the terrorist attacks of September 11, seeking to become an independent partner in the "war on terror" by holding repeated meetings with the transitional government in Afghanistan, during one of which an agreement for thousands of KamAz trucks from Tatarstan to be shipped to Afghanistan was signed (*RFE/RL Tatar-Bashkir Service* January 10, 2001). Shaimiyev most recently reiterated this Tatarstani aspiration in August 2005 on the occasion of Kazan's 1000th anniversary celebration, in conjunction with which the republic played host to a full-scale CIS summit, touted by Shaimiyev and other Tatarstani elites as proof of the republic's "essential" historical and contemporary role in helping Russia flourish and fulfill her "Eurasian destiny" (*Kommersant-Vlast* August 29, 2005, 32–35). Eager not to lose the momentum built up over the past years, in September 2005 Tatarstan hosted what it touted as the first ever Islamic film festival ("The Golden Minbar International Muslim Film Festival"), a joint project between Russia's Council of Muftis, the Islamic World television company and Tatarstan's Presidential Administration that featured films from Egypt, Iran, Jordan, Malaysia, Britain, and Canada as well as CIS countries (*RFE/RL Tatar-Bashkir Service Daily Report* July 18, 2005 and September 6, 2005). The festival was so successful that it has become an annual event in Tatarstan, with the 2007 iteration boasting a nearly $1 million budget and the attendance of legendary French film actress Catherine Deneuve (*RFE/RL Newsline* September 6, 2007).

Tatarstan's energetic and successful "Islamic diplomacy" has not only brought economic benefits to the Russian Federation in the form of contracts for military hardware, oil and other commodities, but has also raised awareness in Moscow about the potential utility of using Russia's large Muslim population as an additional way to increase Russia's influence in the international community in the post-Communist era. As such, the Putin administration piggybacked on to the relationship that Tatarstan had cultivated with the OIC and in October 2003 announced Russia's own intention to apply for membership to the organization. This is a perfect illustration of the way in which allowing sub-state units to exercise more sovereignty even in the international arena benefits states; as Putin himself commented, observing the changed international climate that fostered such a novel turn of events for Russia, "Our cooperation with the OIC may become a most important element of a fair and secure world" (*Pravda.Ru* October 16, 2003). In the wake of Russia's participation in the 32nd Conference of the Foreign Ministers of the OIC in Yemen in June 2005, the Russian Foreign Ministry issued special recognition of Ekzam Gobeidullin, one of Tatarstan's senators to the Russian Federation Council, for his help in fostering Russia's ties with the Islamic world and the OIC in particular (*RFE/RL Tatar-Bashkir Service Daily Report* July 19, 2005).

If the federal government in Moscow has become aware of the potential utility of allowing some functional regional autonomy in the international arena, the republics themselves have likewise learned that they often need the mediation of the central Russian state for their initiatives to succeed. When Tatarstani elites embarked on efforts to build direct political and economic contacts with the international community immediately after the republic declared sovereignty, they soon realized that no foreign state outside of the C.I.S. countries was willing to commit fully to economic or diplomatic ties with the republic while its relationship to Russia was still unclear legally. Tatarstani officials thus needed to convince foreign audiences that the republic's economic and political relationship with Russia was stable and regularized while also attaining the maximum level of foreign policy-making authority and sovereignty for Tatarstan in the international arena. The goal of the Russian Federal government, on the other hand, was to simultaneously encourage the development of the international economic ties of its sub-state units while still conducting a unified Russian foreign policy and presenting a unified sovereign presence in the international arena.[15]

The concept of a bilateral agreement between Tatarstan and Russia, which would include international relations powers for Tatarstan far beyond those afforded by the Russian Federal treaty, became the vehicle for the realization of both sides' goals. The aforementioned February 1994 agreement achieved an ambiguous if strategic alliance between Tatarstan and Russia in the sphere of international political and economic activity. Tatarstan received the right to make foreign economic policy "independently," to participate in international organizations, and to sign treaties and agreements that do not contradict Russia's Constitution or its international agreements. Yet the agreement also allowed for the preservation of the integrity of Russia's transportation, currency, and tariff systems by relegating decisions in these areas to the joint jurisdiction of Russia and Tatarstan. The levels of Tatarstan's yearly oil export levels also fell under joint jurisdiction, while the Russian Federation alone retained the right to make decisions on war and peace.[16]

The February 1994 agreement allowed Russian officials to declare that the fundamental unity and integrity of the Russian state had been preserved, especially in the areas of military and defense policy. It also enabled Tatarstani officials to assure potential foreign economic partners both that Tatarstan possessed the right to conduct its own foreign policy independently *and* that the basic unity of Russian economic and political space was legally ensured. Since the signing of the agreement, Tatarstani officials have characterized their foreign activities as "fully independent" but still "coordinated with," and "in the same channel" as the Russian Federation's foreign policy (*FBIS Report on Central Eurasia* August 19, 1994, 27 and July 5, 1995, 42). Russian federal officials have echoed these reassurances, which appear to be aimed at international audiences (potential investors, international organizations); in April 2002 then Russian Foreign Minister Igor Ivanov asserted that Russia and Tatarstan had "complete and mutual understanding" that their foreign policies were "unified," and that Moscow was "grateful" to Tatarstan for its cooperative approach to foreign policy making (*RFE/RL Tatar-Bashkir Service Daily Report* April 23, 2002). This evolving and mutually-beneficial cooperation between Moscow and Kazan in the realm of foreign policy was formalized by the Russian Ministry of Foreign Affairs in May 2003, when Ivanov announced the signing of a three-year "Protocol on Cooperation between the Ministry of Foreign Affairs of the Russian Federation and the Republic of Tatarstan in the Realm of International and Economic Relations," the first such agreement of its kind in Russia (*RFE/RL Tatar-Bashkir Service Daily Report* May 19, 2003). In 2005, further proof of the utility of the joint Kazan-Moscow efforts in the international system was produced, the republic became the recipient of two separate $125 million loans—one from the World Bank for social development in Kazan (*RFE/RL Tatar-Bashkir Service Daily Report* August 31, 2004), and one from the EBRD to "increase Kazan's attractiveness to foreign investment" (*RFE/RL Tatar-Bashkir Service Daily Report* May 23, 2005). These successes led Russian Foreign Minister Sergei Lavrov in 2005 to praise Tatarstan's "experience in developing international and foreign economic relations" and urge other Russian regional leaders to follow the republic's example (*RFE/RL Tatar-Bashkir Service Daily Report* July 8, 2005).

Autocracy and Ethnocracy in Tatarstan and Beyond

While I have attempted to highlight here the positive impact that Tatarstan's domestic and international efforts to project sovereignty have had for Russia's overall political and economic development and its development as a federation, the less salubrious aspects of these state-building efforts must also be addressed. One of the strongest critiques of the republican sovereignty projects, as noted in the previous chapter, is that the republics, including Tatarstan, have tended to use their new powers and authorities to build autocratic and indeed ethnocratic regimes. The most forceful of these critics is Henry Hale, who argues that the domestic sovereignty projects in the republics have led to the consolidation "not of democracy, but rather an ethnically exclusive autocratic system of machine politics: ethnocracy" (Hale 1998). Critics point to the fact that the new legislative and executive institutions in the republics are even more biased towards the titular ethnicities than were their Soviet predecessors, and argue that regional elites have used these ethnic networks to fully dominate civil society, becoming in the process among the worst human and civil rights abusers in the entire country (Hale 1998, 2003b; Kahn 2002, chapter 7; Opalski 2001). Soviet-era rationalization of ethnic affirmative actions for titular elites have been transformed by the republics in the post-Soviet era into legitimizing rhetoric that serves to mask the worst type of "cronyism and autocratization" in Tatarstan and other republics, especially Bashkortostan (Hale 1998, 2003, 244).[17]

There is no denying that the titular ethnic group has maintained, and at times even increased, the Soviet-era elevated levels of representation in political institutions into the post-Soviet period. For example, in 1997 ethnic Tatars occupied over 75 percent of the slots in the executive branch in Tatarstan (as compared with 56.2 percent in 1990), while ethnic Bashkirs composed 67.5 percent of the Cabinet of Ministers of Bashkortostan (as compared with 27.7 percent in 1990) (Guboglo et al. 1997, 129, 152; Kaiser 1997, 20). This pattern was also evident in legislative institutions—in Tatarstan, the first corpus of the State Council, elected in 1993, was 73 percent Tatar and 25.1 percent Russian (as opposed to the ethnic composition of the 1990 Supreme Soviet in the Tatar A.S.S.R., which was only 58 percent Tatar and 38 percent Russian) (Kaiser 1997, 20).

The potential for ethnocracy is not the only pathology present in the republics—Tatarstani President Shaimyev has installed his sons and nephews in important political and economic positions over the past decade. He has been outdone in this case only by Murtaza Rakhimov, president of neighboring Bashkortostan, whose son Ural has been particularly well-treated in this regard—in January 2003 he was announced as Chairman of the Board of four of Bashkortostan's largest companies—Bashneft, the oil giant, Bashkneftkhim, another oil products firm, Bashkirenergo, the republic's energy firm, and Salavatneftorgsintez, another oil firm.

This last fact points to an important characteristic of the very real and important political ills that plague the republics; that they may not in fact be a consequence of the pursuit of "sovereignty" per se, but rather reflect a universal trend towards authoritarianism, cronyism and the concentration of executive power in Russia, and that the central government in Moscow has played an important role not in fighting, but rather in propagating these types of political pathologies. It is not clear that the ethnic and in some cases kin networks that dominate political and economic institutions in the republics are that much different from the crony and "family" networks that dominate the same institutions in St. Petersburg, Moscow, or anywhere else in Russia. Indeed, the two sets of networks seem to overlap and reinforce one another, as is demonstrated by the fact that the percentage of Tatarstani State Council deputies elected in 2004 who pledged allegiance to Putin's United Russia party (85 percent) was much higher than the percentage of deputies identified as ethnic Tatars (52 percent).

Likewise, while there is ample evidence to support the characterization of the Tatarstan government as routine violators of civil rights, particularly the right to free speech, it is not clear that the Moscow Kremlin's record on this account is much better than that of the Kazan Kremlin. The manipulation of local media and harassment of political opposition in the republics would seem to differ from that which occurs on the federal level or elsewhere in Russia only in degree, if at all—for example, the harassment of "alternative" media and alternative candidates during the 1998 and 2003 presidential elections in Tatarstan's neighbor Bashkortostan was so heavy-handed and widespread that at times it bordered on the farcical, particularly in December 2003 as one after another television and radio stations were shut down for various "technical" reasons (Hale 1998).

I do not mean to exonerate Tatarstan or the other republics for the absence of democracy in their sovereignty projects, but rather I want to argue that to require the absolute dismantling of republican sovereignty projects like Tatarstan's, in part because of their antidemocratic nature, as the Putin administration has done of late, is, to lay on the metaphors, both a case of the pot calling the kettle black and throwing out the baby with the bathwater. Rather, the problem of democratic reforms and the protection of civil rights is a common one for both federal and regional actors. While in federal systems like the United States it is left to the central government to protect civil rights and liberties and enforce state compliance with these norms, in Russia, unfortunately, Moscow has shown neither the will nor ability to use the Constitutional Court or federal legislation to really force the regions to adhere to democratic practices, instead indulging regional violations while engaging in plenty of its own (Stepan 2000, 150).

Evaluating Domestic and
International Sovereignty Projects in Tatarstan

Despite the failures of democratization in the republics, citizens of Tatarstan on the whole seem satisfied with the results of the efforts of their leaders to "act like states" domestically and internationally. Residents of the republics consistently rate their regional governments as being more effective than the federal government in a whole set of policy spheres and view their local governments as being more reliable and trustworthy than Moscow (Debardeleben 2003, 348). Overall, in 2003 a strong majority of citizens in Tatarstan (65 percent) voiced the belief that the pursuit of sovereignty had led to "a good and calm situation" in the republic, while only 32 percent said the same about the Russian Federation as a whole (*RFE/RL Tatar-Bashkir Service Daily Report* April 11, 2003). Furthermore, despite the holdover of Soviet-era over-representation of titular ethnic groups in political institutions, few Russian residents of the republics felt that their economic rights had been violated in the republics because of their ethnicity, and in fact income and wage data reflect a systematic *ethnic Russian* advantage in the republics, indicating that there has not been a concomitant attempt to "ethnicize" the economic or public sectors in the republics in the name of sovereignty in the post-Soviet period (Bahry 2002, 681, 688). Less scientifically, ten years of fieldwork in Tatarstan and Kazan in particular confirm that in general citizens are appreciative of the efforts to beautify Kazan and transform it into a capital city worthy of a "sovereign" republic.

Thus to reiterate, while it is imperative to strengthen those aspects of federalism that will ensure that both the federal and regional governments respect human and civil rights and adhere to democratic norms in Russia (an issue I address in more detail in the conclusion), it does not appear that republican sovereignty projects in and of themselves prohibit these reforms. And as this chapter has demonstrated, the sovereignty projects have in fact furthered federal development in Russia in other ways by serving as the means for the development of the real, substantive powers and authorities at the regional level that characterize strong federal systems and enhance the state's overall well-being. The next chapter turns to a discussion of one of the other most important, ways that Tatarstan's sovereignty project has done this—by providing for an adequate level of ethnocultural justice in Russia in the absence of a meaningful federal commitment to do so.

Notes

1. In June 1991, former first secretary of the Communist Party of the Tatar A.S.S.R. Mintimer Shaimiyev was elected to the post of Tatarstani president. As was discussed in the previous chapter, Tatarstan has clauses in both its constitution and presidential electoral legislation stipulating that the president of the republic must know both Tatar and Russian, the two official state languages of the republic.

2. Survey data on attitudes towards the state symbols of the republic is not available, making it difficult to assess the results of this strategy.

3. For an interesting discussion of the importance of such symbols to the construction of a sense of "banal" nationalism, see Billig (1995).

4. Significantly, Wagenaar (2000, 3) notes that the two things most associated with "upgrading" of Paris aped by other European capital cities in the nineteenth century were slum-clearance programs and public transportation projects.

5. In August 1993, the government of Tatarstan introduced its own individual privatization checks or vouchers (IPC's), which were worth 30,000 roubles each (the all-Russian IPC's were worth 10,000 R each). The Tatarstani IPCs could not be bought or sold outside of Tatarstan, effectively protecting Tatarstan from "foreign" investors from the Russian Federation (*Sovetskaya Tatariya* August 1, 1993, 1; *Kommersant-Daily* April 26, 1995, 3). The end result of the multiphase Tatarstani privatization regime, which the Russian central press criticized as "economic autarky" was that the Tatarstani government maintained a larger share in the major enterprises of the republic (oil, automobile, and chemical industries) than did the federal government with respect to Russian businesses, with the republican government holding an average 30–40 percent stake in these enterprises (*Kommersant-Daily* April 26, 1995, 3; *Rossiya* June 7–13, 1995, 6).

6. On December 27, 2004, Shaimiyev announced that the republic would double the previously announced cash payments for veterans and victims of state repression, while Tatarstan's Deputy Prime Minister Zilya Valiev noted that the action meant Tatarstan's program for social support "would have no equal in the Russian Federation" (*RFE/RL Tatar-Bashkir Daily Report* December 27, 2004). Tatarstan's total supplemental outlays during the transition to monetized benefits amounted to 1.1 billion rubles ($40 million) (*RFE/RL Tatar-Bashkir Daily Report* January 26, 2005).

7. Magarif's director defines his publication house's mission as that of enabling Tatarstani citizens "to know their own history, the history of Tatarstan and the Tatar people *objectively* for the first time" (emphasis mine) (Pyatletnii 1996; Valeev 1995).

8. The protocol for Tatarstan's conduct of foreign economic activity was outlined in a separate agreement, also signed on February 15, 1994. In this agreement, the two parties agreed to "coordinate" their formation of foreign economic policy. According to this document, the determination of export quotas, payment-credit regimes with foreign partners, and licensing of the sale of Tatarstani products abroad belong to the "joint authority" of Tatarstan and the Russian Federation. Tatarstan itself has

exclusive authority to: conclude trade and economic agreements with foreign states; to guarantee and oversee the usage of foreign state, bank and commercial credits; to form a currency fund of the Republic of Tatarstan; to develop a separate policy of attracting foreign investment to Tatarstan; to participate in the work of international financial organizations; and to establish free economic zones in Tatarstan. See *Suverennyi Tatarstan: Sovereign Tatarstan* (Moscow: Plenipotentiary Representation of Tatarstan, 1997), 73–75.

9. For example, two months after the Declaration of Sovereignty, in October 1990, then Prime Minister of Tatarstan M. G. Sabirov led a delegation from Tatarstan's huge oil conglomerate TATNEFT to the United States to discuss economic cooperation. See *Sovetskaya Tatariya* October 31, 1990, p. 1.

10. Tatarstan signed the earliest of these agreements with the Baltic countries and Belarus (in late 1992) and signed others with Hungary and Turkey in 1993. In June 2001, Tatarstan's Minister for Trade and Foreign Economic Cooperation, Khafiz Salikhov, bragged that Tatarstan had the most experience in signing bilateral treaties, both domestic and international, "of any Russian region." See *RFE/RL Tatar-Bashkir Service* June 27, 2001.

11. According to the list published on the official website of the Republic of Tatarstan (www.tatar.ru), accessed May 28, 2008.

12. See the full Program on Social and Economic Development as published in *Respublika Tatarstan: Vremya Bolshikh Peremen* (*Republic of Tatarstan: Time of Great Changes*) (Kazan, 1996).

13. These laws provide large tax breaks to foreign investors, allow foreign partners to own the land that the enterprises they invest in are located on, and provide guarantees against nationalization backed up by Tatarstan's government and national bank. The new laws on foreign investment are reprinted in *Suverennyi Tatarstan: Sovereign Tatarstan* (Moscow: Plenipotentiary Representation of Tatarstan, 1997), 190–99.

14. The survey was conducted by the firm Pioneer First, as reported in the online *OMRI Russian Regional Report*, Volume 1, #17 (December 18, 1996).

15. At a conference about Russian federalism in Kazan in June 1996, a top official of the Russian Ministry of Foreign Affairs admitted that in the early 1990s the Russian regions had surprised the center with their vigorous foreign policy initiatives, forcing the center to try to "make some order" out of the de facto independent foreign policies of the regions, especially Tatarstan (*Tatarstan* October 1996, 15–16).

16. According to one of the related agreements also signed on February 15, 1994, the Tatarstani government is to be consulted about the deployment of Russian Federation troops in Tatarstan and about issues of defense production in Tatarstan.

17. Hale does allow that genuine "protection for the ethnic group" might be "part of the motivation" for keeping Soviet-era ethnic affirmative action institutions, but does not seem to find these claims to be persuasive (Hale 2003, 244). Neither does Kahn (2002), who is even more dismissive of a potential right to self-determination for the titular minorities in Russia.

CHAPTER FOUR

Projecting the Nation: Sovereignty Projects and Ethnocultural Justice in Tatarstan

Liberal Pluralism, Ethnocultural Justice, and the Soviet Ethno-Federal Legacy

One of the most exciting recent evolutions in democratic theory is the attempt, largely initiated by Canadian thinkers grappling with the Quebec question, to bring considerations of ethnic and other minority group rights into discussions about liberal democracy.[1] Positing that traditional liberal theories of justice had overlooked both the "intrinsic value" represented by different cultural and linguistic groups in a society, and that membership in a cultural or language community was for some people the most important context in which they could pursue happiness (Reaume 2000, 246–47), these theorists believe it essential that modern, multiethnic liberal democracies learn to respect and honor the "deep diversity" that often exists in their midst (Taylor 1992).

The resultant "liberal pluralist approach" to ethnocultural diversity "requires the public recognition and accommodation of diversity," arguing that "learning to live with the public expression and institutionalization of ethnocultural diversity is a key precondition for a stable and just democracy" (Kymlicka and Opalski 2001, 1).[2] This vision of liberal pluralism, which envisions "ethnocultural justice" being served only when the internationally-recognized right of self-determination of peoples is "institutionalized in a meaningful way" in democratic polities, together *with* individual rights and liberties

(Tully 2001, 32), is significantly more demanding than an "orthodox" liberal approach to cultural pluralism, which would relegate issues of diversity to the private sphere (Kymlicka and Opalski 2001, 1).

While in some respects the Soviet ethno-federal system addressed some liberal multicultural goals, for example providing for the "public expression and institutionalization" of ethnocultural diversity to an extent unheard of before that point in Russia's history, in other, more important ways, it was obviously deficient as a system for providing ethnocultural justice. The fact that the Soviet state guided and tightly controlled the public expression of ethnicity for its own ideological goals, according to the formulation "national in form, Soviet in content," is the most egregious example of this deficiency. Furthermore, there is the fact that the groups chosen for representation in the Soviet ethnic pantheon and the level of institutional support they were afforded was determined by the Soviet central government and did not reflect the democratically voiced desire for self-determination of the group in question, a requirement that is one of the pillars of a liberal theory of pluralism (Tamir 1995). Ironically, Soviet violations of this tenet of liberal pluralism affected both peoples who wanted greater self-determination than that afforded by their assigned status in the Soviet ethno-federal hierarchy (like the Volga Tatars and the Chechens), and those who received greater self-determination than desired (like several of the North Caucasus peoples who received A.S.S.R. status according to the "divide and rule" principle, despite not having voiced any desire for such a status).

As was discussed in the Introduction and chapter 1 of this book, the Soviet ethno-federal system had significant unintended consequences, chief among them the institutionalization and territorialization of the very ethnic group identities it was meant to transcend (Brubaker 1994). Thus the mobilizations that eventually brought down the Soviet Union were driven by the desire of Soviet ethnic groups to realize more meaningfully the right to self-determination that they had been told for seventy years was theirs while simultaneously being denied the ability to exercise this right in practice. The present chapter examines the extent to which ethno-federal institutions, in their new guise in Tatarstan's sovereignty project, either already do or harbor the potential to provide for the realization of ethnocultural justice in Russia in a way that is more consistent with liberal democratic norms than their Soviet-era predecessors.

There is reason to believe that an ethno-federal system, properly reformed to Russia's newly proclaimed democratic context, could well serve the liberal cause of ethnocultural justice in the country. Several prominent authors argue that a system of federalism, even an asymmetrical one that allowed some members to exercise more attributes of sovereignty than others, is one of the best ways to promote cohesion in a multiethnic society (Kymlicka 2001 27; Requejo 2001, 124; Smith 1998). Not only does federation promote the type of minority self-government that "best secures the loyalty" of ethnic minorities in a multinational state (Kymlicka 2001, 64), in fact ethnic minorities may see federation as "the only available means to cultural self-preservation short of secession," according to Jeff Kahn (2002, 60).

For an ethno-federal system to promote both ethnocultural and liberal justice, however, assiduous care must be taken to ensure that all players in the system—the federal government and the member states alike—are compelled to uphold liberal democratic norms. In other words, group rights in an ethno-federal member-state can never be realized in a way that infringes on the protected rights and liberties of other citizens of the federation who may not belong to the ethnic group in question; according to the "second-order dialectic of nation-building and minority rights," as Kymlicka terms it, sub-state units in ethno-federations must also respect the rights of minorities in their own midst (2001, 48–50). Indeed one of the powers that must be reserved for the central government in a democratic ethno-federation is the protection of individual civil rights and liberties for all citizens (Gagnon and Tully 2001; Smith 1998).

Many critics charge that post-Soviet ethno-federal institutions are not much closer to the ideal of providing for ethnocultural justice while staying true to liberal democratic norms than were their Soviet predecessors. According to this view, the pursuit of sovereignty has allowed the republics to pursue an "aggressive, illiberal form of nation-building" that contradicts both democracy and human rights (Opalski 2001, 301–03). Even a more sympathetic observer such as Graham Smith notes that the ethnic republics are "nationalizing regimes" that "tend to infringe on the rights of others" and thus "stifle the development of civic nationalism" in Russia (Smith 1998, 7–8). Others question the very need for ethnocultural justice in Russia in the post-Soviet period, let alone the utility of ethno-federalism as a way to realize this goal, arguing that the national republics "have no greater right to self-determination" than any other member of the Russian Federation (Kahn 2000, 191). Henry Hale argues that the expressed republican desire to insure a modicum of ethnocultural justice through the sovereignty projects is merely a fig leaf hiding the naked desire of ethnic elites in the republics for personal enrichment, the perpetuation of cronyism and autocracy (Hale 2003, 244).

I want to argue here that, contrary to these accounts, Tatarstan's sovereignty project, from its very inception, has been self-consciously modeled on a liberal pluralist approach to ethnocultural justice, according to which the quest for sovereignty has been justified in the name of the titular ethnic nation's right to self-determination (understood as the right to cultural and linguistic renewal and guaranteed political representation), but wherein this ethno-nationalist rationale for sovereignty has been accompanied by an equally strong commitment to civic multiculturalism, both rhetorically and in practice. Tatarstani elites have endeavored to make their new sovereign republic the simultaneous ethnic homeland of the Tatar people (both those Tatars who live in the republic and those in diaspora), *and* the legitimate civic, multicultural homeland of all the different peoples that make up the multinational "Tatarstani" people. In this sense, the architects of Tatarstan's sovereignty project have attempted to transpose old Soviet nationalities policies, which also attempted to balance an overarching commitment to the "Friendship of Peoples" that exemplified the Soviet Union with the commitment to certain privileges for the titular nationalities of the republics, by updating them and adapting them to the new post-Soviet, liberal multi-cultural context.

The results of this complex nation-building strategy have been mixed, but on the whole the efforts of Tatarstani elites have been more successful and beneficial in terms of providing for ethnocultural justice and building a framework of liberal pluralism in Russia than is generally recognized. The Shaimiyev administration's strong and visible commitment to using the state resources captured during the quest for sovereignty to improve and secure the cultural and ethnic health of the ethnic Tatar nation has been matched by analogous efforts to provide for the cultural and ethnic rights of the other ethnic groups in the republic, including Russians, Chuvash, Udmurts, Maris, and Jews. As the Tatarstani government itself has often pointed out, it has undertaken these efforts on its own initiative, and has done so in the absence of any type of analogous legal or financial commitment to ethnic minorities on the part of the Russian Federation. As such, Tatarstan provides a useful model of how to pursue ethnic and civic nation-building simultaneously in one political space, and of how other member units of the Russian Federation might serve the needs of ethnic minorities in their own polities.

While of course there are shortcomings to this multicultural program-ming in Tatarstan, it is important to emphasize that, largely because of the absence of any real effective leadership or demonstrated commitment to the provision of ethnocultural justice for non-Russians on the part of the federal government in Moscow, Tatarstan has, in the name of its sovereignty project, taken the lead in providing for the ethnocultural needs, not only of its own titular Tatar population, but of the other non-Russian minorities living in the republic. Tatarstani elites argue, and historical experience seems to confirm, that national minorities seeking ethnocultural justice in Russia, titular or otherwise, have no alternative to the type of bottom-up, sovereignty-project oriented form of ethno-federalism that Tatarstan is trying to create. Absent some type of ethno-federal system, and especially in a climate of growing xenophobia and anti-Muslim sentiment, it seems unlikely that Moscow will make the cultural and linguistic needs of non-Russians a priority. Indeed, particularly in the post-Beslan era, the Putin administration has seen fit to deny the ethnic nature of the "nationality question" entirely (demoting it to the status of "regional policy"), in favor of "preserving the integrity of the Russian state," which he sees as being "under threat" exactly from multicultural "separatism" (see chapter 5). In this centralizing, Russifying context, sovereignty projects like Tatarstan's are perhaps the only hope left for the realization of any sort of liberal politics of cultural pluralism in post-Soviet period.

However noting the potential utility of the republics' nation-building efforts for the creation of regimes of liberal multiculturalism in Russia does not mean ignoring or excusing the fact that there are significant illiberal aspects to the republican sovereignty projects themselves. As was noted in previous chapters, violations of civil liberties and individual rights in Tatarstan are as prominent as they are elsewhere in the Russian Federation, and while the rhetorical commitment to democracy may be stronger among elite leaders of the sovereignty project in Tatarstan (who consistently frame their support of federalism and civic multiculturalism as a "democratic" bulwark against the growth of a "great Russian" form of unitarism in Moscow), in reality the Tatarstani elite is not really any closer to providing true democratic freedoms or protections than either elites in Moscow or in the other member states of the federation. What I am suggesting here, however, is that given the absence of a real commitment to providing civil liberties and individual rights and liberties *anywhere* in Russia, the provision of ethnocultural justice for both the titular ethnic groups *and the other ethnic groups in the republics, including Russians*, is a positive benefit of Tatarstan's sovereignty project that must be preserved and extended, one that will not otherwise be accrued in Russia at all.

That said, it is also clear that for an ethno-federal system that accommodates republican sovereignty projects like Tatarstan's to be an effective way to purvey a liberal form of ethnocultural justice in Russia, methods will have to be found and implemented for ensuring that *both* the federal government and the republics respect *both* individual rights and liberties *as well as* group rights to national self-determination. While this goal may seem impossibly idealistic, the alternatives, according to which either the titular groups in the republics continue to pursue narrow, ethnic nation-building strategies at the expense of other citizens' rights or the federal government dismantles the ethno-federal system entirely and does not provide any type of meaningful "public expression or institutionalization" of ethnic diversity in Russia at all are equally unacceptable, leaving the international community and community of post-Sovietologists with little choice but to think deeply about and push strongly for continued (ethno)federal reforms in Russia.

The Nationality of Sovereignty: Declarative Ambiguities

The delicacy of the task of promoting national revival for the titular ethnic group while also fostering civic multiculturalism for all of their citizens is clearly reflected in Tatarstan's declaration of sovereignty itself. The preamble of Tatarstan's 1990 Declaration states that it was being issued out of a feeling of responsibility for "the fate of the multinational people of the republic" but also simultaneously in order to "realize the inalienable right of the Tatar nation and all the peoples of the republic to self-determination." The document goes on to guarantee equal rights for citizens *regardless* of nationality and guarantees the preservation and development of the national languages of *all* other national minorities in Tatarstan, but names only Tatar and Russia as official state languages in Tatarstan (article 3). That both Russian and Tatar were named as official languages (as opposed to Tatar alone, as some ethnic Tatar nationalist activists had wanted), and that respect for other national languages in the republic was enshrined in the declaration furthermore indicate how important the question of ethnic/civic multicultural balance was for the newly-sovereign republic in 1990. In the years following the declaration of sovereignty, Tatarstan's ambitious Tatar-language promotion projects, and its policies on state symbols, public spaces and holidays all became the means through which the republic pursued the complex task of reviving the ethnic Tatar nation while simultaneously creating a civic sense of "Tatarstani" nationalism that included a strong multicultural component.

Whose Sovereign Nation? Tatarstan as Ethnic Homeland *and* Multicultural Republic

The nationalities policy pursued by the Tatarstani government during the early years of sovereignty illustrates both the difficulty of the task of simultaneously fostering and balancing ethnic and civic conceptions of the nation and the seriousness with which the republican leadership approached this dilemma. For example in May 1992, even before the adoption of the new constitution, the republican government spent lavishly on a "Congress of Peoples of Tatarstan," an event aimed at showcasing the multicultural credentials of the new republic and demonstrating the loyalty of all the peoples of Tatarstan to their new "sovereign" homeland—the congress's widely publicized resolution asserted that "the multinational people of Tatarstan" were the only true bearer of state sovereignty in the republic (*Materialy* 1993, 148). Article one of the Tatarstani Constitution, adopted six months later, codified this formulation, which has since become the core of official discourse and policy on the subject in Tatarstan.

Beginning with the celebration of Republic Day in August 1994, public officials began to refer to the collective civic and multiethnic people in whose name sovereignty had been declared as the "Tatarstani" people (*Respublika Tatarstan* August 30, 1994, 1). This reference to the Tatarstani people and "Tatarstanis" has since become ubiquitous in official parlance and the mass media. In just one example, during his annual address to the republican legislature in February 1996, President Shaimiyev asserted that Tatarstan was building a "poly-ethnic and poly-cultural" society based on civic and not ethnic criteria of citizenship, and that evidence of the growth of this civic society was the growth of patriotism and pride for Tatarstan "among all Tatarstanis" (*Vremya i Dengi* February 10, 1996, 1). In an attempt to insure the hegemony of the official discourse about civic nationality, the President established a special Department of Inter-Ethnic Affairs under his personal administration that is responsible for ensuring the national cultural development of and civic equality for all different ethnic groups in Tatarstan. This department oversees the activity of the Association of National-Cultural Organizations of Tatarstan (A.N.K.O.) and together they are to provide for the national cultural needs of the republic's multiethnic population.[3] The multicultural credentials of the republic are also part of official ceremonies and public displays—any "national" (Tatarstani) holiday in the republic now is marked by the presence of representatives from the entire pantheon of nationalities that live in Tatarstan (Chuvash dancers, Mari singers, and Udmurt children along with Tatar celebrities), and the triumvirate of Tatarstan's Chief Mufti, Gayaz Ishaki, the republic's Chief Rabbi Berl Lazr, and the Patriarch of Kazan, Anastasi, are also omnipresent at "official" events in Tatarstan.

A prominent and interesting element of the state's efforts to create a civic and multiethnic Tatarstani sense of nationness is the *feminization* of all the peoples of Tatarstan and the location of all Tatarstan's ethnicities in a position of subordination to the paternalistic (and subtly patriarchal) leadership of the state, embodied first and foremost by its President Mintimer Shaimiyev (though also variously by any other high-ranking male officials, most often former Prime Minister and current speaker of the Tatarstani State Council Farid Mukhametshin) (Graney 2004). For example, the most common representation of ethnic nationality at events like Republic Day are folkloric groups which prominently feature young, attractive, conventionally feminine women wearing "ethnic" costumes.[4] When the "multiethnic Tatarstani nation" is displayed for outside consumption the images again are invariably of attractive young women, from all the different ethnic groups of the republic, either dancing with or serving bread and salt to one of the "wise fathers" of the Tatarstani nation. These multicultural displays bear more than a passing resemblance to Soviet-era "friendship of peoples" with the patriarchal, paternalistic, all-embracing father-figure of the Communist Party now played by Shaimiyev and the new "sovereign state" of Tatarstan.

Alongside these vigorous efforts to mold a civic sense of Tatarstani nationhood, republican elites in Kazan have also actively promoted ethnic Tatar conceptions of nationhood. Indeed, it seems that the one policy, identifying Tatarstan as the multicultural home of all the peoples of Tatarstan, is aimed at "buying" legitimacy or space for the other policy, promotion of Tatarstan as the ethnic homeland for Tatars both in and outside of the republic. Again, here we see a potential similarity with the Soviet period, where the commitment to official multiculturalism, embodied in ethno-federalism, legitimated a simultaneous policy of Russians as "first among equals" and "big brothers" to the other members of the Soviet family of nations (Martin 2001). In the new sovereign republics, a policy of official multiculturalism legitimates a concurrent policy of ethnic nation-building for the titular people. This idea is based on the assertion that if there is a formal legal and civic equality, and if the state is committed to providing for the "national-cultural" needs of all ethnic groups in the republic, claims of a special spiritual role for the Tatar nation in Tatarstan are not discriminatory and therefore not incompatible with a civic Tatarstani nation (Apparat Prezidenta Respubliki Tatarstan 1993, 5–7). These arguments are not unlike those made about the potential compatibility of liberal democracy with special minority group rights, (usually referring to the Quebecois case), made by theorists like Taylor and Kymlicka.

In its first and most visible identification of the new sovereign republic of Tatarstan as the ethnic homeland of Tatars, the government of Tatarstan sponsored the first ever "World Congress of Tatars" in Kazan in June 1992, with over 1000 Tatar delegates from around the world, the C.I.S. and the Russian Federation participating. President Shaimiyev attempted to downplay the ethnic significance of this event by noting that it took place *after* the Congress of Peoples of Tatarstan and asserting that it in essence was really just "a continuation" of that multiethnic event" (Mustafin and Khasanov 1995, 118–24). However he also noted triumphantly that the event marked the first time that Tatars "were gathered here in our own homeland, in our own state!" (*Sovetskaya Tatariya* June 20, 1992, 1). Afterwards, the Department of Inter-Ethnic Affairs continued to claim that sovereignty in Tatarstan "did not have ethnic coloring," but also asserted that, as evidenced by the World Tatar Congress, Tatarstan had "accepted to fulfill the role as the spiritual center of the entire Tatar people" (Apparat Prezidenta Respubliki Tatarstan 1993, 7).[5]

The idea that the civic, multiethnic Tatarstani concept of nationhood could and should also afford a special role for ethnic Tatars as a sort of "first among equals" nationality has since been elaborated on and codified into official state policy. In August 1993 the Department of Inter-Ethnic Affairs asserted that despite the fact that the republic was home to many ethnic groups, "history has conspired such that the Republic of Tatarstan is the spiritual center for the entire Tatar people" (*Tatarstan* 1993, 8: 20). Even more explicitly, in November 1996, the department outlined the "basic priorities" of nationalities policy in Tatarstan; first on the list was the assertion that Tatarstan was the "cradle of the Tatar people and its culture and language," and that as such Tatarstan had a special obligation to help Tatars in diaspora (*Informatsionno-Metodicheskii Byulleten'* 1996, 8: 15), an obligation that was reaffirmed in August 2002 when the third "World Congress of Tatars" was held in Kazan and in January 2004 when amendments including an increased commitment to fostering the teaching of the Tatar language in the diaspora were added to Tatarstan's Law on Languages.

Giving Voice to the Sovereign Nation: Language Policies in Republican Sovereignty Projects

Language is widely recognized as one of the most important markers of membership in a national community, thus a state's official policy on language illuminates its nation-building priorities and helps to determine the boundaries of the national community under construction. State support for the preservation and revival of the Tatar language has been a crucial part of the domestic nation-building project in Tatarstan since the beginning of the sovereignty era. A main complaint of Tatar intellectuals during glasnost' was the poor state of Tatar language instruction and low rates of Tatar language knowledge and use among urban Tatars in the republic. For example, in 1989 while 95 percent of urban ethnic Tatar residents claimed Tatar as

Figure 4.1. The statue "Khurriyat" ("Freedom") flies over the new Tatarstan Museum of National Culture in Kazan, formerly the Lenin Memorial Museum.

their "native language," further surveys revealed that only 36 percent of them actually used Tatar on a daily basis with their spouses, only 25 percent used it daily with their friends, and only 21 percent with their colleagues.[6] Most urban Tatars used either a mixture of Tatar and Russian or only Russian in these different situations (*Sovremennye* 1991, 27–29). Furthermore, Tatar was not used at all in the central governing institutions of the Tatar A.S.S.R., but was only used in local governing institutions and local party organizations in rural areas of the republic that had purely Tatar populations (*Sovremennye* 1991, 33–34).

Claiming the status of a sovereign state was seen as a way to remedy the deteriorating situation facing the Tatar language in the late 1980s. As we have seen, the Tatarstani Declaration of Sovereignty itself made both Tatar and Russian official state languages in Tatarstan, and Shaimiyev's speech on the day of the adoption of the declaration stated that a main goal of the new sovereign republic was to make "true bilingualism of Russian and Tatar" a reality for all citizens in Tatarstan (*Sovetskaya Tatariya* August 30, 1990, 1).[7] Even before it passed the new republican constitution, the Supreme Soviet of Tatarstan promulgated the "Law on the Languages of the Peoples of Tatarstan" (in June 1992) (*Zakon* 1996, 3–15). To establish its multicultural credentials, the law guaranteed freedom of language use for all citizens of the republic, banned discrimination on the basis of language, and committed the government of Tatarstan to protecting each citizen's right to use and develop their own native language. But according to article 6, another main goal of the law was to make Tatar and Russian "equally functioning state languages" in the republic. Specifically, the law stipulated that all the official governing organs of the republic, including the State Council, the Cabinet of the Ministers, the President's Office, and the courts in Tatarstan should conduct their business and publish their official decisions, documents and decrees in both Tatar and Russian (articles 11–13). Furthermore, all business pertaining to foreign affairs, industry, and transportation was to be conducted in "both state languages of the Republic of Tatarstan." Finally, the law introduced the mandatory study of the Tatar language and literature at an average of three-and-a-half hours a week for all students in Tatarstan, regardless of nationality, starting from grade one—a number that has been steadily increased and is set to be increased again in 2005 (MORT 1991b; Zaripov 2005). To further make bilingualism a reality in Tatarstan, in April 1993 a controversial clause in the new "Law on Judges" which stipulated that all judges must know both Russian and Tatar, because citizens of Tatarstan were entitled to use either language in the courts of Tatarstan, caused some Russians in Tatarstan to worry that only ethnic Tatars would be able to serve as judges (*Sovetskaya Tatariya* April 6, 1993, 3; April 22, 1993, 2).

Two years later, in July 1994, a comprehensive "State Program for the Preservation, Study and Development of the Languages of the Peoples of Tatarstan" aimed at implementing the June 1992 law was developed and adopted by the Supreme Soviet of Tatarstan (*Zakon* 1996, 16–39). It called for the increased study of the Tatar language both in general educational and in professional scientific institutions in the republic, including a recommendation that a Tatar-language university be established in the republic. The program also contained several points aimed at making Tatar a "true" state language in the republic, especially by efforts to increase Tatar language knowledge among non-Tatars in Tatarstan. As such, it called for a whole series of new "minimum knowledge" Tatar dictionaries to be published and "basic knowledge" Tatar language classes to be established in government and workplace establishments around the republic (*Zakon* 1996, 18).

The implementation of these new policies has been pursued vigorously in Tatarstan. A new department opened at Kazan State University to produce teachers who will teach Tatar to Russian-speaking children in Tatarstan (*Izvestiya Tatarstana* September 24, 1993, 3). An even more extraordinary development was the creation of a new bureaucratic office, the Assistant Directors for National Education, which was established by the Ministry of

Education of Tatarstan in October 1994. These officials, one of whom is now present in every Russian-speaking school and mixed Russian-Tatar school in Tatarstan, are charged with overseeing and facilitating the implementation of the new Tatar language and literature classes and the classes on the culture, literature, and history of Tatarstan (MORT 1994). More recently, in November 2003, the Tatar parliament introduced revisions to its 1992 language law that introduced monetary penalties for bureaucrats and schools that violated the republic's bilingualism policy, and which offered 15 percent monthly salary bonuses for employees who could "effectively employ bilingualism" in their work—the amendments passed in January 2003 (*RFE/RL Tatar-Bashkir Service Daily Report* November 12, 2003, November 24, 2003, December 10, 2003, December 16, 2003). Textbooks and pedagogical aids for teaching Tatar to Russians have also been continuously updated and revised in the republic since 1992, with the aim of helping Russians to "really learn Tatar, not just to pretend to" (Gibatitdinov 2005; Zaripov 2005).

The results of these various Tatar-language promotion efforts are considerable.[8] During the years of sovereignty, 700 different new Tatar language textbooks have been developed for use in the republic, the number of Tatar language teachers in Kazan alone has increased from 400 to 1800, "every institution of primary and middle school study in the republic now teaches both state languages" in Tatarstan, and the number of secondary schools providing instruction exclusively in Tatar (with Russian as a separate subject) has increased from 3 to 47 (*RFE/RL Tatar-Bashkir Service Daily Report* October 30, 2002; *Vremya i Dengi* December 25, 2002). Similarly, the percentage of children in the republic who study all subjects in Tatar continues to rise, from 45.9 percent in 1996 to 52 percent in 2005, and Tatarstan Ministry of Education officials have recently developed a new "intensive model" of Tatar-language instruction for young school children, introduced in 90 of the republic's schools in September 2005, which is aimed at getting all students in Tatarstan to the point where they will be able to learn even a non-Tatar language subject, such as the history of Tatarstan, entirely in the Tatar language by grade six (Zaripov 2005). Tatar-language promotion efforts not limited to Tatarstan's borders, either; in 2002 Tatarstan that it would provide tuition-free entry quotas allowing each region of the Russian Federation to send 10 students to study in Tatarstan's institutes of higher-education, so that they could in turn become teachers of the Tatar language in their region—in 2005 that yearly quota was raised to 70 students (*RFE/RL Tatar-Bashkir Service Daily Report* May 14, 2002).

Tatarstani officials insist that the promotion of the Tatar language (which also includes a controversial decision to switch to the Latin script for the

Tatar-language, a policy that is discussed further later in this chapter) have not come at the expense of a multicultural commitment to promoting the languages of "all the peoples of Tatarstan." As Deputy Prime Minister Zilya Valeeva told the Council of Europe in October 2002, a higher percentage of Chuvash and Udmurts study their own languages in Tatarstan than anywhere else in the Russian Federation, and the republic funds over 220 regular "nation-language" schools for peoples other than Tatars or Russians, as well as sponsoring "Sunday Schools" for 22 other indigenous languages in Tatarstan (*RFE/RL Tatar-Bashkir Service Daily Report* October 7, 2002; *Vremya i Dengi* December 25, 2002). The amendments to the 1992 Law on Languages that were passed in 2003 include increases in funding and personnel for schools that teach languages other than Tatar as well (*RFE/RL Tatar-Bashkir Service Daily Report* January 30, 2003). The updated 2004–2013 Program on State and Other Languages in the Republic of Tatarstan also includes measures aimed at promoting the development of Mari, Udmurt, and other languages in the republic, aiming to continue the positive growth the republic has already achieved in this area (for example, five new Udmurt language schools opened in the republic between 1996–2005, raising the total in the republic to 45; 3 new Mordvin language schools opened during the same period, raising the total to 5) (Zaripov 2005). Finally, in a move that seemed calculated to demonstrate the poverty of Russia's nationalities policy and the robustness of Tatarstan's multicultural efforts, on April 26, 2004, the republic held its first "Day of Native Languages," which celebrated all the languages spoken and taught in the republic, arguing the republic created this official, legal holiday in order to "help spur Russia to adopt the European Charter on Minority Languages" (*RFE/RL Tatar-Bashkir Service Daily Report* September 24, 2003; April 26, 2004).

To further illustrate the nondiscriminatory nature of the republic's language law, Tatarstani officials point out that the law was upheld by the Russian Federation Constitutional Court in November 2004, when it rejected the claim in a suit brought by both Tatar and Russian citizens in Tatarstan that mandatory Tatar language study was a violation of their children's rights. The court argued that because the Russian Constitution contains provisions for republics to establish state languages, Tatarstan's provisions for the equal teaching of Tatar and Russian as joint state languages were legal, a ruling Tatarstani State Council Chair Mukhametshin called "the biggest event of 2004" (Gibititdinov 2005; Zaripov 2005; *RFE/RL Tatar-Bashkir Service Daily Report* November 18, 2004 and December 30, 2004). Supporters of Tatarstan's language law also point to the fact that the republic agreed to strike down the provisions of the law calling for mandatory use of both

Tatar and Russian to conduct business in foreign affairs, industry, and transportation, because according to the Russian Federation Constitution, these are considered areas of federal concern, and thus are reserved for Russian-language use only (*RFE-RL Tatar-Bashkir Daily Report* May 30, 2003).

Shaping Sovereign Nations: Public Spaces and Museums as Elements of Nation-Building in Tatarstan

An important way of situating citizens physically in a given national community is through the creation of official sacred spaces such as national monuments and historical landmarks. Other policies on the use of public space, such as the naming and renaming of streets or the regulation of religious buildings also mark the boundaries of the national community for citizens. In Tatarstan in the post-Soviet period, the politics of nationhood have been negotiated in all of these arenas—physical space is in fact intensely "socio-political" in this context (Verdery 1996, 63).

The most prominent public space in Tatarstan is the ensemble of the Kazan Kremlin, where the Presidential Administration and many republican ministries have their offices (see cover photo). The complex is home to a monument thought to have been built in the early 16th century which traditionally identified with a dead Tatar queen (Suyumbike Tower), as well as two Russian orthodox churches, the larger of which is known as the Blagoveshchenskii Sobor (Cathedral of the Annunciation). The Kazan Kremlin is an inherently politicized space not only because it is where the president sits, but also because it is historically identified by Tatars as the former site of both the Great Bulgar state and the Kazan Khanate, which was destroyed by Ivan Grozny and occupied by Russian invaders in 1552. Until 1552 the Kazan Kremlin was said to have contained several mosques, the largest of which had eight minarets and was destroyed by the Russian invaders and used as the basis for the Blagoveshchenskii Sobor. Thus, the way this space is treated in the post-Soviet period has great significance for the construction of a national community in Tatarstan.

The importance of the Kremlin as a symbol of the new sovereign republic was revealed in November 1992 when several Tatar nationalist and Muslim organizations wrote an open letter to President Shaimiyev reminding him that the churches in the Kazan Kremlin were built "on the graves of Tatars and their mosques," and demanding that the government provide a more "national face" for Kazan by rebuilding the former mosques inside the Kremlin walls (*Izvestiya TOTs* November 1992, 11: 2). They also demanded that the administration erect a monument on the Kremlin wall dedicated to those Tatars who died defending the Kremlin from Russia in 1552 (a monument to the Russians who died in 1552 already exists near the Kremlin in the Kazanka River).

The government of Tatarstan did not respond immediately to either of these requests, although a commission to study a possible monument to the Tatar dead from 1552 was founded. Despite the views of the republic's Minister of Culture, who stated publicly in a 1994 interview that "of course we need such a monument" (*Idel* 1994, #1/2, 56), it was clear that other members of the Tatarstani government were in no hurry to undertake such a potentially inflammatory act. Eventually, in November 1995, the Shaimiyev administration indicated its intention to restore parts of the Kremlin and, significantly, to build one new mosque within the Kremlin walls (to be named Kul Sharif, after one of the Tatar defenders of Kazan in 1552) (*Izvestiya Tatarstana* November 15, 1995, 1). But the Presidential plan for the restoration of the Kazan Kremlin firmly reflected the administration's official discourse about a civic, multi-cultural nation in Tatarstan—in addition to building the new mosque, the plan also contained provisions for the refurbishing of the Blagoveshchenskii Sobor in the Kremlin. Furthermore, the plan pointedly did not contain provisions for a Kremlin monument to the Tatars who died in 1552 at the hands of Ivan Grozny. Only in December 2002, after years of agitation from ethnic Tatar activists, and perhaps in response to the Kremlin's decision to pass a controversial law banning non-Cyrillic alphabets for non-Russian languages in Russia earlier that week, did Shaimiyev apparently finally give in to the long-standing demand that a monument to the Tatars who fell in defense of Kazan in 1552 be built inside the walls of the Kazan Kremlin (*RFE/RL Tatar-Bashkir Service Daily Report* December 9, 2002). Significantly, however, the monument still has not been built.[9]

Since the adoption of the plan to restore the Kremlin in November 1995, President Shaimiyev has emphasized on numerous occasions how the simultaneous restoration of Blagoveshchenskii Sobor and building of the mosque of Kul Sharif in the Kazan Kremlin are evidence of Tatarstan's "poly-ethnic, poly-cultural, civic society" and the republic's commitment to "balancing the interests of the different ethnic groups in Tatarstan."[10] The Tatarstani Ministry of the Interior's new complex, under construction in the Kazan Kremlin, will include a memorial to fallen Tatarstani law-enforcement officers that features both a mosque and an Orthodox church, further illustrating the Shaimiyev administration's strategy of explicitly identifying Tatarstan's most prominent public place with the official discourse about the civic and multiethnic Tatarstani nation.[11] This multiculturalist strategy has not endeared the regime to Tatar nationalist actors, who protested Shaimiyev's recognition of Blagoveshchenskii Sobor as a national landmark of Tatarstan by carrying signs that read "Shaimiyev will be punished by Allah!" (*Altyn Urda* January 1996, #1, 1)

Despite the government of Tatarstan's sensitivity to the official discourse of civic multiculturalism regarding the issue of the Kul Sharif mosque, the mosque is also seen as an important symbol which serves to link ancient ethnic Tatar statehood with the modern state of Tatarstan, in this case identifying Tatarstan with the Kazan Khanate, under whose rule the original Kazan Kremlin mosques were built. Both state and societal actors in the republic have agreed that the new mosque should be "a symbol of the rebirth of the statehood of Tatarstan" and "a unique monument to the sovereignty of the republic" (*Respublika Tatarstan* February 15, 1996, 1; April 16, 1996, 3, 5; *Vremya i Dengi* June 29, 1996, 1, 6–7). Tatarstani TV has referred to the new mosque as "a monument to all Tatars who died defending their homeland," further identifying modern-day Tatarstan with the ancient Tatar state of the Kazan Khanate (Tatarstan State TV Broadcast, September 21, 1998). However, despite general agreement that the new mosque was an important symbolic link between past and present Tatar statehoods, there was deep controversy between state and societal actors over the design of the new building. That the street leading up to the Kazan Kremlin, which was formerly called Lenin Street, was renamed Kremlin Street, and not Suyumbike Street, as some Tatar nationalists had wanted, also reflects the government's desire to construct civic Tatarstani identifications with these most prominent national political spaces.[12] These instances reveal the limits of ethnic Tatar identifications of statehood within the broader civic and multiethnic discourse about the nation in Tatarstan.

Subsequent evolutions in the use of the space of the Kazan Kremlin have further demonstrated the republic's commitment to maintaining a fundamental balance of ethnic and civic understandings of nationhood in "sovereign" Tatarstan in the post-Soviet period. In 1994 the entire territory of the Kazan Kremlin and all its contents was "museumified" by a series of Presidential and Ministerial decrees that created the "State Museum Preserve of the Kazan Kremlin." The stated goals of this new museum complex were to: "first, preserve and develop the historical-cultural legacy of the peoples of Tatarstan contained within the Kazan Kremlin; second, to restore the Kazan Kremlin to a state fit for the historical, cultural, and political-administrative center of the Republic of Tatarstan; and finally, to restore the Kazan Kremlin to a state fitting its significance of an object of historical-cultural importance, for the republic, the Russian Federation, and the international community" (*Kazanskii Kreml'* 2005). I would add a further goal—the restored Kazan

Kremlin museum complex is clearly meant to demonstrate to multiple audiences (Tatarstani, Russian federal, international) just how well Tatarstan historically has, and currently does, play the role of modern, democratic, multiethnic nation-state. The fact that from 1994–1998 the Republic worked tirelessly to get the Kazan Kremlin listed on UNESCO's list of "World Cultural Heritage Sites," an honor it now relentlessly publicizes both on the Kremlin walls and in all official publications about Kazan and the Kremlin, demonstrates clearly how the administration sees the Kazan Kremlin museum complex—the calling card of the modern, cultured, multiethnic, and indeed, civilized, state of Tatarstan (*Kazanskii Kreml'* 2005).

But what is the nature of this calling card? What stories are told in the new "museumified" Kazan Kremlin? Does it, as it claims to, represent the "complicated historical and cultural heritage of all the peoples of Tatarstan" and reflect its history as a product of "the interaction of three great civilizations—Tatar, Russian, and European" (*Kazanskii Kreml'* 2005)? To a significant degree, the answer is yes. The museums and historical buildings that have been restored and newly-opened in the Kazan Kremlin do reflect this professed creed of civic multiculturalism, though there is a pronounced current of ethnic Tatar pride running through many of the complex's offerings as well. For example, the Museum of Islamic Culture of the Volga Region that is part of the Kul Sharif mosque is paralleled by a planned Museum of Culture of the Slavic Peoples of the Volga, which is to be opened under the auspices of the Blagoveschenskii Cathedral elsewhere on the territory of the Kremlin complex. The planned Museum of Silver-working and Silver Art, devoted to the works of the Kazan Tatars of the Kazan Khanate period (fifteenth–sixteenth centuries), will be counterbalanced by the planned "Weapons Hall of the Kazan Armory" and "Museum of the Garrison of the Kazan Kremlin," whose exhibitions will be devoted to the history of the Russian Imperial Army and its foundry-works in the Kremlin during the eighteenth and nineteenth centuries.

Accompanying the attempt to present an ethnically-balanced and multicultural view of Tatarstan's cultural history through the museums of the Kazan Kremlin is the creation of a prestigious "national gallery" for the Republic of Tatarstan along the lines of the National Portrait Gallery in Washington or the National Gallery in London. According to the conceptual plan for the new National Gallery of the Republic of Tatarstan, the intention is to establish a "unique and unrepeatable" institution, one that will "bear the national character of Tatarstan, distinguishing itself from all the other art museums in Russia."[13] However, being located in the Kazan Kremlin, the "national" character reflected in this gallery is specifically based on a *territorial* understanding of

the national community, and as such, will "reflect the unity of artistic process that have taken place in Tatarstan," featuring "the best Russian artists
who in some way are connected with Kazan or Tatarstan," along with "the
history of the development of Tatar decorative arts in Tatarstan." The main
exhibition gallery, on the third floor of the museum space, reflects this civic
nationalism, devoting two rooms to Russian artists of the eighteenth and
nineteenth century, two rooms to Tatar artists of the Kazan Art School, one
room to "Tatar people's decorative arts" and the rest of the rooms to "the art
of Tatarstan during the twentieth century."

Other elements of the Kazan Kremlin complex also reflect the government's desire to incorporate residual elements of Soviet patriotism into this
new "Tatarstani" civic multicultural nationalism. For example, the second
floor of the new National Gallery is devoted to one Tatar artist, Kh. Yaku-
pov, whose works are solidly in the socialist realist vein and do not portray
any ethno-nationalist elements. Relatedly, one of the most prominent of
the new museums in the complex is the Museum of the Great Fatherland
War (WW II), which opened for the sixtieth anniversary of V-E day in May
2005. Furthermore, in August 2005 the Kazan Kremlin also became home to
a new Tatarstan filial of a great *Russian* art institution, the State Hermitage
Museum in St. Petersburg, which debuted with a "once in a millennium"
exhibit about the material culture of the Golden Horde. State Hermitage
Director Mikhail Piotrovskii praised the Tatarstani government's efforts to
raise the level of culture in the republic, which he said made the opening of
the Hermitage filial in the Kazan Kremlin possible, adding that there were
no other places in Russia at Kazan's level, and as such, no plans to introduce
other regional Hermitage branches anywhere in Russia (*RFE/RL Tatar-
Bashkir Service Daily Report* August 24, 2005).

However within the civic and multicultural fabric of the Kazan Kremlin museum complex is woven a prominent threat of ethnic Tatar pride,
much akin to the Russocentrism that marked the ostensible "Friendship of
Peoples" of the Soviet era. For if the Kazan Kremlin is meant to represent
the historical-cultural legacy of all the peoples of Tatarstan, there is little
doubt that the greater part of that legacy is most closely identified with the
ethnic Tatar people. This subtle, but clearly discernible, ethnic-Tatar bias is
present both in the official self-descriptions of the Kazan Kremlin museum
complex, whose uniqueness is based first on it being "the only intact for-
tress of the Kazan Tatars," second on it being "the only operational center
of Tatar state power in the world," and only third on being "the product of
cooperation and interaction of many different cultures." Thus it is perhaps
not surprising that in the planned "Museum of Statehood of the Tatars and

Tatarstan," the entire first floor will be devoted to the history of the Kazan Khanate (the last independent Tatar state formation before the coming of the Russians in 1552) while the entire second floor will be an exhibit entitled "1000 years of Tatar Statehood" (Khalitov 2005). This museum then seems pointedly not to include any reference to the Russian imperial or Russian Soviet influence on the seemingly purely-Tatar identified state-building history of the republic.

Moreover, the creation of another new museum in the republic, entirely separate from those currently being erected in the Kazan Kremlin, a museum explicitly designed to be a *purely Tatar* "national" institution, further under-scores the existence of a competing ethnic Tatar understanding of the nation embedded within the civic Tatarstani variant.

In late 1990, a group of ethnic Tatar cultural intelligentsia sent the Tatarstani government an appeal in which they called on the state to show its support for the revival of ethnic Tatar culture through an act that would have both symbolic and material impact—converting the recently completed Lenin Memorial Museum in Kazan into a "National Cultural Center" for the republic. The Cabinet of Ministers of Tatarstan complied with this request, creating the National Cultural Center "Kazan" on January 6, 1991. While quickly "nationalizing" the former Lenin Museum did certainly give the impression of a convincing break with the communist past, the goals and aims of the new center remained obscure until the following year, when on September 16, 1992, another Tatarstani ministerial decree announced the creation of a "Museum of National Culture" (MNC) as the centerpiece of the "Kazan" complex (Valeeva-Suleymanova 2002, 121).

The MNC was the brainchild of those same Tatar intellectuals who had sent the original appeal to the government of Tatarstan about its cultural obligations to the ethnic Tatar nation, and who made more clear just what they felt those obligations were in the "Conception of the Development of Tatar Culture" that was published in a moderate nationalist newspaper in the republic in June 1992.[14] According to this influential document, one of the lynchpins of the revival of Tatar culture was the creation of what it called a "national museum," defined as a museum of a "new type" that would be organized on an ethnic Tatar, not a territorial Tatarstani, basis. The intellectuals argued that without such a museum to showcase the "highest forms of spiritual and artistic culture of the Tatar people," Tatars "can't be considered a civilized nation." As such, they called on the government to create a "national fund" for the acquisition of the best of Tatar art and artifacts from private and museum collections across the former Soviet Union and the world to form the basis of the new Museum of National Culture.

In the years following the decree creating the MNC, as unease about sepa-ratism and non-Russian ethnic nationalism in Russia grew, theorizing about what role this new type of ethnic-identified national museum should play in Tatarstan continued. In an interview in October 1993, Tatarstan's then Min-ister of Culture, Marsel Taishev, tried to calm fears about the ethnic revival in Tatarstan, arguing that this was a "natural process of a people returning to the culture, a process that was not allowed to function normally during the totali-tarian period." He added that opening "new type" museums such as the MNC was a "priority" of the government in aiding this process of revival (*Izvestiya Tatarstan* October 22, 1993, 3). Later that year, one of the most prominent ethnic Tatar art historians in Tatarstan, Guzel Valeeva-Suleymanova, further elaborated the conceptual framework underpinning the MNC, arguing that it "must be distinct from all other museums in Tatarstan, such as the State United Museum [later to be renamed the National Museum of the Republic of Tatarstan—NMRT], which remain organized on the principles of Russian imperialism." Instead, the MNC, under the direct patronage of the govern-ment of Tatarstan, must serve to "unify the Tatar nation in all countries" and act as the "cultural center and basis for cultural revival" of the entire Tatar nation, wherever it be located (*Tatarstan* #12, 1993, 36).

The ethnic aspirations of the MNC have only intensified in the years since its founding. Its assistant director proudly told this author that the MNC has the distinction of being "the first ethnic museum in the whole world," distinguished from other museums in that it is neither the "product of colonial plunder nor the desire for exotica," but rather that it is inspired by the lofty goal of "transmitting the contents of the Tatar national soul" to the world (Shageeva 2005). She added that the MNC's great achievement is that it has "attempted to present all components that make up the Tatar people's culture," including ethnography, history, decorative arts, linguistics, and "mentality." It is also unique in that it has "begun to reimagine Tatar history outside of the categories the Soviets had used" (*Tatarstan*, #1, 1997, 84–5). By the early 2000s, the MNC had refined its organizing principles down to three: accurately presenting the history and culture of the entire Tatar people, including the Siberian, Mishar and other sub-ethnoses; ac-curately presenting the ethnocultural history of the Tatar people within its proper place in Turkic, Muslim, and world civilization; and finally, present-ing the best of Tatar fine arts, including especially contemporary Tatar art (Valeeva-Suleymanova 2002, 119).

If the conceptual apparatus behind Tatarstan's MNC has evolved in so-phistication and sharpness since 1990, actually realizing this vision of an ex-clusively ethnically-defined national museum in the republic has been more of a challenge for its staff. Having to start virtually "from scratch" during the extremely lean first post-communist years, the MNC staff struggled to mount its first temporary exhibits in 1993, managing to open studies of prominent nineteenth-century author Gayaz Ishaki and a show of rare Tatar genealogical scrolls from the eighteenth and nineteenth centuries (*Izvestiya Tatarstan*, February 22, 1994, 3). Plans for the MNC's permanent installations have been hampered by the difficulty of acquiring artifacts from private collections and other museums, forcing the MNC to rely on reproductions, such as that of the famous "Kazanskaya Shapka" (a sixteenth-century bejeweled Mongol Khan crown that sits in the Kremlin Armory in Moscow) and on other creative means, such as the set of clay busts of the nineteen Tatar khans that ruled the Kazan Khanate in the fifteenth and sixteenth centuries that the museum commissioned in the mid-1990s (Shageeva 2005; *Tatarstan*, #1, 1997, 84–85). Despite the challenges, by 2004 the MNC's collection fund had grown to almost 30,000 exemplars, and the museum was gearing up at last to unveil its first permanent installations, including a "Hall of Tatar Khans" with a reproduction of a sixteenth-century Mongol-style throne (the MNC administration has also tried supplement its state revenues with such entrepreneurial, but also ethnic-inspired, measures like holding Tatar pop music disco nights along with more traditional Tatar song festivals, and renting out the center for conferences) (*Vsye Musei Kazani*, 2004, 10; Zakirov 1996).

The government of Tatarstan has continued its initial patronage of the MNC, including most prominently the funding in 1996 of a nearly 200-foot tall statue on its premises by Moscow-born Tatar sculptor Kamil Zamitov. The statue, called "Khurriyat," which means "freedom" in the Tatar language (and which replaced a huge bust of Lenin), is meant to symbolize the rebirth of the Tatar people (see figure 3.1) (Shageeva 2005). More recently, Tatarstani President Shaimiyev, who is described by MNC staff as being a frequent visitor and great patron of the MNC, chose the museum to be the site of the prestigious "History of Kazan" exhibit, which was mounted in accordance with the 1000th anniversary of the city in August 2005. "He chose us because we know that Tatars founded Kazan and that we'll present the real history of Kazan," an MNC staff member told me in June 2005, two months before the exhibit was to open (Shageeva 2005). The MNC also figures prominently in the international relations of the republic. When Tatarstan hosted the second and third "World Congresses of Tatars" in Kazan in 1997 and 2003, the MNC hosted many of the events, and the government makes sure that a visit to the MNC is on the agenda of all foreign delegations (most recently, in summer 2005, the MNC hosted part of the EU-sponsored "Days of European Heritage" in Kazan, the logic of which makes one's head spin).

Representing the Tatarstani and Tatar Nations in Other Public Spaces
Other aspects of the use of public space in post-Soviet Tatarstan also seem to
indicate that while the civic, multinational Tatarstani discourse is dominant
in the republic, there is significant space for the accommodation of ethnic
Tatar formulations of nationhood within that framework. This is particularly
evident in the politics of the recognition and restoration of national historical landmarks and in the politics of recognizing and restoring religious buildings. The Ministry of Culture's Department for the Preservation of Historical
Landmarks and Monuments shares the government's official commitment
to supporting the civic and multiethnic Tatarstani nation. As the director
of the department said in an interview in 1996, "monuments are not about
politics, but about culture, and work on them should be purely scientific"
(Valeev 1996). Yet an examination of the activities of this department since
1990 reveals a clear emphasis on the restoration of the historical landmarks
and monuments of the ethnic Tatar nation as opposed to those of the other
"multiethnic" peoples of Tatarstan.

While the department's first book was a catalogue of the historical monuments of the entire republic of Tatarstan,[15] it has subsequently published
two books exclusively about ethnic Tatar monuments. Furthermore, the
department has made the restoration of the cities and mosques of the ancient
Great Bulgar state its main priority in the post-Soviet period. There are plans
to form a "Silver Ring" tourist complex consisting of the ancient cities of
Bulgar itself (which Tatars often refer to as the "northernmost Muslim city
in the world" and the "Mecca of the North"), Bilyar, Suvar, and Chistopol
(expressly modeled on the Russian "Golden Ring" of cities around Moscow),
and to restore the "Old Tatar Quarter" of Kazan where many mosques used
to be located. The director of this department has also asserted that it has a
responsibility to the entire Tatar nation, even in diaspora, and has pledged to
catalogue Tatar monuments outside the republic as well (*Sovetskaya Tatariya*
March 18, 1993, 3; *Idel* 1994, 1/2: 51–57).

While the restoration of these important Tatar historical monuments
has been a priority of the Ministry of Culture since 1990, ethnic Russian
activists in Tatarstan who are concerned about the Volga River island of
Sviyazhsk, where Ivan Grozny's troops stayed as they planned their siege of
Kazan in 1552, and which as a result is home to a number of extremely old
and rare Orthodox churches, had to wait until 1996 to get the attention of
Tatarstan's Ministry of Culture (which did, however cosponsored a conference on Sviyazhsk in October 1996). In interviews with activists involved in
the campaign to restore Sviyazhsk, there emerged a common belief that the
administration had been dragging its feet on this project because it was an

ethnic Russian historical monument and moreover, a space identified with
the painful memories of the loss of Tatar statehood when Kazan was seized
by Russia in 1552.[16] In response to these protests, however, the Shaimiyev
regime recently has increased the priority of the restoration of Sviyazhsk,
dedicated more funds to the project, and asked UNESCO to include the island, along with the ancient city of Bulgar, in its list of World Heritage Sites
(*RFE/RL Tatar-Bashkir Service Daily Report* June 3, 2002).

Despite the priority placed on restoring monuments of the ethnic Tatar
nation, the government of Tatarstan has made significant public gestures of
good will towards all religious communities in Tatarstan, such as returning
a synagogue to Kazan's Jewish community in a high-profile ceremony which
was attended by the Israeli Ambassador to the Russian Federation, and returning a church to Kazan's Lutheran community (*Sovetskaya Tatariya* May
6, 1990, 10–11; *Respublika Tatarstan* December 10, 1996, 1; *Vremya i Dengi*
December 11, 1996, 4). The situation regarding the restoration of Orthdox
churches is a bit more complicated—in an interview given in early 1994, the
director of the Tatarstani Ministry of Culture's Department of Preservation
of Historical Landmarks and Monuments admitted that the department was
spending more funds on the restoration and construction of mosques than on
Orthodox churchs, but justified this policy by saying:

> Churches didn't live badly before, church coffers were never empty before.
> Therefore, our first priority is to develop Tatar national architecture. We have
> earmarked 60 percent of our funds for this goal. Patriarch Anastasii (of Kazan)
> complains, as if we are putting all our money for the revival of mosques, while
> churches are falling apart. But we tell him, that we are also putting resources
> towards Russian architecture, however, more attention is being paid to na-
> tional architecture at this point (*Idel* 1994, #1/2, 54).

Since 1992, the number of mosques in Tatarstan has increased from
around 100 to almost 700 (*Vremya i Dengi* July 24, 1997, 11), while Russian Orthodox activists in Tatarstan report that the Ministry of Culture has
repeatedly delayed the return of several churches in downtown Kazan to
the Orthodox community. When activists from Kazan's Russian Cultural
Society and the Patriarch of Kazan went to visit the Minister of Culture in
winter 1995 to talk about speeding up the return of these religious buildings, the Minister reportedly told them that in his personal opinion, as a
Tatar, he felt that "there is not room in the center of Kazan for another
church, there are already so many there" (*KRIS* January 6, 1996, 2; January
20, 1996, 1).[17] However, despite these disappointments, Patriarch Anastasi
of Kazan has maintained good relations with the Shaimiyev administration,

choosing in public to accentuate positive developments such as the restoration of the Blagoveschenskii Sobor in the Kremlin and the Orthodox Raefskii Monastary outside Kazan (Seminar 2001).

The Shaimiyev administration also supported the construction of a huge Catholic cathedral in Kazan, despite the republic's miniscule Catholic population, in the hopes that Pope John Paul II would visit the republic and return the Holy Mother of Kazan Icon directly to Kazan. Some in Tatarstan speculate that this bit of religious multicultural fervor may have been inspired as much by the desire to raise Tatarstan's profile on the international scene as to provide for the needs of its religious minorities (*RFE/RL Tatar-Bashkir Service Daily Report* November 28, 2003, April 27, 2004). Ultimately, the Mother of God icon was returned to Russia in August 2004 and then to Kazan in July 2005, in conjunction with the celebration of the to "Days of the Orthodox Religion in Tatarstan" and 450th anniversary of the establishment of the Kazan Eparchy Board, The Monastery of the Blessed Virgin in Kazan is being reconstructed to be the permanent home of the icon (*RFE/RL Tatar-Bashkir Service Daily Report* July 4, 2005).

Evaluating Nation-Building Efforts in Republican Sovereignty Projects: Promoters of Ethnocultural Justice, or "Nationalizing Regimes"?

To what extent do the nation-building efforts the Tatarstani government has pursued as part of their sovereignty project reflect the priorities of liberal multiculturalism presented at the beginning of this chapter? Has the republic followed through on its stated commitment to promoting the development of the ethnic Tatar nation simultaneously with the civic, multiethnic Tatarstani nation and the needs of the other individual communities that make up that larger community? Are Russian and other ethnic minority group rights being violated as a result of the pursuit of ethnocultural justice for Tatars in their new "sovereign" homeland? I would argue that the evidence presented in this chapter demonstrates that republican elites have made a good faith effort to create a balance between ethnic understandings of the Tatar nation and civic, multicultural understandings of the "Tatarstani" nation, and that they have achieved at least the semblance of a functional and useful equilibrium between providing for the cultural and linguistic needs of the titular Tatar population and those of the other ethnic groups in Tatarstan, including Russians. A similar conclusion was reached by Council of Europe Human Rights Commission Alvaro Gil-Robles in April 2005, when he declared that Tatarstan's initiatives aimed at promoting harmony between ethnic groups had "made a strong impression" on him, leading him to state that in his opinion, "Tatarstan can fairly be titled a laboratory for cooperation between different nationalities" (*RFE/RL Tatar-Bashkir Service Daily Report* April 27, 2005).

While it is clear that the ethnic Tatar nation does occupy a privileged place in the multinational pantheon that makes up the "Tatarstani" nation, the republican government has not prohibited other ethnic groups from pursuing their interests in the Tatarstan, and in fact has provided them with the legal and material resources to do so (to a much greater extent than the federal government has, in fact). Thus the Tatarstani government has supplemented its claim, imminently defensible according to liberal multicultural theory, that Tatarstan is the proper, natural, and indeed, only state structure in Russia (or the world) that can adequately provide for the linguistic and cultural revival of the Tatar nation[18] with a significant, if not necessarily equal, commitment to recognizing the legitimacy of and fulfilling the cultural needs of the other ethnic groups on its territory, including Russians (who nevertheless, as Tatarstani officials often point out, do in fact have powerful patrons in the cultural and political institutions of the Russian Federation and the Russian Orthodox Church). This reality should be acknowledged as a useful corrective to the common portrayal of Tatarstan as rabidly ethno-chauvinist "nationalizing" regime.

The significance and utility of the form of cultural pluralism Tatarstan has developed as part of its sovereignty project to the provision of any type of liberal pluralist regime or any modicum of ethnocultural justice in Russia is magnified when the poor record of the Russian Federation on nationalities issues in the post-Soviet period is considered.

The December 1993 Russian Constitution enshrined the principles of cultural pluralism in the new Russian state in many significant ways, including the following: the constitution was issued in the name of the sovereignty of the "multinational" people of Russia and not the ethnic Russian nation (article 3); it did not give the Russian Orthodox Church any special privileges in Russia but rather declared Russia to be a secular state (article 14); it gave the republics the right to have their own constitutions and state languages (articles 66 and 68); and it gave the republics significant representation in the upper legislative chamber in Russia, the Federation Council (article 95).

Yet as the next chapter discusses in some detail, in the intervening late Yeltsin and Putin years, mostly due to the continued war in Chechnya and the attendant rise in terrorist violence on the territory of the Russian Federation, the federal government has moved inexorably to erode and invalidate almost all of these multicultural protections, most recently in the name of "preserving Russia's territorial integrity." In addition to denuding the republics' representation in the Federation Council (and now, it appears, in the Duma as well), and attacking the legal bases of republican sovereignty projects through legislative and judicial means, the federal government has also demonstrated through both passive and active means that it does not intend to provide for the cultural and linguistic needs of Russia's ethnic minorities in any meaningful way.

For example, while the Russian parliament did adopt a "Law on National Cultural Autonomies" in Russia, which gives ethnic minorities the right to form associations in Russia, it has never funded this law or the activities of any of Russia's national cultural autonomies, leaving the groups to rely on the handouts of their "kin-state" patrons instead (*RFE/RL Tatar-Bashkir Service Daily Report* December 4, 2002, April 11. 2003; Zaripov 2005). Furthermore, Moscow has been reluctant to commit the bureaucratic resources necessary to make nationalities policy a priority at the cabinet level. During the Yeltsin era, there was a cabinet-level "Minister of Nationalities," but that post has been downgraded to a "Minister without Portfolio" status, which does not include the bureaucratic resources necessary to make or implement effective nationalities policy. For example, in April 2003, Vladimir Zorin, the most recent occupant of the position in question, asked Tatarstani President Shaimiyev to develop and present a draft program for a "Russian Federation State Nationalities Policy," which Shaimiyev did. However, Zorin then proceeded to table Shaimiyev's program without enacting any part of it (Hahn 2003, 2004; *RFE/RL Tatar-Bashkir Service Daily Report* March 11, 2002, April 11, 2003). This willed passivity led one of Tatarstan's representatives in the Russian Duma to label Zorin "a bum minister with no staff, no finances, and no power"(*RFE/RL Political Weekly* Volume 3, #15, April 17 2003), and spurred Shaimiyev himself to lament that "Russian Federation bodies have done nothing to resolve the national-cultural development issues for Tatars," and that "national republics and peoples in Russia have no real chance of solving these problems with the help of the Russian Federation"—indicating, of course, that republics like Tatarstan had no choice but to seek solutions to these problems themselves (*RFE/RL Tatar-Bashkir Service Daily Report* February 16, 2004). As will be discussed in the next chapter, the events in Beslan in September 2004 would motivate the Putin administration to take up the question of non-Russian needs more seriously, but with few concrete results.

More disturbingly, the federal government's neglect of non-Russian nationalities policy has been accompanied by an active pro-ethnic Russian, anti-multiculturalist agenda. In January 2002, the Russian Duma proposed a draft "Law on the Russian People" that would introduce special protections and programs for ethnic Russian language and culture, a move that engendered heated opposition from ethnic minorities across the federation, including Tatars in Tatarstan, who proposed an analogous "Law on the Tatar People" to demonstrate that "Russia was not just the home of Russians but of over one hundred different peoples" (*Vremya i Dengi* January 18, 2002, 1). The Russian Federation Duma has also proposed introducing a mandatory "Orthodox Culture" class into all secondary schools in the country, although after an outcry from Tatarstan and other republics, it appears to have conceded that republics with non-Russian populations, such as Tatarstan and Bashkortostan, will be allowed to introduce teachings about other religions into their curriculum as well (*RFE/RL Tatar-Bashkir Service Daily Report* February 6, 2004, May 28, 2004). More egregious, in the view of ethnic Tatars and other minorities, were the amendments to the Law on Languages of the Russian Federation passed in December 2002, which forbade ethnic minorities from using any alphabet other than Cyrillic for their indigenous languages. These restrictions have led deputies and ethnic intelligentsia from Tatarstan to appeal to international organizations such as the European Union and UNESCO to "protect" them from Moscow's "incursions" against the rights of ethnic minorities, and from the overall thrust of Moscow's nationality policy, which they describe as "having the goal and contents of reforming the Russian federation into a "unitary, mononational, and monolinguistic state" (Tatar Latin Front Appeal 2005).

A new draft nationalities policy circulated by the Russian Federal Ministry of Regional Development in late 2005 seemingly confirmed Tatar fears about the direction of Russian federal nationalities policy. While the draft did define a main goal of Russia's nationalities policy as "strengthening the formation of a united, multinational society" in Russia, it also called for the Russian people and the Russian language to play a "consolidating role" in that process, and stressed that the ultimate goal of any nationalities policy was to "strengthen the power vertical in Russia" (*Kommersant* October 11, 2005; *RFE/RL Political Weekly* Volume 6, #6, March 10, 2006). The "leading role" envisioned for Russians in this plan was criticized not only by ethnic minorities in Russia, but by Emil Pain, head of the Center for the Study of Extremism and Xenophobia at the Russian Academy of Sciences, who asked rhetorically, "Do you remember the Stalinist idea of the elder Russian brother? If Russians do not, people in Chechnya, Tatarstan, Yakutia, and elsewhere certainly do" (*Window on Eurasia* March 13, 2006). Further underlining the low priority Moscow places on the provision of cultural needs for national minorities in Russia is the fact that when asked about potential funding for non-Russians' concerns in fall 2005, Federal Minister of Regional Development Vladimir Yakovlev felt it necessary to assuage potentially outraged Russians by assuring them that his ministry would instead ask for funds for building more housing units in Russia, as he felt this was a better use of scarce federal funds (*RIA Novosti* October 12, 2005).

Given Moscow's lack of commitment to cultural pluralism and the considerable and successful efforts of Tatarstani sovereignty-seekers in constructing multiple civic and ethnic national identities in Tatarstan that aspire to "respond to the needs of all national and peoples residing within the state's borders" (Harty and Murphy 2005 37), the Russian Federation's considerable efforts to obstruct and even dismantle the sovereignty project in Tatarstan that has generated these innovations, the subject of the final two chapters, is ill-advised from both a political and a normative point of view.

Notes

1. The most influential thinkers in this debate are Charles Taylor (1992), Will Kymlicka (1995), and James Tully (1995).

2. I am following Kymlicka and Opalski's use of the non-hyphenated adjective "ethnocultural" here, but prefer to use the hyphen for the adjective "ethno-federal," as there seems to be less of a consensus surrounding the spelling of this word in the relevant literature.

3. The A.N.K.O. was officially created at the first Congress of Peoples of Tatarstan. Despite being the centerpiece of the Shaimiyev administration's nationalities policy for the multiethnic population of Tatarstan, only in 1998, six years after its founding, did the group and its member collectives of different national-cultural associations receive a building from the government of Tatarstan (*Vremya i Dengi* February 27, 1997).

4. Based on author's fieldwork observations in Kazan 1996, 1997, 2000, 2001, 2005. Also see Mustafin and Khasanov (1995) for a collection of pictures which illustrate this tendency.

5. For more discussion of Tatarstan's adoption of a "kin-state" role in relation to the Tatar diaspora worldwide, a role it continues to embraced today, see Graney (1998).

6. Overall, 96.6 percent of Tatars in Tatarstan claimed Tatar as their native language in 1989. Among rural Tatars, 99.98 percent claimed Tatar as their first language. However for Tatars in the Russian Federation as a whole the native language retention rate in 1989 was somewhat lower—83.2 percent (Frank and Wixman 1997, 167–68).

7. While virtually all urban Tatars and most rural Tatars consider themselves bilingual in Tatar and Russian (whether or not this claim is actually true), only 1.4

percent of urban Russians and 4.6 percent of rural Russians in Tatarstan consider themselves bilingual in Tatar and Russian (Drobizheva et. al. 1996, 289). Thus Shaimiyev's pledge to ensure that every citizen of Tatarstan becomes bilingual is in actuality a pledge to increase the knowledge and use of the Tatar language among Russians in the republic.

8. For two opposing views of the impact of a decade and a half of Tatar language promotion policies in Tatarstan, see Faller 2006, and with a less sanguine take on the issue, Gorenburg 2006.

9. The plans called for a monument composed of three pillars with a glass dome to be erected opposite the North tower of the Kazan Kremlin complex in time for the 1000th anniversary of Kazan celebrations, to be held in summer 2005. Ironically, the funding for these lavish celebrations came largely from Moscow—which means the monument to the defenders of Kazan would have been built with money from their "conquerors." However, the monument did not materialize in time for the August 2005 celebrations, and its future is unclear (*Tatar-Inform* June 10, 2004; *RFE/RL Tatar-Bashkir Service Daily Report* June 11, 2004).

10. These occasions included the ceremony in January 1996 naming Bla-goveshchenskii Sabor an official national landmark (*Vremya i Dengi* February 24, 1996) his annual appeal to the State Council in February 1996 (*Vremya i Dengi* February 15, 1996), and his address to the country on Republic Day in August 1996 (*Respublika Tatarstan* August 30, 1996).

11. Besides the Kazan Kremlin's role as the most politicized public space in Tatarstan, the emphasis on civic equality in this project may also be a function of the fact that the Russian Federation government has pledged a large sum of money to help complete the restoration of the Sobor and the Kremlin (*Izvestiya Tatarstan* August 9, 1994, 3).

12. While the Tatar intelligentsia and nationalist community lost their bid to have the main street renamed after a Tatar heroine, other streets in Kazan have been renamed in honor of Tatar poets (Sajidi Suleymanova) and Tatar social activists (Mushtari), as well as after the German historian who taught at Kazan State University and wrote the first "objective" history of the Kazan Tatars, Karl Fuchs (*Kazanskiye Vedemosti* October 9, 1996, 3). The committee on the renaming of streets in Kazan expressed its understanding of the delicacy of their task considering their location "in the multinational republic of Tatarstan." In the city of Naberezhniye Chelny, the former Lenin Prospect was successfully changed to Suyumbike Street, while other important streets were also given Tatar names (*Sovetskaya Tatariya* May 13, 1993, 2).

13. All references to the new National Gallery in Tatarstan are from the document entitled "Kontseptsiya Ekspositsii Nationali'noi Kartinnoi Galerei," a copy of which I acquired from the new director of the gallery in Kazan in June 2005.

14. See the special issue of *Izvestiya TOTs* (#8a, June 16–21, 1992), devoted entirely to the "Concept of the Development of Tatar Culture."

15. In this book, the editors assert that the basic foundation layer of the historical culture of Tatarstan is "above all" the physical monuments of the Tatar people. The

monuments of Russians and other peoples of Tatarstan are "secondary aspects" of the republic's culture. See *Respublika Tatarstan: Pamyatniki Istorii i Kul'tury (The Republic of Tatarstan; Monuments of History and Culture)* (Kazan: Aidos, 1993), 6.

16. This analysis is based on interviews conducted by the author August 16–17, 1997 on the island of Sviyazhsk during the time of President Shaimiyev's visit there.

17. This event prompted the head of the Society of Russian Culture in Kazan to write an editorial complaining that all aspects of Russian culture had suffered in Tatarstan since the adoption of the Declaration of Sovereignty in 1990, and that Russian cultural needs never received "adequate understanding" in official policy organs intended to ensure the equality cultural rights for all of Tatarstan's ethnic groups, such as the A.N.K.O. (*KRIS* March 5, 1997, 4).

18. For an eloquent articulation of this claim by the speaker of the Tatarstani State Council, Farid Mukhametshin, see speech reprinted in the *RFE/RL Tatar-Bashkir Service Daily Report* from January 1, 2002, where Mukhametshin laments that the Russian Federation "neither wishes to nor can develop Tatar language and culture," leaving Tatarstan with the "exclusive duty to do so." Mukhametshin adds that it would be proper for Russia to at least subsidize Tatarstan's efforts in this regard if it won't take up the responsibility itself.

CHAPTER FIVE

The End of Russian Federalism?
Tatarstan's Sovereignty Project
under the Putin Administration

In August 2000, the Tatarstani government staged an elaborate celebration of the tenth anniversary of the adoption of the Declaration of State Sovereignty, which included a special session of the republican parliament, art exhibits, academic conferences, and a three-day public holiday and festival, all capped by an extravagant fireworks display over the city of Kazan. During the celebrations, the rhetoric praising the achievements of the decade-long Tatarstani quest to fulfill its declaration of sovereignty flowed freely. Government officials referred to the August 1990 declaration as the "fulfillment of the Tatar people's centuries-long desire for self-determination" and the "first and most important step on the on-going road to restoring Tatar statehood," while also stressing the various concrete benefits a decade of sovereignty had brought to Tatarstan's population. These included establishing "treaty-based relations with Russia," fostering an above-average standard of living, the transformation of Kazan, the revival of Tatar and other national cultures, and giving Tatarstan "a high profile on the European and international stages."[1]

It is difficult to fault the leaders of Tatarstan's sovereignty project for marking the tenth-anniversary of the Declaration of Sovereignty in this lavish way, for the achievements of the previous decade were both real and remarkable. Tatarstan's persistent, creative, and multifaceted pursuit of sovereignty in the federal, republican, and international arenas was far more ambitious, well-organized, sustained, and energetic than that of any other republic, and the results of its sovereignty project far more apparent. The republic's boasts, repeated many times over the tenth-anniversary weekend, that it was the "unmatched leader" in "bottom-up federation building" and sovereignty-seeking, and that it had achieved its goals in an "entirely peaceful way," unlike Chechnya, were indeed supported by the facts on the ground in Kazan in August 2000.

Perhaps the sole damper on the festive mood in Kazan in August 2000 was that, according to decisions of the Russian Federation Constitutional Court issued two months previous under the watchful eye of new Russian President Vladimir Putin, Tatarstan's much-celebrated claim to be a sovereign state was wholly unconstitutional and thus illegal under Russian federal law (*EWI RRR* Volume 5, #25, June 28, 2000 and Volume 5, #27, December 7, 2000). Though the republic chose to very publicly deny the validity of the Constitutional Court rulings by holding the tenth-anniversary of sovereignty celebrations, Tatarstani leaders could not deny or evade the collective impact of the other salvos that were part of the Putin administration's much broader and comprehensive attack on regional sovereignty projects. Indeed, reversing the republics' sovereignty projects, chief among them Tatarstan's, ending the "legal anarchy" that marked center-periphery relations during the Yeltsin era, and reestablishing "vertical authority" from Moscow were the main stated goals of the new Russian president. Putin in fact seemed to view this task as an almost spiritual obligation, arguing that the "super-centralization" of government in Russia is "inherent in the genetic code, tradition, and mentality of Russia's people" (*EWI RRR*, Volume 5, #25, June 28, 2000).

The Putin administration's attempt to recentralize Russia's federal system by halting and reversing Tatarstan's sovereignty project can be divided into two main periods. The first, ranging from 2000–2004, included the following measures: an ambitious set of legislation known as the "federal package"; the introduction of the post of presidential envoy, each of whom had responsibility for one of seven new federal districts; a collection of coordinated ministerial initiatives designed to reestablish unilateral federal control over a broad spectrum of policymaking and administrative arenas; and the use of the Russian Federal Constitutional Court and regional high courts as well as so-called "harmonization commissions" to attack the legal bases of regional sovereignty, equalize the powers of all Russia's regions, and bring regional constitutions, bilateral treaties, and other legislation in line with federal norms.

The second wave of Putin's centralizing attack on the regions, comprised of a new set of presidential legislative initiatives, was introduced as a response to the wave of horrific terrorist attacks that culminated with the Beslan massacre of September 2004. This more vigorous attack on federalism in Russia, which cancelled the popular election of regional governors and presidents and replaced them with presidential appointments, provoked substantial criticism, with the Putin administration standing accused of fostering an "anti-federative takeover" of the country and returning it to "the Soviet system of government" (*Nezavisimaya Gazeta* September 14, 2004). In an editorial responding to the fall 2004 reforms, former U.S. National Security Advisor Zbigniew Brzezinski called Putin's moves "Stalinist" and referred to Putin himself as "Moscow's Mussolini" (*Wall Street Journal* September 20, 2004). Significantly, Putin's post-Beslan federal reform initiatives were couched in a much more alarmist rhetoric which openly equated regional sovereignty with ethnic separatism and the imminent break-up of the Russian Federation, and which both fed off and fed into the growing and sometimes violent Islamophobia, xenophobia, and Russian nationalism that increasingly characterizes Russian society in the first decade of the twenty-first century.

Unsurprisingly, the architects of Tatarstan's sovereignty project did not acquiesce silently to the Putin administration's attempts to dismantle the republic's hard-fought gains and to portray all regional sovereignty projects as ethno-nationalist separatist movements bent on breaking up Russia. Instead, Tatarstani elites greeted Moscow's initiatives with the same familiar pragmatic attitude and flexibility combined with steadiness of purpose, namely to continue to seek as much sovereignty as possible under any given set of (ever-changing) circumstances in Russia. In fact, Tatarstan used the Putin-era attacks by Moscow to defend even more forcefully its right to possess sovereignty, and to position itself even more directly as the chief guardian of federalism, the principles of rule of law and constitutionalism, the principles of cultural pluralism and self-determination, and the rights of non-Russian peoples in Russia. In doing so, it accused the Putin administration in Moscow of running roughshod over the Russian Federation's Constitution, of willfully destroying the ethno-federal system called for in that document, of denying Russia's history and present as a multicultural entity, and the commitment to cultural pluralism embodied in the constitution, and finally of ignoring what common sense requires of a country as complex as Russia attempting to compete in the modern globalized world, namely flexibility and decentralized regional initiative, not hyper-centralized statism.

The present chapter traces the turbulent course of relations between a Moscow Kremlin pursuing vigorously the "dictatorship of law" and "power vertical" in Russia by curbing regional sovereignty and autonomy and the Kazan Kremlin's attempt to repel those overtures by recasting its own battle to hold onto its sovereignty as a fight undertaken in the name of preserving the last remnants of federalism, democracy, and cultural pluralism in Russia. The situation resulting from this most recent engagement between Moscow and Kazan is somewhat more complex and the implications to be drawn from it somewhat more sanguine than might be expected given the dire predictions about Putin's "Stalinist" intentions for federal reform in Russia in the wake of Beslan. Indeed, as a result of Tatarstan's resistance, the Putin administration was, to an unanticipated degree, forced to compromise its overall vision of establishing unitarism and a renewed power vertical, and found itself in many important instances acquiescing in particular to Tatarstan's sovereignty-based claims of "special status." Tatarstan, for its part, was able to retain the majority of its most important legal, symbolic and policy attributes of sovereignty in the face of strong pressure from Moscow to relinquish them.

In the end, the process of grappling over Putin's controversial reforms in many respects actually helped to institutionalize the type of iterated, institutionalized push and pull, back and forth type of negotiation and compromise between the Moscow and Kazan Kremlins that is one of the essential and defining features of federalism. In other words, the vigorous response that Tatarstan mounted to the Putin administration's equally powerful challenge to regional sovereignty actually generated a federation-building process that has powerful positive implications for Russia's future development. More specifically, Putin's overtures forced Tatarstan to comply more completely with a growing federal legislative and regulatory framework, while Tatarstan's spirited defense of regional sovereignty forced Moscow to adopt a more flexible and responsive attitude towards federalism and the regions in general, particularly regarding issues of cultural pluralism and autonomy. Thus, the evidence presented in this chapter supports my overall argument that Tatarstan's sovereignty project has helped to midwife an intriguing kernel of real, functioning federalism and ethnocultural justice in Russia.

Putin's First Attempt at Restoration of Central Power (2000–August 2004)

Even before the appointment of Vladimir Putin as acting president of Russia, the Russian Duma had taken steps towards curbing the sovereign power of the regions. For example, the Law on the Establishment of Regional Political Institutions, which was passed by the Duma in June 1999, stated that all bilateral treaties between the center and the regions must be adjusted to comply with Russian Federal legislation by July 2002, while the Law on Federal Relations, passed in October 1999, stated that regional executives could not serve more than two consecutive terms (*EWI RRR* Volume 5, #1 January 12, 2000 and Volume 5, #7, February 24, 2000). However it was only after Putin's inauguration as Russia's new president in May 2000 that legal and institutional attacks on the power of Russia's regions began in earnest.

In the first major offensive against the regions, Putin issued a decree imposing a new administrative layer over Russia's existing territorial structure by creating seven large federal districts, each to be run by a special presidential envoy and to be endowed with a large bureaucracy charged with "ensuring the exercise of the Constitutional powers of the President of the Russian Federation, making the work of federal bodies more effective and improving compliance with their decisions" (*ITAR-TASS* May 13, 2000). In other words, the basic mission of the new Federal Districts was to help Putin keep a closer watch on Russia's restive regions, chief among them Tatarstan. While observers in both Moscow and the regions predicted that the new presidential envoys would prove to be a potent weapon in the quest to curb regional sovereignty drives, in fact the record of the presidential envoys in terms of their ability to pressure the regions into compliance with federal norms is decidedly mixed, with one author going so far as to label the envoys a "failing experiment" (Nudelman 2003).

The main weakness of the new envoys is that they have not been given the proper tools with which to carry out the agenda they have been charged with—in particular, they have been denied control over the financial flows between the center and regions, a power the Russian Federal Finance Ministry still wields from Moscow (Nudelman 2003; *RAS* #8, May 2002). As such, regional governors and presidents like Shaimiyev have properly deduced that the most important decisions, namely those regarding the distribution of resources from the center, are still made in Moscow, and thus have chosen, mostly successfully, to sideline the presidential envoys by "continuing to lobby the central government and Duma directly" (*RAS* #8, May 2002). As a result then, while the presidential envoys may have at first fulfilled one of their original purposes, namely to "scare" the regional elites and act as a "heavies" helping to keep strong regional leaders like Shaimiyev in line (*EWI RRR* Vol. 7, #20, June 17, 2002), even this limited effectiveness has dwindled and now most important issues between regional elites and Moscow are still resolved, as they were during the Yeltsin era, by means of direct negotiation with the president in Moscow (*RAS* #8, May 2002).

Less than a week after announcing the creation of the new federal districts and presidential envoys, Putin made a dramatic television appearance in which he addressed the nation directly and announced his intention to introduce a supplementary package of laws designed to help strengthen the "unity" of the Russian state. Putin's "federal package" directed against the separatism of the regions like Tatarstan consisted of three bills (*AP* May 31, 2000). They first sought to remake the Federation Council by depriving regional governors and legislative heads of their automatic seats and replacing them with full-time, appointed representatives from the regions. The second bill, an amendment to the Law on Principles for Legislative and Executive Government bodies, sought to give the Russian president the power both to dissolve local legislatures and to remove regional executives in the case that they were found guilty of violating federal laws. The third proposed bill of the federal package sought to give both the president and regional executives the right to remove mayors and other local officials in their domain in the case of violations of federal laws. A final part of the package was a revised tax code shifting the balance of both collection and distribution back in the favor of the federal government.

On May 31, 2000, the Duma approved all three bills on the first reading, with the two-thirds majority that would be necessary to overrule any future Federation Council veto action. As expected, the Federation Council initially rejected Putin's federal package, although it did eventually vote to form a conciliatory commission with the State Duma to try to hammer out a compromise. On July 19, the Duma overrode the Federation Council's veto and passed the new compromise versions of the three bills in Putin's federal package (*RFE/RL Newsline* July 19, 2000). On July 26, the Federation Council approved the bills, the current members in effect voting themselves out of a job. The consolations for the Federation Council members included the fact that they were given the right to appoint and dismiss their own representatives to the new Federation Council, and that regional executives, and heads of parliament were offered seats in a new "State Council," whose powers remained unclear but were certainly less than those of the Federation Council (*EWI RRR*, Volume 5, #29, July 26, 2000). Tatarstani President Shaimiyev was one of those who lobbied hardest to extract the ambiguous concession of the State Council from the Putin administration, and as will be discussed later in this chapter, while the new State Council by no means carries the same weight as the old Federation Council, its few meetings have had a disproportionate impact on federal reform, and Shaimiyev has had a disproportionately large influence within that body.

Many of the post-2000, appointed members of the Federation Council have tenuous, if any, links with the regions they are representing, and instead seem to have been chosen for their loyalty to Moscow and their ties to oligarchs close to the Kremlin. Scholar Thomas Remington estimates that

75–80 percent of the new Federation Council members seem to have been "recommended or cleared" by the Kremlin in Moscow, a situation that is uncomfortably close to the old Soviet-era *nomenklatura* system (Remington 2003, 673–74). Perhaps unsurprisingly, the new Federation Council is less apt to challenge the Kremlin's initiatives than its predecessor—if between 1996–1999 the Federation Council rejected 20 percent of executive initiatives, from 2000–2003 it rejected only 3 percent, with the vast majority of legislative votes being approved by "sizable affirmative majorities" (Remington 2003, 683).

The Putin-era Federation Council has also, as might be expected, shown great unwillingness to entertain independent thought from the regions about the appointment or removal of members from their territories. For example, in April 2003 Tatarstani President Mintimer Shaimiyev sought to recall one of the republic's representatives to the Federation Council, independent-minded Tatar businessman Refget Altynbaev, and replace him with a more loyal Shaimiyev appointee, Filze Khemidullin. The Federation Council rejected Shaimiyev's motion on the first vote, though they would approve it on the second. This encroachment on what Shaimiyev perceived as one of the few imperatives of regional autonomy left under Putin enraged Shaimiyev, who accused the Federation Council of "excluding Tatarstan from Russia" and "depriving the Republic of Tatarstan of its constitutional right to represent its interests in the Upper Chamber" (*RFE/RL Tatar-Bashkir Service Daily Report* April 24, 2003). This was not to be the last time Shaimiyev or other Tatarstani elites would criticize the "reform" of the Federation Council—in December 2003 Tatar State Council Speaker Mukhametshin lamented the demise of the "old" Federation Council and pointed out that "even in the Soviet era the national minorities had direct representation in the Duma through quotas" (*RFE/RL Tatar-Bashkir Service Daily Report*, December 12, 2003). Shaimiyev himself charged in June 2006 that Federation Council members had no ties or loyalty to the regions they were meant to represent, and instead were "moneybags senators" who had openly "bought" their seats by bribing federal and regional elites, most to the tune of $2 million (*Moscow Times* June 9, 2006).

The second element of Putin's federal package, the bill giving Putin the right to remove regional executives from power and to disband local legislatures, was unpopular with the ethnic republics, including Tatarstan, from the beginning. As Ingush Republic President Ruslan Aushev asked after the July 26 vote, "What kind of federation is it if the president can remove the popularly elected head of a region or disband the regional legislature?" (*EWI RRR*, Volume 5, #29, July 26, 2000). In fact a number of republics, including

Tatarstan, sought to challenge this new law, but it was upheld by the Russian Constitutional Court in an April 2002 decision, albeit with the caveat that these new Presidential powers could only be invoked after a minimum of three jurisdictions, including the Russian Constitutional Court, had passed rulings supporting such an action (*RIS* Moscow April 4, 2002).

Despite this legal victory, the Putin administration did not move immediately to wield this new power against regional elites, apparently choosing to use the carrot rather than the stick with this group—indeed, Putin supported another new law, passed in December 2000, which allows most regional executives to pursue third and even fourth legal terms in office.[2] Shaimiyev, who was elected to a third term in office in March 2001, was a beneficiary of the Putin administration's seemingly contradictory decision to support this legislation, a decision which demonstrates how vulnerable Putin's recentralizing overtures are to the harsh political realities of post-Soviet Russian politics—namely the power of regional elites and Putin's need to appease them.

A crucially important piece of Putin's federal package is a revised tax code, which was approved by both the Federation Council and the Duma in July 2000, particularly when the favorable tax regime Tatarstan achieved with its February 1994 treaty with Russia is considered. The new code, aimed at simplifying Russia's byzantine and oppressive tax system, introduced a 13 percent flat federal income tax, established a minimum 5 percent unified federal social tax, increased excise taxes on alcohol and tobacco and, most importantly, revised the law on value-added tax, dictating that 100 percent of the VAT must be turned over to the federal budget (*RFE/RL Newsline*, Volume 4, #138, July 20, 2000; *Reuters* July 19, 2000 and July 25, 2000). Later, separate acts would also revise the division of excise taxes on oil and natural resources, again in favor of the federal government.

Many regional elites bemoaned the fact that the new tax code would decrease the amount of money that would be collected by and left in the regions, with some estimating that the new plan would send 70 percent of revenue to Moscow, leaving only 30 percent for the regions, a figure disputed by Russian Finance Minister Aleksei Kudrin, who claimed that the regions would retain 52.5 percent of revenue under the new plan (*EWI RRR*, Volume 5, #29, July 26, 2000). It was not immediately clear if the new tax plan would apply to regions like Tatarstan and Bashkortostan, which in the past had negotiated separate budget deals with Moscow allowing them greater financial sovereignty.

In practice, the impact of the new tax code in Tatarstan has been mixed. Tatarstan has agreed to comply partly with the new code, allowing a branch of the Russian Federal Treasury Board to open in the republic for the first time in spring 2001. This has been a costly concession for Kazan—in 2001 Tatarstani officials estimated that they sent approximately 50 percent of all tax revenue collected in the republic to Moscow, whereas under the Yeltsin administration the figure was closer to 15 percent (*RFE/RL Tatar-Bashkir Service Daily Report* January 18, 2001). In the following year, 2002, Tatarstani budget officials estimated that the new revised tax code had cost the republic "3 billion rubles in lost revenue" (*RFE/RL Tatar-Bashkir Service Daily Report* October 20, 2003). Tatarstani complaints about the new tax regime would intensify in April 2004 when Putin announced both higher taxes on domestic oil extraction and refining and a new division of those collected taxes between the center and regions, one that was considerably less favorable to Tatarstan (*RFE/RL Tatar-Bashkir Service Daily Report* April 30, 2004).[3]

While increased Tatarstani compliance with the new federal tax code, including the opening of a federal tax collection office in Kazan, may seem to be a great victory for the center (and also for fiscal rationality in Russia), a closer look at budget relations between Kazan and Moscow during this period demonstrates the continued weakness of the federal center vis-à-vis powerful regions like Tatarstan, and the one step forward, two steps back nature of federal reform in Russia. For example, in a classic case of robbing Peter to pay Paul, the "victory" of getting Tatarstan to "give up" its favorable tax regime and allow federal tax collection at high rates was "bought" for a stiff price by the Putin regime. In a speech in July 2001 Tatarstani President Shaimiyev announced that because "joining the Russian Federation's economic space" by participating in the new tax code would "severely damage the standard of living of Tatarstan's citizens," Tatarstan had requested that Moscow compensate the republic by funding a special five-year "Program of Social and Economic Progress for Tatarstan" (*RFE/RL Tatar-Bashkir Service* July 16, 2001). This demand was met by the Putin regime—in the 2002 Russian Federal Budget Tatarstan received the equivalent $408 million in federal funds, while the rest of the 88 regions combined received only $176 million. This blatant pandering to Kazan led one Moscow newspaper to quip that "while we have nothing against Tatarstan, which is a fine republic, it seems to us that Moscow has not been a tributary of the Kazan Khanate for some time, but may be again now" (*RFE/RL Tatar-Bashkir Service* February 19, 2002).

Thus Moscow's "success" in bringing Tatarstan back into a uniform tax code was a pyrrhic victory in some regard, and is emblematic of the challenge the Putin regime faces in trying to create a more uniform economic space in Russia. As political scientist Yoshiko Herrera has observed in her analysis of Putin's effort to create a more homogenized set of rules governing economic activity in Russia, a "formidable set of obstacles" including "the very deep differences in the economic development and programs of economic reforms across the territorial spaces of the federation" hinder Moscow's quest (Herrera 2002). Tatarstan's effectiveness in negotiating a "special deal" in the 2002 federal budget will serve as an example to other regions to continue to seek their own personalized economic relations with the center and thus exacerbate the underlying economic differences that already complicate this important aspect of Putin's recentralization initiative. As will be discussed later in the chapter, this trend seems to have lessened somewhat in the post-Beslan era, but remains a counterweight to Moscow's centralizing tendencies.

Ministerial Initiatives

Individual Russian Federation ministries have also been employed in the drive to curb regional quests to exercise state sovereignty in Russia, with various initiatives aimed at reasserting central federal control over the activities of the regions emerging early in the Putin era. Among the most important of these are: the Russian Interior Ministry's moves to bring all criminal policy units and FSB units under direct control of the Russian Federation and strip regions of the right to block federal appointments of regional police chiefs (*RFE/RL Russian Federation Report*, Volume 2, 38, February 23, 2000; *EWI RRR*, Volume 5, #18, May 10, 2000); the Russian Prosecutor General's desire to "establish more federal control over local prosecutors, who are currently too close to regional leaders," and to abolish regional constitutional courts (*RFE/RL Newsline*, May 25, 2000); efforts to bring all distilleries and alcohol distributors into a centralized and state-owned holding company (*RFE/RL Newsline* May 23, 2000); and the Russian Press Ministry's demand that all regional publications henceforth be licensed and financed from the center (*RFE/RL Russian Federation Report*, Volume 2, #2, January 12, 2000; *EWI RRR* Volume 5, #23, June 14, 2000). However perhaps most directly targeted at and thus most egregious to Tatarstan's sovereignty project was the Russian Foreign Ministry's attempt to rein in "foreign policy freelancing" by denying the regions the right to establish foreign economic ties or borrow money from abroad without prior approval from Russian Federal officials (*RFE/RL Russian Federation Report*, Volume 2, #9, March 1, 2000; Volume 2, #15, April 19, 2000).

As was their experience with the new federal package of legislation, central elites in Moscow have discovered that declaring a policy change regarding the regions and actually seeing that policy change enacted institutionally in the periphery are two different things. Even when the federal center has been able to engender the types of recentralizing institutional changes it desires in the provinces, these changes have come with regional caveats attached. For example, while acquiescing to the demand that the "Republic of Tatarstan KGB" rename itself the "Federal FSB Board in Tatarstan," the Deputy Chair of this entity in Tatarstan held a news conference to assure the republic that "the Tatarstani KGB is not gone, only renamed" and that "it would continue to do the same things and report first to the Tatarstani cabinet, not just to Moscow" (*RFE/RL Tatar-Bashkir Service Daily Report* May 11, 2001).

Similar regard for maintaining the pretense, if not the actual reality, of continued republican control over local institutions was voiced by Deputy Prime Minister of Tatarstan Zilya Valeeva in June 2001 upon the opening of a new Tatarstani branch of the Russian Federal Justice Ministry on Freedom Square in Kazan. Valeeva remarked that citizens should realize that the Federal Ministry would be operating "alongside the existing Tatarstani Justice Ministry" and that there would be "a formal agreement" in place about how to divide powers between them—thus asserting that the local institution would retain some sovereign control in the republic despite the presence of a new analogous federal representation (*RFE/RL Tatar-Bashkir Service Daily Report* June 7, 2001).

Even regarding foreign policy, perhaps the most sensitive ministerial area for battles over sovereignty, Tatarstan has fought to retain its hard-won achievements, and in fact has forced the Putin regime to compromise to some degree. As was discussed in chapter 3, Tatarstani elites worked hard to create an "international personality" for Tatarstan and placed much weight on their success in this regard. Thus unsurprisingly, the republic has refused to acquiesce to federal demands to give up their representations abroad or to cease engaging in "foreign policy freelancing"—the Tatarstani representations abroad remain open, and foreign heads of state continue to visit Kazan regularly, the most recent example being the CIS summit held in Kazan upon the 1000th anniversary of the city in August 2005 (discussed later in this chapter). Instead, Tatarstani elites have continued to stress to Moscow the mutually-beneficial nature of working together *with* the republics in the international arena—the "piggy-backing" of Moscow on Tatarstan's initiation of closer ties with individual Islamic countries and the OIC is one of the best examples of this phenomena.

Constitutional Court Decisions and "Harmonization" Commissions

In addition to using the legislative process and ministries to attack the ongoing regional sovereignty projects, the Putin regime has worked to force the regions to bring their constitutions and legislation into line with federal legal norms, a process referred to as "harmonization." The Russian Constitutional

Court, the seven presidential envoys to the new federal districts, and several different Putin-initiated "harmonization commissions" have all been mustered to the cause of ironing out legal differences between regional and federal legislation and forcing the republics to abandon legal claims to sovereignty that Moscow deems inappropriate and threatening to Russia's legal and territorial integrity.

Besides republican constitutions and legislation, another main target of the harmonization offensive is the treaty-type agreements that Yeltsin signed with several of the regions in the 1990s—the Putin administration has been upfront about its desire to see these treaties consigned to the dustbin of history, this being a major theme of Putin's April 2002 "State of the Union" address, despite the fact that the Russian Federal Constitution allows for exactly this type of treaty relationship with federal subjects (in article 5.3). In his speech, Putin argued that regardless of the formal legal possibility of treaties with the regions, in practice they had been signed "behind the back" of other federation members and only "gave rise to inequality between regions," thus necessitating that they either be abrogated entirely (his preference) or amended and submitted for approval to the entire Federal Assembly (*RFE/RL Tatar-Bashkir Service Daily Report* April 19, 2002). In response to Moscow's pressure, many of Russia's federal subjects have repealed their declarations of sovereignty, changed their constitutions as directed by the Constitutional Court and the harmonization commissions, and a great number have even rescinded the treaties they had previously signed with Yeltsin—as of April 2002, 28 of the 42 treaties with Moscow had been annulled (*RFE/RL Newsline* April 24, 2002). Unsurprisingly, however, Tatarstan has resisted the harmonization process, attempting to shape it to its own interest in preserving sovereignty and blatantly rejecting or ignoring any demands from the federal center which it finds unacceptable. Most significantly, Tatarstan has refused to give up the claim to possess state sovereignty, has insisted that the "treaty-type relations" established in February 1994 remain the basis of its legal relationship with the Russian Federation (about which more below), and has continued to make provocative legal and policy moves aimed at asserting its sovereignty and statehood.

In the early months of the Putin regime, Russia's Constitutional Court issued two key decisions that were directly aimed at curbing regional claims to possess state sovereignty. First, on June 7, 2000, the court declared several clauses in the Altai Republic's constitution illegal, clauses that are almost identical to those found in the Tatarstani constitution. The court objected to provisions in the Altai constitution that declared the republic to be sovereign, stating plainly that "the subjects of the Russian Federation do not possess any state sovereignty, which belongs to the Russian Federation alone" (*RFE/RL Russian Federation Report*, Volume 2, #22, June 14, 2000; *EWI RRR* Volume 5, #25, June 28, 2000). The court also objected to the clause in the Altai constitution which claimed that all the land and natural resources of the republic were reserved for "the people of the Altai Republic," and to those passages which gave the republic the authority to conclude international agreements and to set up its own court system.

Lest the court's strong message be lost on the other republics, the Russian President's Representative to the Constitutional Court Mikhail Mityukov publicly praised the decision and said that it "obliged all Russia's regions which have made similar claims to sovereignty in the past to drop them" (*RFE/RL Russian Federation Report*, Volume 2, #22, June 14, 2000). Three weeks later, on June 27, 2000, Russia's Constitutional Court held a secret session in which it expanded on its earlier decision by declaring similar parts of the constitutions of the republics of Bashkortostan and Tatarstan, along with those of Adygeya, Ingushetia, Komi, and N. Ossetia also to be illegal.[4] The court argued that because these aspects of republican constitutions contradicted the Russian Federal constitution, the republics should henceforth consider them to be "no longer in force" on their territory.

The Russian Constitutional Court's rulings against republican sovereignty were unambiguous, and since their issuance, forcing the regions to rescind their declarations of sovereignty and purge their constitutions of any reference to sovereignty and claims to natural resources has been a main priority of Moscow's harmonization initiative. Armed with this new legal ammunition, in summer 2000 former Russian Prime Minister Sergei Kirienko, the presidential envoy to the newly created Volga Federal District, which contains both Tatarstan, formed a "working group" on harmonization with the Tatarstani leadership. Moscow apparently believed that given the clear-cut nature of the Constitutional Court rulings against republican declarations of sovereignty and constitutions, they could force the republics to bend to those decisions and produce "harmonized" versions of the Tatarstani constitution and other republican legislation very quickly. Thus the initial deadline for wrapping up the work of the harmonization commissions and introducing the new legislation was set for November 2000.

Such optimism proved grossly misplaced in the Tatarstani case. For example, upon the very establishment of the Kirienko-led harmonization commission in fall 2000, President Shaimiyev noted that Tatarstan would be a willing participant in the process of "gradually" bringing republican legislation into "conformity" with federal norms, but only with the understanding that the bilateral power-sharing treaties between Moscow and the regions would be "obeyed" during this process (*RFE/RL Tatar-Bashkir Service* October 18, 2000). The real, and limited, extent of Tatarstan's willingness to participate in the harmonization process became clear in November 2000, when the supposed deadline for the submission of harmonized legislation came and went, and it was announced that the commission's work in Tatarstan had "stalled" and would be extended into spring 2001. At the same time, in January 2001 Russian Deputy General Prosecutor for the Volga Federal District Aleksandr Zvyagintsev filed suit against forty articles of the Tatarstani constitution in that republic's Constitutional Court, thus supplementing the soft, conciliatory approach of the harmonization commission with the threat of legal reproach (*RFE/RL Tatar-Bashkir Service Daily Report* January 12, 2001). Zvyagintsev's challenges to the Tatarstani constitution were focused on the clauses about republican sovereignty, republican citizenship, Tatarstani ownership of natural resources, the requirement that presidential candidates in the republic speak both Tatar and Russia, and Tatarstan's claim to international subjecthood. Significantly, Tatarstan's "declarative position" in its constitution that the republic categorically rejects violence, the means of war and weapons of mass destruction as policy-making tools also made their way into Zvyagintsev's complaint, as Moscow saw such matters of state-craft being "within the purview of the Russian Federation alone" (*RFE/RL Tatar-Bashkir Service Daily Report* April 19, 2002).

The Tatarstani Constitutional Court refused to consider Zvyagintsev's challenge to the Tatarstani constitution, arguing that only the Russian Federal Constitutional Court could rule on the legality of republican constitutions. This strategy of avoidance only worked for a short while—in May 2001 the Russian Constitutional Court upheld Zvyaginstev's suit against the Tatarstani constitution, and ordered the Tatarstani Constitutional Court to "review and harmonize" Tatarstan's constitution without delay (*RFE/RL Tatar-Bashkir Service Daily Report* May 24, 2001). In an act apparently aimed at bolstering the republic's legal arsenal as it embarked on this endeavor, the Tatarstani legislature immediately submitted to the Russian State Duma a proposed amendment to the Russian Federal Constitution which would allow regions like Tatarstan to legally have their own separate citizenship—an amendment that was soundly rejected by the Duma when it finally got around to voting on it in February 2002, garnering only 21 votes (*RFE/RL Tatar-Bashkir Service* May 28, 2001; *RFE/RL Newsline* February 21, 2002).

After the May 2001 Russian Constitutional Court ruling ordering Tatarstan to proceed with harmonization, the Shaimiyev administration did demonstrate more willingness to cooperate with the Putin administration, meeting with Deputy Russian Presidential Administration Head Dmitrii

Kozak, who had recently been named by Putin as the head of yet another twenty-two-member special "Presidential Commission on Power Sharing Between the Federal Center and the Subjects of the Federation," which was charged with "equalizing the rights of all federal subjects and restricting as much as possible relations based on bilateral power-sharing treaties." The meetings were tense, as Kozak vehemently rejected Shaimiyev's ideas on center-periphery power-sharing, claiming that they would in effect "destroy the integrity of the legal system in our country and its economic space . . . and bring separatism even to those federal subjects which are now calm" (*RFE/RL Tatar-Bashkir Service Daily Report* June 28, 2001). Despite these differences, Shaimiyev pledged that the Tatarstani parliament would finally develop "harmonizing" amendments to the Tatarstani constitution and hold hearings on them by September 2001. Unsurprisingly, the reluctant Tatarstani parliament failed to produce an amended constitution by the appointed September 2001 deadline, though it did announce at that session that a new Constitutional Commission was being formed to develop amendments to be voted on at a future date. However only after several personal, bilateral meetings between Shaimiyev and Putin in fall and winter 2001 and after the passage of the 2002 Russian Federal Budget in January 2002, with its incredibly generous outlays to Tatarstan, did the Tatarstani Constitutional Commission actually get down to work. At this point, the Commission quickly produced a new draft constitution that was presented to the local legislature and passed in its first reading on March 4, 2002 (*EWI RRR* Volume 7, #7, February 20, 2002; *RFE/RL Newsline* March 4, 2002). The timing of these events cannot but give the impression that Tatarstan's complicity in the harmonization process was bought by the Putin administration—yet an analysis of the new constitution shows that Moscow perhaps did not get the better end of this expensive transaction.

The newly amended Tatarstani Constitution, which passed its third reading and was signed into law in April 2002, was a pared-down version of the November 1992 original, containing 124 paragraphs as opposed to the 167 in the earlier document. The most important changes concerned the plain assertions of sovereign statehood that the republic had made in articles 61 and 62 of the original November 1992 document, which stated that Tatarstan was a "sovereign state and subject of international law *associated* with the Russian Federation on the basis of a treaty on mutual delegation of powers" (emphasis mine) and that the republic "shall have relations with other states, conclude international treaties, exchange diplomatic, consular and commercial and other missions, participate in international organizations, and take its guidance from international laws, which take precedence in the republic."

The new April 2002 Tatarstani basic law replaced these frankly contro-versial claims with what apparently seemed to be the less vexing claim that the republic was now "*united*" with the Russian Federation (emphasis mine) "by the authority of the Constitutions of the Russian Federation and the Re-public of Tatarstan and the 1994 Treaty on the Delimitation of Authorities and Powers Between the Russian Federation and the Republic of Tatarstan" (article 1).[5] The new document also plainly stated that the republic was "a subject of the Russian Federation," but that it retained for itself "all sover-eign powers (legislative, executive, and judicial) that are not explicitly given to the Russian Federation" (article 1). The previous claim to international subjecthood was replaced in the April 2002 Constitution by the statement that Tatarstan "independently participates in international and foreign eco-nomic ties" (article 1) and that it "can conclude international agreements, exchange representatives, and participate in international organizations" (article 6).

In addition to these revisions, which are clearly more semantic than sub-stantive, the amended Tatarstani Constitution also retained several clauses that various federal actors in Moscow had previously found objectionable, including the following: the assertion that the republic's borders could not be changed without its agreement (article 5), the claim that Tatar and Rus-sian held equal status as official state languages in the republic (article 8), the rejection of the use of violence and war as a way to "solve problems between states" (article 15), provision for a separate republican citizen-ship (article 21), the assertion that the 1994 treaty between Moscow and Tatarstan "formed the basis for the legal system of Russia and Tatarstan" (article 25), and the requirement that the president of Tatarstan "be fluent in both the state languages of the republic, Tatar and Russian" (article 91). The amended April 2002 constitution even staked out provocative new attributes of nation-statehood for the republic of Tatarstan—in article 14 Tatarstan is described as a state which is committed to "helping to revive the national culture, language, and traditions of Tatars living outside the repub-lic," reflecting the adoption of a "kin-state" identity in relation to the Tatar diaspora which was wholly absent from the original document.[6]

Thus the new Tatarstani basic law of April 2002 did not actually limit the republic's claims to sovereignty in any meaningful way, despite the months of negotiation with various federal "harmonization" commissions. This makes the initial favorable reaction of Russian federal actors to the amended Tatarstani Constitution quite surprising—Putin publicly thanked Tatarstan for "harmonizing its constitutional space" with that of the Russian Federation, while even Dmitrii Kozak, the head of Putin's Commission on harmonization, offered that "to a large extent we have settled all our issues with Tatarstan" and denied that Moscow sought to annul the 1994 treaty with Tatarstan (*RFE/RL Tatar-Bashkir Service Daily Report* April 23, 2002; *RFE/RL Newsline* April 24, 2002).

Yet less than six weeks later Deputy Russian Federation Prosecutor General Aleksandr Zvyagintsev formally filed a protest against the new Tatarstani constitution, targeting its assertion of sovereignty, and its calls for separate citizenship, bilingual presidential candidates and "treaty-based federalism" (*RFE/RL Tatar-Bashkir Service Daily Report* June 17, 2002). Tatarstan's President Shaimiyev has defended the republic's revised constitution, arguing that the authorities Tatarstan had claimed in it were well within the limits provided for in the Russian Federal Constitution itself. He also told Tatarstani citizens that, in the face of Moscow's opposition to the new document, the republic should "have enough courage to formulate and defend its own principles for the benefit of the future of the Russian Federation" (*RFE/RL Tatar-Bashkir Service Daily Report* April 29, 2002).

When the tenth anniversary of the signing of the February 1994 treaty between Kazan and Moscow arrived in spring 2004, it provided a very public opportunity for Tatarstan to defend the principle of bilateral, treaty-based relations between the regions and the center in the face of the Putin administration's attempt to nullify the treaties and harmonize regional legislation with federal norms. While the treaty had been renewed in March 1999 by representatives of the Yeltsin and Shaimiyev administrations, through both its tough anti-treaty rhetoric and legal actions (as described above), the Putin administration cast doubt on the legal force of the treaty, and put continual pressure on Tatarstan to abrogate the document, as so many other regions had already done with their bilateral agreements with Moscow. Tatarstan's leadership, however, continued to resist pressure to repudiate the bilateral treaty throughout the early 2000s, and continued to insist that its relations with Moscow were governed by the agreement, arguments it made publicly and loudly on the tenth anniversary of the document in February 2004, when the republic held a ceremonial meeting marking the occasion. Shaimiyev used the opportunity to point out again that the Constitution of the Russian Federation itself allows for bilateral agreements between the center and regions as a way of regulating federal relations and to assert that "the main principles of power-sharing enshrined in the treaty with Moscow—such as the Republic of Tatarstan's sovereignty and statehood—remain in force," despite the Putin administration's ongoing attempts to cast legal and practical doubt on them (*RFE/RL Tatar-Bashkir Service Daily Report* February 16, 2004).

Other statements made on the tenth-anniversary of the February 1994 treaty indicated, however, that Tatarstan was willing to bring its position on the matter "into greater conformity with the present political situation," namely the federal reforms and legal harmonizations initiated by the Putin administration and the newly amended Tatarstani constitution (*RFE/RL Tatar-Bashkir Service Daily Report* February 13, 2004). For example, Tatarstani State Council Speaker Mukhametshin noted that while Tatarstan "was not going to give up on treaty-based relations with Russia," the republic did agree that a new version of the treaty needed to be negotiated with Moscow, one that would "establish strict judicial relations between Tatarstan and the federal authorities," and one that would "become Russian Federation law," that is, be approved by the Russian Federation Duma, as Putin desired (*RFE/ RL Tatar-Bashkir Service Daily Report* February 17, 2004). The treaty issue remained at an impasse until the Beslan crisis and Putin's response to it engendered a new round of negotiations on the issue, events that are discussed later in this chapter.

The overall scorecard regarding the Putin administration's early attempt to erase the legal formulations underpinning claims to sovereign statehood by forcing the process of "harmonization" on Tatarstan is decidedly mixed. While Moscow succeeded in getting Tatarstan to join the new uniform tax code, to harmonize much of its legislation with their federal counterparts and to revise its constitution, the tax concessions were bought at the price of generous subsidies to Tatarstan, and Tatarstan's new constitution retains almost all of the republic's most controversial claims to sovereignty and statehood, and Kazan refused to budge on the abrogation of the February 1994 Treaty. The refusal of regional elites in Kazan to purge the constitution of meaningful legal claims to sovereignty or to give up the concept of bilateral relations with Moscow demonstrates how engrained the commitment to sovereignty and statehood have become in the republic during the post-Soviet period. Thus, in response to Putin's early initiatives, adherence to the sovereignty project spurred Tatarstani officials to successfully sidestep Putin's new presidential envoys, to exert some local control over new federal institutions in the republic, and to manipulate the process of legal harmonization to their advantage as well, producing with great fanfare new constitutional wineskins which contain the same brew of sovereignty.

At the same time, Moscow did gain some important concessions from Tatarstan during the early Putin era that ultimately advanced the cause of federalism in Russia by strengthening federal legal norms and policy frameworks. Much Tatarstani legislation was harmonized with Moscow's variants, federal ministries achieved a new prominence and authority in Tatarstan,

Moscow imposed a much more center-friendly tax regime on the republic, and was successful in getting Tatarstan to acknowledge that some aspects of the February 1994 Treaty were no longer acceptable to Moscow and would have to be renegotiated. Thus at the time of the Beslan tragedy in September 2004, events which would provide the impetus for Putin to again shake up the legal and political foundations of relations between the center and the regions, Tatarstan's sovereignty project, while bent into somewhat different and slightly chastened form by the first Putin centralizing initiatives, was by no means broken completely. Indeed, it would prove to be well-positioned to survive and even help shape the course of the second, post-Beslan set of Putin federal reforms, forcing the center to recognize the political autonomy of the regions and the political and cultural needs of non-Russians to a degree unthinkable in the absence of Tatarstani pressure to do so.

The Second Wave of Federal Reforms: Beslan and After (September 2004–Present)

The horrific attacks on the school in Beslan in the Republic of North Ossetia in September 2004, which would ultimately claim over 330 lives, many of them children, and which was only the latest and worst in a series of damaging terrorist acts on Russian soil since the second Russian invasion of Chechnya in September 1999, not only riveted world attention on Russia, they galvanized Russian President Putin into restarting and indeed ramping up his campaign to "restore the power vertical in Russia" by replacing Russia's federal structure with a more unitary state system. On September 13, in a speech in front of the Russian government and the heads of all the Russian regions, Putin laid out what one NTV commentator would later dub his "September Theses," a series of policies and policy rationales that would set the tenor for all subsequent center-regional relations in Russia.[7] Putin began by offering his administration's view of the ultimate aim of the terrorists who were behind the Beslan attacks, namely that "in their far-reaching plans," those who had committed the atrocity aimed for nothing less than "the disintegration of the country, the break-up of the state, and the collapse of Russia." In the face of such a grave and immediate threat to the country's unity and territorial integrity, Putin argued, "it is clear that a unity of actions of the entire executive power vertical must be ensured here unconditionally." In his remarks at the end of the session, Putin repeated the claim that the terrorist attacks were a result of the failure of the center to build a truly unified system of executive power in Russia, that the Russian state's weakness resulted from its inability to "tug the blanket" totally away from the regions and unify the power vertical in Moscow (Putin 2004b). In subsequent days and weeks Putin would again reiterate the connection between terrorism, regional separatism and the threat to the unity and integrity of the Russian state. For example, in a speech at a meeting of the Russian Presidential Council for Coordination with Religious Organizations on September 29, 2004, Putin again stated that "there must be no doubt" that terrorist activity in Russia "follows separatist political goals" and aimed to "deal a blow to the unity of Russia" (Putin 2004c).

In his "September Theses" Putin introduced a number of initiatives meant to establish the "unified system of executive power" whose absence had allowed the Beslan and other terrorist attacks to occur, including most prominently (and most controversially), the end of election of regional executives by popular vote. Instead, Putin proposed, Russia's governors and republican presidents were to be elected by the regional parliaments, with candidates for these posts to be nominated by the President of the Russian Federation himself (thus rendering the legislative "elections" more like confirmations) (Putin 2004a). To further cement the links in the chain of vertical executive power, the regional heads of state would gain the power to appoint heads of local administration in their territories. The second policy initiative was the conversion of all elections to the State Duma to the proportional representation and party list system (previously 50 percent of the State Duma seats had been first-past-the-post contests). Third, Putin created a Special Federal Commission on the North Caucasus, a rare concession to the reality that terrorist activity in Russia was linked particularly to the political conditions in that area of the country and not merely the result of the "international terrorist network" that threatened the rest of the world as well. Fourth, Putin announced the creation of a Ministry for Regional and Ethnic Policy, further indicating his understanding that the terrorist violence in Russia was not unlinked to domestic issues, including problems of cultural pluralism. Finally, Putin charged all elements of the Russian Federation government, including the ministries, the departments, the regions, and local authorities, to develop an "anti-crisis management system" that would be able to act effectively "in the conditions of the terrorist war that is being conducted against Russia."

Putin's September Theses had the impact of a political earthquake, provoking a loud, sustained, and mostly negative reaction from politicians and political observers both in and outside of Russia. Many criticized Putin's plan for executive appointment of regional leaders, pointing out that Putin was in effect restricting citizens' voting rights, thus violating the Russian constitution. Others complained that Putin's moves directly contradicted the January 1996 Russian Constitutional Court decision that specifically ruled that regional executives in Russia could not be appointed by regional parliaments but had to be directly elected by the local population (*Gazeta.ru* September 14, 2004). Several prominent observers argued that Putin's reforms meant simply "the end of federalism in Russia" and its replacement with a unitary state on the Soviet model,[8] while others lamented that Putin's moves amounted to the "destruction of the last vestiges of Yeltsin-era democracy" (*Christian Science Monitor*, September 14, 2004). Some used even stronger language to criticize the September Theses, such as the Center for Strategic Studies analyst Andrei Piontkovsky, who argued that "steps to transform a federation into a unitary state in a multiethnic country like Russia are suicidal" (*Moscow Times* September 16, 2004), and the leadership of the Russian opposition party Union of Rightist Forces (SPS), which issued a statement calling these moves "a fatal mistake canceling all the achievements of the past few years" (*ITAR-TASS*, September 16, 2004). The argument that Putin's centralizing moves would provoke the exact opposite of their intended effect by creating even more resentment and separatism amongst the country's ethnic minorities and national republics was also voiced by several commentators in and outside of Russia.

A few voices did defend the September 2004 proposals, including Dmitry Rogozin of the ultra-nationalist Motherland Party, who argued that "Russia has always been a single state and always been structured from the centre outwards to the regions," and praised the reforms because they would "make it possible to avoid blackmail of the federal center by overwheening regional barons and oligarchs" (*ITAR-TASS* September 13, 2004). The potential utility of the new reforms in curbing regional corruption was also noted by analyst Stanislav Fedulov from the Baring-Vostok Captial Group, who added that the increased centralization called for in the reforms could inspire increased foreign investment in Russia's regions (RIA-Novosti, September 16, 2004). Others countered with the opinion that increased centralization of power in the Moscow Kremlin would only ease the path to analogously centralized forms of corruption that could potentially come back to haunt Putin, who would become, under his new plan, the only plausible target for public outrage in the regions.[9]

The fact that commentators warned that both Soviet-style hyper-centralization and increased ethnic fractionalization of Russia were potential impacts of Putin's post-Beslan reforms reflects the contradictory imperatives imbedded in those proposals. On the one hand the reforms clearly convey that Putin held there to be a deep connection between ethnic difference, regional separatism, and terrorism in Russia, one that threatened the very existence of the Russian state and therefore had to be more closely controlled by the central state. On the other hand, Putin's proposal to create a new ministry of regional and ethnic affairs, and his comments in a speech to the country's religious leaders a few days after the Beslan events, in which he stressed the multicultural and religiously plural nature of Russia's past and present demonstrates that Putin respects, at least to some degree, the impossibility of managing Russia's ethnic diversity through the forceful imposition of unitarism alone.

Tatarstan's reaction to the September Theses, and its interactions with the Moscow Kremlin since September 2004, reflect an understanding of the contradictory impulses inherent in them, and an appreciation that Putin's simultaneous fear of and begrudging respect for Russia's cultural diversity and federal structure meant that there was both danger and opportunity for the republic lurking in the new policies. The danger for Tatarstan was located in Putin's renewed rhetorical emphasis on the threat to Russia's territorial integrity posed by "separatists," language that brought Tatarstan's sovereignty project under even greater scrutiny, while the opportunity lie in the hope that Putin's admittedly weak concessions to cultural pluralism in the September Theses could be exploited and transformed into more robust protections of Tatarstan's sovereignty. While other observers found cause for great alarm in Putin's post-Beslan actions, Tatarstan by contrast saw in them the chance to continue to pursue the same strategy that had brought them such success in the past—keeping the sovereignty project as robust as possible while accommodating it to new political and economic realities in Russia.

Tatarstan approached the task of shaping Putin's new federal agenda to suit the imperatives of its own sovereignty from two angles—using its own republican parliament and the Federation Council as public tribunes to effect region-friendly changes in the new legislation and using the United Russia party structures behind the scenes to do the same. It also would become clear later that Tatarstan's rather quick approval of the new legislation, which its republican State Council endorsed by a vote of 57–19 on October 25, 2004, was secured at the price of several important concessions, both public and private, by Moscow. In his speech to Tatarstan's State Council about the impending vote on the September Theses, Shaimiyev began by chastising Putin, saying that if the Russian Federation's house had been in as good political order as that of Tatarstan, "he never would have had to go through with these initiatives."[10] While calling the proposed changes "painful," and acknowledging that they amounted to a "decrease in democracy" in Russia, Shaimiyev argued that they would help make Russia into a more "civilized" country (presumably one more like Tatarstan!). He also sought to reassure Tatarstan's parliament that he had secured guarantees from Putin about his respect for the "rights of national-territorial foundations in Russia, especially Tatarstan," and attempted to disarm any potential skepticism about his support of the reforms by saying that "If I was not convinced that Putin and the Russian Federation had taken our needs into account, I would not be asking you to take any steps to support these new laws." After the parliament assented to the new legislation, Tatarstani State Council Speaker Farid Mukhametshin sought to further reassure Tatarstanis by claiming that the parliament had "only agreed to the new legislation in theory"—"Now," he continued "we will argue over the details, revisions, and amendments to the program" (*Vechernaya Kazan* October 26, 2004).

The aspect of Putin's September Theses that Tatarstan found most objectionable was the provision that a regional parliament could be disbanded if it failed two consecutive times to confirm the center's proffered candidate for regional executive. In his October 25 speech to Tatarstan's parliament, Shaimiyev boldly asserted that "Tatarstan will never agree to the dismissal of the State Council of Tatarstan—it is elected by and is the voice of the people." He also stated that regional parliaments should be able to "elect" and not just "confirm" the center's candidates for regional executive posts. This, according to Shaimyev, would "conform to democratic practice." Tatarstani Parliamentary Speaker Mukhametshin wanted regional parliaments to have another perogative as well—not just to elect the candidates offered by the center, but to actually nominate those candidates themselves, a change he offered in his post-vote commentary on October 25 in Kazan.

To formally enact these suggestions, Tatarstan proposed two amendments to the new legislation through the Russian Federation Council. First, it called for "conciliatory procedures" to come into effect in the event that a regional legislature should reject the center's candidate two consecutive times. The second proposed amendment would "permit regional legislatures to participate in selecting candidates for the post of head of the executive authority of the subjects of the Russian Federation" (*ITAR-TASS* November 9, 2004). Shaimiyev also used his position as head of the United Russia party organization in Tatarstan and one of the cochairs of that body's national organization to push a regional agenda, particularly opposition to the dissolution of regional legislatures and a suggestion that the appointment of regional executives be made a time-limited policy, points that Shaimiyev stressed, "must be listened to" by the national United Russia apparatus (*Nezavisimaya Gazeta* November 11, 2004). Ultimately, some elements of Tatarstan's proposed amendments were accepted by Putin—the center agreed that regional parliaments and elites should be "consulted" in the period proceeding nominations of candidates for regional executive, and a month-long "conciliation" period was introduced before the dissolution of any regional parliament in the event of two consecutive candidate rejections (*Rossisskaya Gazeta* December 15, 2004). Shaimiyev, while praising the changes as a "reasonable compromise," continued to argue against the provision allowing for the dissolution of regional parliaments in the event that the conciliation measures should fail (*RFE/RL Tatar-Bashkir Service Daily Report* December 8, 2004). However his continued disapproval of this point was not strong enough for him to prevent the Tatarstani State Council from changing the republic's constitution to reflect the new federal legislation, an action that, according to State Council Speaker Mukhametshin, would surely be interpreted by Moscow as a "political ultimatum" that would certainly bring "punishment" upon the republic (February 28, 2005). Instead, on February 25, 2005, amendments bringing Tatarstan's constitution in line with the new federal legislation by "freezing" those articles calling for the election of the republic's president were passed by a handy margin in Tatarstan's State Council.

Very shortly after the passage of these changes, the concessions that Tatarstan had exacted from the center for the republic's surprisingly painless acquiescence to the September Theses began to make themselves manifest. First, on March 10, 2005, Volga Federal District Presidential Envoy Sergei Kirienko revealed to reporters that the working group on revising and renewing the February 1994 Tatarstan-Moscow bilateral treaty, which had been set up in October 2004, almost immediately after the Beslan events, had nearly finished its work on a new draft treaty, which, if passed by both the Tatarstani and Russian federal legislatures, would gain full legitimacy as "federal law" in Russia (*RFE/RL Tatar-Bashkir Service Daily Report* March 11, 2005).[11] The timing first of the establishment of the treaty working group itself and then the announcement of the new treaty leaves little doubt that Tatarstan's support for Putin's post-Beslan reforms was bought at the price of a new bilateral treaty for the republic, thereby further institutionalizing one of the most central aspects of Tatarstan's sovereignty project. The following day, on March 11, Shaimiyev himself held a news conference to announce that, despite his (supposed) reluctance to do so, and citing the "high price of stability in Tatarstan" as his motivation, he had fulfilled the "expressed wish" of both President Putin and Presidential Envoy Kirienko by asking Putin to nominate him to the post of President of Tatarstan under the new system of central appointments to regional executive offices (Shaimiyev's candidacy was confirmed by the Tatarstani parliament on March 28) (*RFE/RL Tatar-Bashkir Service Daily Report* March 11, 2005). Thus a new five-year term for Shaimiyev as president of Tatarstan seems also to have been part of the deal made by Putin to secure the republic's support for his post-Beslan federal reforms (as it seems also to have been for many other of the regions—as of June 2005 about one-quarter of Russia's regions had had their chief executive appointed under the new system, while in only three of those twenty-odd cases was the incumbent replaced with a new candidate) (*RFE/RL Political Weekly* Volume 5, #23, June 9, 2005).

As was the case with earlier Putin-era "pacts" between Tatarstan and Moscow aimed at winning the former's increased compliance with centralizing federal reforms, Tatarstan has, in spite of making some concessions to the center, also continually sought to use both rhetoric and policy to exercise, protect, and even expand its sovereignty within the new legal confines of the post-Beslan era. In an example of rhetorically protecting the republic's sovereignty, both Shaimiyev and Mukhametshin have publicly reiterated their conviction that the policy of central naming of regional executives must only be a temporary concession, and that in the future "democratic processes will force federal authorities to return to a procedure of electing heads of the Russian Federation entities by popular vote" (*RFE/RL Tatar-Bashkir Service Daily Report* March 25 and March 31, 2005). They also have reminded Tatarstanis that the constitutional provisions calling for the election of the president of Tatarstan had only been "suspended" by the new amendments, while Shaimiyev has also asserted that Tatarstan has no intention of ever giving up its own presidency, as North Ossetia did in May 2005, arguing that Tatarstan does not suffer from the same "erosive" processes that plagued the North Caucasus, which in any case was "in no way a model for Tatarstan" (*RFE/RL Tatar-Bashkir Service Daily Report* May 26, 2005).

Despite their assertive rhetorical attempts to defend the republic's sovereignty in the face of Putin's post-Beslan reforms, Tatarstan's leaders could not have missed the broad anti-region, anti-federalism message delivered by chief United Russia ideologist (and Deputy Head of the Russian Presidential Administration) Vladislav Surkov during the presentation of the party's platform in February 2005. Offering a strong defense of Putin's post-Beslan agenda, Surkov's speech defined federal relations in Russia during the Yeltsin and early Putin eras as an arena where "chaos reigned" and a situation "that can only be described as threatening the territorial integrity of Russia" (Surkov 2005). Furthermore, he offered, thanks to the sovereignty-seeking of reckless regions like Tuva and Chechnya (Tatarstan was not mentioned by name in Surkov's speech), Russia itself was "practically on the brink of losing its own state sovereignty." Hence, Putin had no choice but to "normalize the situation in the country" by again asserting "the predominance of federal law over regional law" (Surkov 2005). While the platform also asserted that United Russia supported the concept of a Russia that was for "all the peoples of Russia" and not just Russians, the anti-region, pro-Moscow agenda of the party was explicit throughout the speech. As a member of United Russia's national executive committee, the platform had Shaimiyev's tacit approval, and indeed no public criticism of the speech came from Kazan in the weeks after the speech. As events leading up to the Kazan Millennium celebrations, scheduled for August 2005, were to show, however, it is clear that behind the scenes Shaimiyev and other regional actors were applying pressure on federal elites to soften the anti-region stance of United Russia and Moscow.

Celebrating Kazan's Kremlin: More "Dan" For the Khan?

The lavish, and partially federally-funded celebrations of the 1000th anniversary of the founding of Kazan, held in late August 2005, provided a prominent national and international tribune for Shaimiyev and the republic to use to promote and defend both Tatarstan's sovereignty and the general principles of federalism and cultural pluralism in Russia. Even before the events in Kazan, which included both a session of the State Council (the organization of Russia's regional executives set up in the wake of the reform of the Federation Council in late 2000) and a CIS summit, Putin showed signs of retreating from the extreme centralizing rhetoric and agenda he had proposed in the wake of the Beslan events. For example, at a meeting of the State Council in Kaliningrad in July 2005, Putin "for all intents and purposes admitted that in its current form, the deregionalization policy adopted nearly a year and half earlier was both unworkable and incompatible with the ongoing transformation of the economy, politics, and social sphere," and as such, announced that he was transferring over 100 additional powers to the regions (Petrov 2005). Indeed, at Kaliningrad Putin announced that he largely agreed with regional leaders who claimed that "the number of federal bodies is constantly growing in the provinces without any improvement in quality," and that therefore, he felt it best to transfer to the regions "all powers which don't infringe on Russia's wholeness," including the power to name the heads of regional branches of federal ministries (except the Ministry of Defense and the FSB), and certification of educational institutions (*Gazeta. ru* August 24, 2005; *Kommersant* August 24, 2005).[12]

The degree of Putin's personal involvement in the August 2005 Millennial celebrations in Kazan is both interesting and revealing in terms of his administration's understanding of multiculturalism and federalism in Russia. The lavish cost and scale of the events in Kazan in August 2005 suggests the importance both Kazan and Moscow placed on them. The cost of the Kazan Millennium, what Putin himself called "a holiday not only for all Russia but for the whole world" (*Kommersant Vlast'*, 29 August 2005, 32–35), is estimated to have run over 50 billion rubles, or slightly less than two billion U.S. dollars. As might be expected, the expense, and high profile given to the Kazan millennial made the events the subject of great controversy both in Tatarstan and in Moscow (as well as the target of some rueful humor—one popular t-shirt selling in Kazan in August 2005 read "I survived the Kazan Millennium!") (*Itogi*, September 5, 2005, 20–21). Indeed, many aspects of the Kazan millennial celebrations, from the origins of the idea itself to the way the events were interpreted and spun by both the Russian and Tatarstani press after the fact, provides unique insight into the relationship between Moscow and its most powerful region and that between Putin and Shaimiev.

First and foremost, the Kazan Millennium must be understood as evidence of how truly interdependent, even symbiotic, relations between those who sit in the Moscow and Kazan Kremlins actually are. The degree of mutual obligation, need and dependence demonstrated by the case of the Kazan Millennium provides an important corrective to the popular argument that Putin's "assault on the regions" reduced even the most important regions like Tatarstan to the status of purely administrative appendages, as they were during the Soviet era. The millennial celebrations also suggest two other surprising things regarding Putin and his relations with the regions. This case illustrates clearly the importance that Putin puts on using both the persuasive carrot as well as the punitive stick in dealing with the regions. Furthermore, it demonstrates that Putin seems to be more sensitive to issues of cultural pluralism in Russia than he is often given credit for. Ultimately, the Kazan case suggests that Putin may have softened the "hard-line" he took against the regions in the early part of his regime, and that through a combination of both necessity and desire, he is and in the future will remain ready to concede more to and buy more into Tatarstan's bottom-up form of federalism that emphasizes the essentially culturally plural nature of the Russian Federation than was ever imagined earlier that he would.

For its part, the Shaimiev administration's actions in the run-up to the Kazan Millennium amount to a continuation of the tactics that it has engaged in since the beginning of the drive for sovereignty in 1990— attempting to find a modus operandi with Moscow by granting it something it wants (the signing of a document "locating Tatarstan irrefutably within Russia's legal space" or agreeing to new financial arrangements that benefit Moscow), while also extracting from Moscow its own concessions of either a political or symbolic nature that it can "take home" and use to forward the idea that the Tatarstani sovereignty project lives on and has not been compromised during the transaction. In the case of the Kazan Millennium, the extravagant celebrations and Putin's direct and significant monetary and personal investment in them were the concessions made by Moscow in exchange for the Shaimiev administration's agreement to a new and less-economically favorable set of relations with Moscow negotiated with Putin in the year 2000 (*Izvestiya*, August 26–28, 2005). From this angle, then, the Kazan Millennial celebrations intimate that while Tatarstan certainly is not in danger of becoming infected with the *Chechen variant* of the virus of separatism (which Putin famously suggested would sweep up the Volga from the North Caucasus were the Chechen "problem" not dealt with accordingly thoroughly) (Evangelista 2002, 5–6), it also has not rolled over and given up its dreams of cultivating as much sovereignty and statehood within the Russian Federation in the post-Soviet era as it is able to at any given moment. Indeed, for many Tatarstanis, the Kazan Millennium represented "A celebration of federalism and regionalism, the culmination of the epoch of sovereignty, the sum total of fifteen years of development of the Republic of Tatarstan, demonstrating the success of our independent path" (*Zvezda Povolzhe*, August 18–24, 2005, 1).

How did August 2005 come to be designated as the historically appropriate and politically necessary time to mark the Kazan Millennium, a celebration that pointedly amounts to a very public, very official, and very noticeable acknowledgement on the part of Russian President Putin that Kazan is at least 150 years older than Moscow, and a good seven centuries older than Russia's capital of the North (Moscow celebrated its 850th anniversary in 1997, St. Petersburg its 300th in 2003)? If one believes some of the more cynical elements of the Muscovite press, the story behind the August 2005 celebrations is only the last in the long string of instances since the first mid-thirteenth-century Mongol invasions that Russia has been "bamboozled by the clever Tatars into paying them the Khan's tribute (dan)"; if one chooses Kazan's interpretation, it is the first time since 1552 (when Kazan fell to the forces of Ivan Grozny) that Kazan has been given something even approaching an appropriate level of acknowledgment, tribute, and respect (Khasanova 2005).

During the State Council meeting held at the Kazan Kremlin as part of the Kazan Millennium, Putin's public speeches contained surprising refederalizing rhetoric and policy initiatives. He asserted his earlier call for the strengthening of the "power vertical" in Russia did not mean "the unlimited consolidation of powers within the federal government" and that Moscow intended to keep "only a small amount" of administrative and policy duties under federal jurisdiction (*RIA Novosti* August 26, 2005). Yet despite Putin's conciliatory and region-friendly actions and talk, Shaimiyev used his perogative as host of the Kazan Millennium State Council meeting to chastise Putin for his historical lack of trust in the regions, imploring him to "trust them more," as they had "great potential to solve the many questions that can only be solved there."[13] Shaimiyev also took the opportunity to criticize Putin's power vertical concept, calling it a "negation of federalism," to remind Putin that Russia was a "huge and multinational state with many peoples who have their own traditions and ways and cultures," and to reiterate Tatarstan's conviction that *only* the republics could develop and finance the cultural development of their own (non-Russian) populations, singling out Russian federal television programming and history textbooks that exclude any reference to non-Russians as specific examples of how Moscow continued to neglect its obligation to foster cultural pluralism in the country. Shaimiyev also used his position as host of the August 2005 festivities to show off the "world-class" capital city of Kazan and to play up the "international personality" of Tatarstan, clearly relishing the fact that as host of the CIS summit, he was the only regional leader to share the stage of with Putin and the CIS presidents.

In the wake of the Kazan Millennium celebrations, both Kazan and Moscow pursued somewhat contradictory policies regarding federalism and cultural pluralism in Russia, with Moscow at times appearing to act on the more pro-region and pro-federalism approach Putin had articulated in Kazan in August 2005, while Tatarstan sought to build on the momentum it had gained during Kazan 1000th anniversary to continue with various aspects of its sovereignty project. Tatarstan also made some conciliatory gestures signaling its willingness to work with Moscow to build a more integrated federal system of governance in the country. In October 2005 Putin sent a bill to the Duma that would allow parties who had won regional parliamentary elections to nominate candidates for regional executive, who would then be subject to the approval of the Russian executive and finally the regional legislature (*Moscow Times* October 4, 2005). The implication of this change for federal relations is somewhat unclear. On the one hand, Putin attempted to portray the bill as increasing the say of the regions in the process of picking their executives, while critics pointed out that the bill was just a way to strengthen Putin's United Russia party and to lay a mask of false democratization over a process that in essence still left the choice for regional executive in the hands of the Russian president. As Nikolai Petrov pointed out in the *Moscow Times*, nearly 75 percent of the current regional executives in Russia professed loyalty to United Russia, and in many cases the regional executive also served as the local United Russia party boss, "much like in the Soviet era" (*Moscow Times* February 22, 2006).[14] For Tatarstan and for Shaimiyev, who has consistently used his leadership roles in both the local and federal branches of United Russia to push a more pro-region agenda,

Putin's October 2005 bill can be seen as a partial victory, one that ostensibly gave some power back to the regions, but only if they agreed to play within the framework set by the party of power in Moscow.

Those who were skeptical of the commitment Putin made in Kazan in August 2005 to truly "re-federalize" Russia by showing more respect for the country's cultural diversity and its regions' autonomy received partial confirmation of their doubts later in October 2005 when the Moscow Kremlin released a draft of a new Russian federal nationalities policy. The document, prepared by order of the President, failed to mention at all the role of Russia's federal system in providing for the needs of non-Russians, and instead called for "the formation of a single multinational society in Russia with a consolidating role to be played by the Russian people in providing the unity of the country and strengthening the power vertical" (*Kommersant* October 11, 2005; *RFE/RL Political Weekly* Volume 6, Number 6, March 10, 2006). The draft policy also referred only to Russians as a "nation" in Russia while referring to non-Russians in the country as mere "ethnic groups." Predictably, Tatarstani Presidential advisor Rafael Khakimov reacted negatively to the draft policy, saying that it echoed the "big brother" role that Russians played during the Soviet era, a criticism shared by former Yeltsin-era Minister of Nationalities Emil Pain, who warned that while dismissing federalism and foregrounding ethnic Russian interests in Russia might not raise the specter of the Stalin era to most Russians, "for people in Chechnya, Tatarstan, Yakutia, and elsewhere, it certainly does" (Goble 2006).[15]

The Putin administration also angered some regional leaders and supporters of federalism in the country in May 2006 when it moved to oust four Federation Council deputies, including two from the Nenets Autonomous Oblast (A.O.) ostensibly in the name of fighting corruption, and when it further targeted the Nenets A.O. by arresting its governor, Alexei Barinov, on suspicion of fraud and embezzlement. The fact that Barinov was the last regional executive to be popularly elected before Putin's post-Beslan reforms was not lost on many locals, however, who were not convinced by Moscow's assertions that concerns for clean governance were behind the arrest. Instead, the actions were interpreted as pure anti-region intimidation measures. As one local politician said of the arrest, "Just because there are only 40,000 people in our region, our big brother in Moscow thinks he can wipe his feet on us. People who live here may be small in number but we are proud in spirit and will not tolerate this" (*Financial Times* May 25, 2006). The fact that what truly lay behind the arrest were Barinov's loud public demands that the Rosneft oil company pay a large sum in "social responsibility" payments to the Nenets A.O. that it had previously promised only served to reinforce the idea that Putin's post-Beslan, anti-region, pro-center agenda was at heart about strengthening not just the "power vertical" but also the power of the state-natural resource complex centered in Moscow.

In this confused situation, where the Putin administration moved back and forth between centralizing and federalizing actions and rhetoric, the Tatarstani leadership likewise sought to navigate the safest course possible, protecting and asserting both its institutional and symbolic sovereignty when possible, while also making concessions to a more unified legal, political and economic space in Russia. Pro-sovereignty rhetoric had flowed liberally out of Kazan during the August 2005 celebration, with Shaimiyev claiming in an interview in *Kommersant* that the pursuit of sovereignty in Tatarstan had not only "raised the status and authority of the Tatar people in the world's eyes," but also had been one of the "only forces" preventing Russia from going "back down the path of totalitarianism, of unitarism" in the post-Soviet era (*Kommersant* August 29, 2005). History, demography, and common sense all dictate, Shaimiyev went on, that only a "democratic federal path," one that could accommodate some form of Tatarstani sovereignty would lead to a "civilized Russia"; any other path, including the "easy and attractive path to a unitary state," would lead to "the destruction of Russia from within" (*Kommersant* August 29, 2005). And yet, the inconvenient fact that the Russian Constitutional Court had declared Tatarstan's state sovereignty to be unconstitutional several times would not go away. Thus, mere weeks after the loud public defenses of sovereignty that accompanied the Kazan Millennial celebrations, the Tatarstani State Council quietly passed amendments to the republic's law on the celebration of Sovereignty Day in Tatarstan, changing the significance of the event slightly. Hence, the August holiday now officially would celebrate only the "proclamation of the Declaration of state sovereignty in Tatarstan" and not the apparently more inflammatory "proclamation of [*actual*] state sovereignty" in Tatarstan (*RFE/RL Tatar-Bashkir Service Daily Report* October 21, 2005).

Another Victory for Tatarstan: The 2007 Treaty

In October 2005, Tatarstan's State Council approved the draft of the long-awaited, revised bilateral treaty with Moscow (the 1999 renewal of the 1994 treaty had expired over a year previously). The new draft treaty recognized both the Russian Federation and Tatarstani constitutions as "governing documents." It did not make explicit reference to Tatarstan's status as a "sovereign state," but did give implicit recognition of this status by referring to the March 1992 referendum, which had declared Tatarstan to be "a sovereign state, a subject of the international law, forming its relations with the Russian Federation, other republics and states on the basis of equal agreements," as one of the bases of legitimacy for the new treaty.[16] The new agreement also acknowledged the importance of the "historical, cultural, economic, environmental, and other specific features" of Tatarstan as impetus for the promulgation of a special agreement (Preamble). In article 2.2, the treaty called on the governments of Russia and Tatarstan to "conclude agreements for the joint resolution" of these "specificities," thus clearly creating the legal framework for separate arrangements in the realm of oil policy, tax policy, and cultural and educational policy to be made later between Kazan and Moscow.

Beyond this broad, if vague, endorsement of the right of Tatarstan to continue to bargain for special economic, political, and cultural arrangements within Russian legal space, the new treaty specifically endorsed the right of Tatarstan to "within its competence, carry out international and foreign economic relations" (article 2.3), to "provide state support and assistance to its compatriots in the preservation of the identity and in the development of national culture and language" (article 2.4), and recognition of Tatar and Russian as the two official state languages in Tatarstan, including the right to require its presidential candidates to speak both Russian and Tatar (article 2.5). Furthermore, the new treaty affirms the current practice of including a separate page for Tatarstani residents in Russian Federal passports, bearing the Tatarstani state seal and holder's personal information printed in the Tatar language (article 3).

In early 2007, President Putin signed the new bilateral treaty and submitted it to the Russian Federal Duma for approval, which it received easily, with a 306–110 affirmative vote. Tatarstani Parliamentary Speaker Farid Mukhametshin greeted the news enthusiastically, telling reporters that the decision implied recognition by the federal center that "we [Tatarstan] are somehow different," and adding, "This is an honorable agreement for us" (RFE/RL Newsline February 13, 2007). The jubilation in Kazan was short-lived, however, as just over a week later, in a rare show of dissention from the Russian president's position, and after hearing the body's speaker, Sergei Mironov, called the treaty "a dangerous political precedent" for the country, the Federation Council voted down the treaty 93–13, with 15 abstentions (RFE/RL Newsline, February 22, 2007). The Federation Council rebellion itself proved to be only temporary, however. After being reintroduced into and again sailing through the Duma in July 2007, the new Tatarstani-Russian agreement this time passed in the Federation Council by a vote of 122–4, indicating that in the five-month interim the (Moscow) Kremlin's unhappiness with the upper chamber's public display of disagreement had been clearly expressed and heard (*RFE/RL Newsline* July 11, 2007).

The fact that the new treaty was finally approved in July 2007, after having gone through all the many legal channels necessary for it to attain full and incontestable status as federal law in Russia (unlike its 1994 predecessor and renewal, which was signed ad-hoc with Yeltsin), is an obvious, significant, and enduring victory for Tatarstan in its quest to keep its sovereignty project alive. Unsurprisingly, therefore, Tatarstan's leaders have portrayed the new treaty as the culmination of the republic's self-portrayed lonely battle to preserve federalism, keep the Russian Constitution alive, and protect non-Russians in the face of growing anti-regional and anti-Muslim sentiment in Russia. As Tatarstani parliamentary speaker Mukhametshin emphasized, approval of the treaty showed that "the Russian Constitution was finally working" and indicated that Russian Federation citizens "could now look forward to real federalism" in Russia (*RFE/RL Newsline* July 11, 2007).

Whether or not the new treaty lives up to Tatarstan's expectations for it, especially in terms of preserving economic and cultural autonomy for the republic, depends on how successfully its leaders are able to continue to translate the various aspects of the sovereignty project that have developed over the past nearly two decades into functional political capital during the Medvedev era. The next chapter assesses the results of the sovereignty project under Russia's first two presidents and speculates about its future prospects under its third, and beyond.

Notes

1. See Mintimer Shaimiev's speech on Tatar TV on August 29, reprinted in *Respublika Tatarstan*, August 30, 2000. Other references are from the speeches made by Tatarstani government officials at the special conference on "Ten Years of Sovereignty in Tatarstan: Results and Perspectives" held in Kazan on August 28, 2000, which the author attended.

2. This law, an amendment to the Law on Regional Political Institutions, renders the change in term limits by considering regional executives to have begun their first terms in office upon the adoption of the Law on Regional Political Institutions, which took place on October 16, 1999. This in effect allows 69 of the 88 regional executives to run for a third term (*EWI RRR* Volume 5, #45, December 6, 2000).

3. The new legislation raised the tax from 347 rubles to 400 rubles per ton of oil, and reserved only 5 percent of that collected revenue for Tatarstan. Previously, 20 percent (2002) and then 14 percent (2003) of that revenue had stayed in Tatarstan. Tatarstani officials estimated that the republic would lose 2.6 billion rubles per year

and result in the closing of 13,000 to 14,000 oil wells in Tatarstan (*RFE/RL Tatar-Bashkir Service Daily Report* April 20, 2004, May 14, 2004).

4. Specifically, the court targeted the same provisions it had objected to in the Altai decision, including republican declarations of sovereignty, claims to natural resources, claims to be subjects of international law, and claims that republican laws have precedence over federal laws in the republics (*EWI RRR* Volume 5, #27, July 12, 2000).

5. The text of the revised Tatarstani Constitution is available in Russian on the government of Tatarstan's website at the following address: www.tatar.ru /constitution .html.

6. For a general discussion of diaspora politics and state-building in the former Soviet Union see King and Melvin (1998). For a specific discussion of these issues as they relate to Tatarstan see Graney (1998).

7. All references to the speech are from the English-language translation of the speech, "Speech at the Enlarged Government Meeting with the Government and Heads of the Regions," September 13, 2004, catalogued at the President of Russia's website at www.kremlin.ru/eng.

8. Including politician Grigory Yavlinsky from Yabloko, who called the plan "anti-constitutional" and "insulting to the people of Russia" as well as "a blow against the foundations of federalism in Russia" (*ITAR-TASS* September 13, 2004) and political commentators such as Dmitry Oreskin from the Mercator Group, Mark Urnov from the Foundation of Analytical Programs, Stanislav Belkovsky from the National Strategy Institute, Georgy Saratov from the InDem Foundation and Lilia Shevtsova and Anatol Lieven from the Carneigie Foundation for International Peace.

9. See for example, the analysis by Aleksander Dianov in the *Moscow Times* on September 17, 2004, and the text of the Carneigie Endowment for International Peace's public forum on "What Has Putin's Russia Become?," held on September 23, 2004, and cataloged on their website at www.ceip.org.

10. All references to Shaimiyev's speech are from the transcription in Russian published on the *e-Kazan* news website on October 28, 2004 (www. E-Kazan-runews/ politics/).

11. As of May 2006 the final points of contention in the treaty had been resolved (Tatarstan was allowed to keep the provision in its constitution naming Tatar and Russian as co-state languages and that required the president of Tatarstan to know both languages and received the right for its residents to carry the supplementary page in their passports designating them as citizens of both Tatarstan and Russia), the treaty had been approved by all necessary parties in the Tatarstan government, and was being sent to Prime Minister Fradkov and then on to Putin himself for final approval (*Kommersant* May 22, 2006).

12. Other powers that the center continued to reserve for itself included the right to issue licenses for alcohol production and branding and the use of natural resources.

13. All references to Shaimiyev's speech are from the transcription that appeared in *Zvezda Povol'zhe*, September 2–7, 2005, 1.

14. According to the *Washington Post*, as of June 2006, 71 of the 88 incumbent regional executives in Russia were supporters of United Russia, while 58 of 88 regional parliaments were controlled by United Russia (*Washington Post*, June 9, 2006).

15. Tatarstan formalized its objection to the new draft nationalities policy in March 2006 when the republic's State Council voted it down, denouncing in particular the part of the program that "obligated" all citizens of Russia to "know" the Russian language, asking rhetorically, "What does it mean to be obligated to know Russian? Will we be imprisoned if we don't?" (*RFE/RL Political Weekly* Volume 6, #6, March 10, 2006).

16. For reportage on the new draft treaty, see *RFE/RL Tatar-Bashkir Service Daily Report* from August 30, 2005, September 6, 2005 and October 31, 2005. A copy of the final version of the treaty approved in July 2007 is available on the Official website of the Republic of Tatarstan, in English, Russian, and Tatar, under the "Documents" rubric (www.tatar.ru).

CHAPTER SIX

Khans and Kremlins Revisited: Assessing the Tatarstani Sovereignty Project and Fostering Federalism and Multicultural Justice in Russia

When Mintimer Shaimiyev hosted Russian President Putin and the heads of the CIS for a summit meeting in the Kazan Kremlin in August 2005, it was a triumphant and richly symbolic culmination of fifteen years of sovereignty-seeking by the Republic of Tatarstan. Given the attacks on regional sovereignty that Putin himself had launched five years earlier, the taste of this success, which put Kazan, however briefly, on the same diplomatic plane as Moscow, must have been even sweeter for Shaimiyev and the architects of Tatarstan's sovereignty project. Showing off the new and improved capital city of Kazan, with its Europeanized streets and the Kazan Kremlin's carefully choreographed tableau of multiculturalism, while also facilitating the important business of the Russian Federation's State Council and the CIS, during the August 2005 Kazan Millennial celebrations Tatarstan had its biggest opportunity yet to "act like a state" on the domestic, Russian federal, and international stages, and it played that role with obvious preparation and relish. The remarkable events in Kazan in August 2005, including Putin's obvious deference to the Tatarstani leadership during the length of his stay (which included beginning his address to the State Council session with a couple of sentences in the Tatar language),[1] couldn't help but evoke in this author a strong image from Russia's distant past—the frequent visits of Russian princes to the Kazan Kremlin during the tumultuous decades of the Kazan Khanate in the fifteenth and sixteen centuries, before that state's final capitulation to Ivan Grozny in 1552.

Flights of somewhat fanciful and speculative historical comparison aside, how in fact should we judge the events in Kazan in August 2005? To what extent do they represent what Tatarstan's leadership claim they are—evidence of the endurance, cohesion, comprehensiveness, and plain success of the Tatarstani sovereignty project and a strong argument that said venture, having brought benefits to both Tatarstan and Russia, should not only be prolonged but emulated as a model for Chechnya and other Russian republics?[2] These questions bring us back to the three-fold goals that prompted me to research and write this book: To document, describe, and analyze the fifteen-plus year trajectory of the Tatarstani sovereignty project; to assess the impact of Tatarstan's sovereignty project on the development of federalism and center-periphery relations in post-Soviet Russia; and finally, to understand how the Tatarstani sovereignty project should inform our understanding of autonomy conflicts and inter-ethnic relations in multicultural states in general. My inquiry has thus been based on the fundamental assumption that we should take the claims of the Tatarstani sovereignty project seriously and treat the republic's sovereignty-seeking efforts as worthy of sustained academic interest. It is my hope that others will be persuaded by the evidence presented here that this is the case.

Tatarstan's sovereignty project, commenced amid the parade of other such declarations in 1990, was premised on the idea that the former A.S.S.R. both could and should possess, inhabit, and embody more of the attributes of sovereign statehood than it had been allowed to during the Soviet era. The Soviet experience did indeed introduce and inculcate the habit among the Tatarstani leadership of thinking about the territory of Tatarstan as possessing some sort of sovereignty, but limited that understanding to a hollow and ersatz form of statehood that did not at all resemble the type enjoyed by full-fledged states in the international system, by sub-state units in other federations (like the German *lander*, Spanish autonomies, or American states), or indeed, by earlier incarnations of statehood on the very territory of Tatarstan (Great Bulgar, the Kazan Khanate). The narrative presented here clearly demonstrates that, unlike the vast majority of other Russian republics that also declared sovereignty in 1990 and 1991, who either let those claims die from neglect or repudiated them formally under pressure from the Putin administration, Tatarstan has by contrast consistently, creatively, and energetically pursued a rich, multifaceted, and ever-evolving vision of what it means for it to possess sovereignty or be a "sovereign state." This vision is simultaneously informed by multiple sources, initially beginning with the Soviet standard of sovereignty for A.S.S.R.s (as discussed in chapter 1), but quickly supplanted by the following: international norms about self-determination and the rights of ethnic nations, international norms about how states act and what powers they possess, understandings of the ancient Tatar tradition of statehood, a deep knowledge of the historical and contemporary practices of federalism in other multinational states, and a keen awareness of the limits the republic faces as a constituent member of the Russian Federation.

The complexity and richness of Tatarstan's vision of itself as a "sovereign" entity, evolving constantly during the post-Soviet era, is such that the republic has consistently sought to realize and perform its understanding of sovereignty in three arenas at the same time: the Russian Federal stage, the domestic Tatarstani polity, and the international arena. As was illustrated in chapter 2, Soviet-era norms of sovereignty for autonomous republics might have initially served as the impetus for Tatarstan's declaration of sovereignty, but were almost immediately judged inadequate and outdated. Instead, beginning with the March 1992 referendum on sovereignty and continuing through the February 1994 bilateral treaty with Moscow, Kazan's understanding of what its claimed sovereignty actually should mean in terms of its relations with Moscow changed rapidly, becoming based on the non-negotiable principles of "real" republican sovereignty and what it called "bottom-up, democratic" federalism in Russia, embodied first and foremost in the principle of "bilateral, equal, treaty-based relations" with Moscow.

As a corrective to those accounts which characterize Tatarstan's sovereignty-seeking activities during the Yeltsin era as pure instruments of self-enrichment on the part of rapacious regions at the expense of a Moscow Kremlin in disarray, the evidence presented in chapter 3 of this book demonstrates clearly that Tatarstan's vision of its potential as a "sovereign" entity in the post-Soviet era reaches well beyond "robbing the center" to a desire to be able to "act the part" of a modern, efficacious sovereign state in both its domestic, internal guises (as a provider of social services and public goods, both material and symbolic) and its international, external guises (as a participant in international organizations as well as a partner in economic and cultural agreements with other states). While instrumental self-interest can of course account for part of the reason Tatarstan has pursued these domestic and international initiatives (fashioning one's own social service arrangements and international contracts for oil, helicopters, and chemicals certainly has its material benefits), its actions in these arenas make it clear that Tatarstan's leadership, beyond desiring increased wealth and power, also desires that the republic begin look and act like "a real state." Such ventures as turning Kazan into a capital city worthy of a "modern, European state," establishing a republican-level Academy of Science and pursuing an "international personality" by establishing foreign representations abroad and fostering independent relations with the OIC and other international organizations are potentially costly ones that have little value beyond their symbolic functions as indicators of increased statehood for Tatarstan.

Similarly, the nation-building initiatives Kazan has undertaken in Tatarstan, as presented in chapter 4, make it clear that a significant element in the republic's evolving understanding of itself as a "sovereign" entity in the post-Soviet period is the modern equation of nationhood with statehood. Seeing the ethnic Tatar nation as a "historically state-bearing entity" that was given only a false and empty form of statehood during the Soviet era, the architects of Tatarstan's sovereignty project see a renewed and more authentic form of sovereign statehood for Tatarstan as both the inherent right of the ethnic Tatar nation (according to international norms of self-determination of peoples, as problematic as those norms may be) *and* as an absolute necessity if that nation is to recover from the neglect and Russification it faced during the Soviet era. Arguing, convincingly, it seems to this author, that the Russian state has been derelict in its professed responsibility to provide for the cultural and linguistic needs of its non-Russian citizens, Tatarstan has instead, in the name of sovereignty, taken on this responsibility itself. However, its ear clearly attuned to the displeasure expressed by the international community towards any polity exhibiting too baldly the desire for purely ethno-national revival of one group in a multinational context, Tatarstani elites have also, equally convincingly, used the sovereignty claim as a vehicle for fostering the civic and multicultural "Tatarstani" nation and providing for the cultural needs of the non-Tatars in the republic as well. The measures Tatarstan has developed towards this end clearly outstrip those of the federal government, whose commitment to multiculturalism in the post-Soviet era has been largely rhetorical, when present at all, and is increasingly overshadowed by growing Islamophobia and xenophobia in the country as a whole.

Together, the varied and wide-ranging activities making up the Tatarstani sovereignty project and chronicled in this book point to an expansive and multifaceted understanding of "state sovereignty" on the part of the republic's leadership that goes well beyond a crude expression of instrumental self-interest. Tatarstan's understanding of its own sovereignty, as presented through its actions and words, is one that has both external and internal, as well as material and symbolic aspects, and one that is clearly influenced both by the domestic and international practices of contemporary states and by the theory supporting the idea of the modern state—that states are fundamentally tied to national communities which are the proper bearers of sovereignty, whether those nations be ethnic or civic in nature (or as is more often the case, some more or less comfortable combination or hybrid of the two).

At the same time that it exhibits evidence of being informed by a much richer and wider set of influences than the falsely sovereign institutions of the Soviet era, Tatarstan's sovereignty project equally obviously has been profoundly shaped by a basic realism or pragmatism on the part of its architects. Throughout the post-Soviet period, while never wavering from the larger desire to model the behavior of "real states" to the extent possible, the leaders of the Tatarstani sovereignty project also have never lost sight of the fundamental fact of Tatarstan's historical and current physical and legal location within the Russian Federation. In other words, in a crucial way, the Tatarstani sovereignty project, while expansive and evolving and sustained, has also been *essentially self-limiting*. Its approach to achieving the attributes of sovereignty has been probing and relentless, but also flexible and compromising. Its strategy both with Moscow and its own domestic audience, as well as with the international community, has been to use negotiation, incremental reform, policy innovation, and trial and error, while avoiding direct confrontations with Moscow. While continuously exploring the potential for and trying to maximize the extent to which the republic can "act sovereign" in different arenas and contexts over the past two decades, Tatarstan's leadership has never made a maximal claim of sovereignty in the sense of declaring the republic to be an *independent* (as opposed to sovereign) state, nor has it pushed for those attributes of state sovereignty that it believes might provoke an overly negative response or even military retaliation from the center in Moscow (thus, Tatarstan has never attempted to raise an army or a border guard, or even to speak of such possibilities).

Rather, while consistently pushing the limits of its multiple performances of sovereignty further and further out, the architects of Tatarstan's sovereignty have also retreated from their most extreme positions when it has been deemed necessary or prudent to do so, for example, acquiescing to some of Putin's proposed federal reforms and changing legislation deemed offensive by the federal center, as was demonstrated in the previous chapter. Throughout the post-Soviet period, the republic has remained a participant in all the various iterations of Russia's federal institutions (however reluctant or problematic that participation might be), thus choosing to act as an engine of pro-region, pro-federalism and pro-cultural pluralist change both from within *and* from outside the federal frameworks set up by Moscow. It has not tried to sabotage federal institutions directly or actively, but rather has tried to shape them through criticism and proposals for reform. Its chief tools have been legislative and policy proposals, active public and private lobbying of both federal and other regional officials, as well as public relations and symbolic politics. Conspicuously absent from its repertoire of sovereignty-seeking are the use of violence, threats of violence or extortion, or ultimatums. My account of the means Tatarstan has used for its sovereignty project, which makes clear Tatarstan's consistent commitment to working within a federal framework in Russia, even as it seeks to shape that framework to its own vision and pursue its own agenda within it, suggests that Kahn (2000), Krasner (2001) and Herrera (2005) are correct in urging scholars to not automatically characterize autonomy conflicts in Russia or elsewhere, even ethnically motivated ones, as zero-sum games prone to escalate to maximalist positions that will inevitably end in secessionist or other types of violent conflict.

Rather, the account of the Tatarstani sovereignty project presented here supports the conclusion of these and other authors such as Keating (1996, 2001) and Biersteker and Weber (1996) that in the contemporary environment, "state sovereignty" should be seen as being fundamentally ambiguous and fungible in nature, not something indivisible or absolute. As such, sovereignty-sharing between entities (within multiethnic states especially) is not something to be feared or avoided, but rather pursued as the best way to devise creative and lasting solutions to autonomy conflicts in multiethnic societies. In other words, the Tatarstani sovereignty project presents a robust defense of the utility of federalism, the essence and *raison d'etre* of which is, after all, the simple premise that states gain benefits both material and normative from the parceling out of sovereignty amongst different administrative units. Tatarstan's experience also supports the contention of contemporary international relations theorists who argue that the principle of the utility of dividing and sharing sovereignty within states also now should be extended into the international arena, with those states that most readily explore the options for maximizing their political and economic ties with international actors (NGOs, MNCs, bilateral ties) by letting their sub-state units adopt some "international personality" achieving the most success in an increasingly complex and interdependent world (Holm and Sorenson 1995; Keohane 1995; Shehadi 1997)).

And indeed, as I have demonstrated here, Tatarstan's sovereignty project has brought clear benefits not only to the republic or its eponymous ethnic Tatar nation, but also to the Russian Federation as a whole. Policy programs initiated in Tatarstan under the auspices of the sovereignty project, such as the slum clearance and housing replacement program in Kazan and the pursuit of foreign direct investment and other overseas trade relationships, have been praised by Russian federal officials as models for other regions. Thus the desire to seek more sovereignty, to act more like a state to the extent possible in any given context, has helped Tatarstan to become exactly the type of "regional laboratory of innovation" that federal theorists hope to see constituent units in federal states become. By maintaining a view of itself as "sovereign" and consistently seeking to enrich that vision and the possibilities it contains, Tatarstan has shaped itself into a leader in all the realms it functions in: it is the foremost advocate of true federal reforms and a roadblock to ill-conceived re-centralization in Russia; it is the leader in regional domestic policy innovation, a role that will become even more important as more and more responsibilities, like the provision of social services, are transferred to the regions, however reluctantly, under Putin; its foreign policy initiatives have not only brought wealth to Russia, but have helped to integrate it back into the world community, in particular with the Islamic world (in particular with the OIC); finally, its attention to issues of ethnocultural justice and cultural pluralism are virtually the only reason those issues appear even at the outer edges of the federal radar in Russia today.

This, I think, is the main conclusion of the study presented here. It is *exactly because* of the consistent organizing claim of being a "sovereign" entity that Tatarstan's leadership has been able to devise the type of creative, innovative, and useful policy initiatives at the federal, domestic, and international level that it has during the post-Soviet decade. Far from threatening Russia's territorial integrity or preventing the "power vertical" from taking the country forward to some radiant future, Tatarstan's sovereignty project has generated the type of innovative and independent policy initiatives that the country needs to truly become more efficient, more productive, more integrated with the global economy and international community, and more just, both in terms of its provision of public goods and ethnocultural justice. Thus, while the conditions that have led to the development of such a strong sovereignty project in Tatarstan may make it a unique case in Russia (such as the historical tradition of ethnic Tatar statehood which makes the organizing claim of sovereignty more appealing and enduring there, the moderate but consistent leadership of Shaimiyev and his team, and Tatarstan's rich resource and industrial base), this does not mean that the positive aspects for federation-building and fostering cultural pluralism derived from organizing regions on the assumption of sovereignty can't be developed elsewhere in Russia (an argument that Tatarstan makes to other republics and regions whenever it can).

Rather than revert to or expand its self-defeating policy of hobbling the development of a more effective and functional form of federalism in Russia by attacking any manifestation of regional sovereignty as a threat to

Russia's territorial integrity or its very existence, the new Medvedev/Putin administration (and future presidential teams) would do well to continue the intermittent practice of actually listening to, learning from, and encouraging Tatarstan's sovereignty project, and attempting to transfer the best elements of that project to the other regions. How might Moscow be enticed to do so, and how might Kazan, for that matter, be encouraged to foster the positive aspects of its sovereignty project both at home and amongst other regions, while limiting the less salubrious parts?

First, Moscow would do well to back off of its obsessive and ill-considered quest to reinstate unitarism at any cost and stop rejecting out of hand the idea that the republics should possess any sovereignty in any form. In other words, Moscow should begin to accommodate itself to the fact that for real federalism to exist in Russia, sovereignty can and indeed must be shared between the regions and the center, and that such a division can help Russia to prosper politically and economically. The center should try to foster those economic, foreign policy, and legal-political initiatives in the regions that help to spur on economic development, heighten Russia's presence in the international community, and constitute the most effective and rational legislative and policy initiatives for Russia. That is, the center must allow the republics to do what they can do well, and must give them the legal, economic, and political means to do this effectively. The Putin administration itself seems to have eventually come to the conclusion that such a strategy could be mutually-beneficial for both the regions and the center—in early 2006 it announced the creation of a new State Investment Fund to fund innovative economic and political policy initiatives emanating from the regions. Significantly, a proposal from Tatarstan to modernize aspects of TATNEFT's oil production was awarded one of the first grants from this program (*Moscow Times* June 9, 2006). While it remains to be seen if the new Medvedev/Putin administration will continue in this direction of a renewed, if mild openness to regionalism, the official transformation of the new treaty with Tatarstan into Russian Federal law in mid-2007 suggests it will.

It is particularly important that the center give the regions, especially the ethnic republics, the legal, political, and economic authority to develop effective policy (that is, allow them to exercise real sovereignty), in the cultural and educational arena. Moscow should realize that republics have the moral high ground here, as both the principles of liberal multiculturalism and ethnocultural justice demand, and current international practice supports, the idea that ethnic minority communities in Russia should be given wide latitude to revive and protect their indigenous national cultures. As Tatarstan has convincingly argued and its practice demonstrated, this is particularly true given that the federal government has repeatedly shown that it has no intention of fostering an acceptable alternative system of cultural pluralism in the country, and indeed, that its overall commitment to the principles of liberal multiculturalism is weak at best. Given this reality, the international community may have some role to play in prodding Russia to adopt some of these attitudes and actions.

For its part, Tatarstan (and this applies to other sovereignty-minded republics such as Bashkortostan) must continue to accept that there are necessary limits to its sovereign ambitions, however fungible and ill-defined those limits may be. The architects of Tatarstan's sovereignty project (including whomever succeeds Shaimiyev when his current appointed term is up in 2009) thus should continue to make a good faith effort to integrate into the Russian Federation's legal, economic, and social space, while also retaining the legal, political, economic, and cultural bases of regional autonomy. Tatarstani elites should work to preserve and expand the good economic, foreign policy, legal-political innovations that have developed out of its sovereignty project and which represent win-win situations for it and the center. Regarding the pursuit of ethnic Tatar national revival in the name of ethnocultural justice, Tatarstan should recognize that while it may possess the right to engage in such ethnic nation-building projects, it must continue do so carefully and fully within the confines of liberal multiculturalism. That is, ethnic Tatar political and intellectual elites must continue to assiduously protect the individual and group rights of the non-Tatar national communities in Tatarstan, who are also after all citizens of the Russian Federation (what Kymlicka refers to as providing for second order ethnocultural justice). This means that the ethnic elite of Tatarstan and the other national republics must continue to attend to civic nation building and to accept that there are limits to what they can do in the spheres of ethnic nation building and national revival in their republics.

The practice of contemporary multinational democracies such as Canada, Belgium, and Spain, as well as of historical entities such as the Austro-Hungarian empire, suggests that citizens of these states can and do learn to live with multiple identities and loyalties, and that learning to manage complex personal and political distributions of identification and authority is becoming increasingly necessary for all of us who seek to live peacefully in an increasingly globalized world (Gagnon and Tully 2001; Harty and Murphy 2005; Keating 2001). In Russia, the example of Tatarstan suggests that skillful management of republican-level sovereignty projects, including their limitation where necessary, combined with both continued federal integration where appropriate and with intensified international pressure on Russia to preserve and expand those few traces of true democracy, federalism and multiculturalism that currently exist in the country, provides a potentially-useful blueprint for developing a political regime that fosters allegiance to both federal *and* local, civic *and* ethnic identities. Both the center and the regions have responsibility for fostering the development and accommodation of these multiple identifications; it is the task of the international community and the community of post-Sovietologists to help them with this challenge

Notes

1. While it might be expected that the Kazan media would interpret the events of August 2005 as a victory for Shaimiyev and the "sovereign statehood" of Tatarstan, it is significant that even some members of the Moscow media felt that Putin was upstaged in Kazan by Shaimiyev during the State Council and CIS summits. See for example, Andrei Koesnikov's article in *Kommersant*, published on August 27, 2005.

2. For this interpretation of the August 2005 Kazan Millennial celebrations see both the interview with Shaimiyev in *Kommersant Vlast'* from August 29, 2005, and the speech of Tatarstani State Council Chairman to assembled dignitaries at the celebrations reprinted in *Zvezda Povol'zhe*, 2–7 September 2005 edition.

Bibliography

Abdullin, Rafkat Fatkullovich. 1997. Head of sector on National Education in the Ministry of Education of the Republic of Bashkortostan. Interview by author. Ufa, June 17.

Adelcoa, Francisco, and Michael Keating, eds. 1999. *Paradiplomacy in Action*. London: Frank Cass.

Afanas'yev, Yuri. 1997. Specialist, Department of Inter-Ethnic and National Affairs, President's Office of the Republic of Bashkortostan. Interview with author, Ufa, June 24.

Agronoff, Robert. 1993. "Inter-governmental Politics and Policy: Building Federal Arrangements in Spain." *Regional Politics and Policy* 1, no.1 (Spring): 10–23.

———. ed. 1999. *Accommodating Diversity: Asymmetry in Federal States*. Baden-Baden, Germany: Nomos Verlagsgesellschaft.

———. 1999a. "Intergovermental Relations and the Management of Asymmetry in Federal Spain." Pp. 94–117 in *Accommodating Diversity: Asymmetry in Federal States*, edited by Robert Agranoff. Baden-Baden, Germany: Nomos Verlagsgesellschaft.

———. 1999b. "Power Shifts, Diversity, and Asymmetry." Pp. 11–23 in *Accommodating Diversity: Asymmetry in Federal States*, edited by Robert Agranoff. Baden-Baden, Germany: Nomos Verlagsgesellschaft.

Akiner, Shirin. 1986. *Islamic Peoples of the Soviet Union: An historical and statistical handbook*. 2nd ed. London: KPI.

Alexander, John. 1969. *Autocratic Politics in a National Crisis: The Imperial Russian Government and Pugachev's Revolt*. Bloomington, IN: Indiana University Press.

Alishev, Salyam Kh., ed. 1993. *Tatarstan Tarikhinan Khikiyaler (Tales from Tatarstan's History)*. Kazan: Magarif.

———. 1995. "Obrazovaniye Tatarskoi Narodnosti. (Formation of the Tatar people)." Pp. 201–23 in *Materialy po Istorii Tatarskogo Naroda* (Material on the history of the Tatar people). Kazan': Institut Yazika, Literatury i Istorii im. G. Ibragimova Akademii Nauk Tatarstana.

Anderson, Benedict. 1983. *Imagined Communities: Reflections on the Study and Spread of Nationalism*. London: Verso Books.

Apparat Prezidenta Respubliki Tatarstan. 1993. *Mnogonatsional'nii Tatarstan. (Multinational Tatarstan)*. Kazan'.

———. 1995. *Tatarskii Mir (The Tatar World)*. Kazan'.

Appiah, K. Anthony. 1994. " Identity, Authenticity, Survival: Multicultural Societies and Social Reproduction." Pp. 149–63 in *Multiculturalism: Examining the Politics of Representation*, edited by Amy Gutmann. Princeton, NJ: Princeton University Press.

Arel, Dominique, and David I. Kertzer, eds. 2002. *Census and Identity: The Politics of Race, Ethnicity and Language in National Censuses*. Cambridge: Cambridge University Press.

Armstrong, John. 1982. *Nations before Nationalism*. Chapel Hill, NC: University of North Carolina Press.

Bahry, Donna. 2002. "Ethnicity and Equality in Post-communist Economic Transitions: Evidence from Russia's Regions." *Europe-Asia Studies* 54, no.5 (July): 673–99.

———. 2005. "The New Federalism and the Paradoxes of Regional Sovereignty in Russia." *Comparative Politics* 37, no. 2 (January): 127–46.

Baltanova, G. R. 2000. "Islam v Sovremennom Tatarstanye (Islam in Contemporary Tatarstan)." Pp. 34–61, in *Islam v Istorii i Kul'turye Tatarskogo Naroda (Islam in the History and Culture of the Tatar People)*, edited by the Institut' Istorii Akademii Nauka Respublika Tatarstana, Kazan: Shkola.

Balzer, Harley. 2003. "Managed Pluralism: Vladimir Putin's Emerging Regime." *Post-Soviet Affairs* 19, no.3 (July–September): 189–227.

Barkin, J. Samuel, and Bruce Cronin. 1994. "The State Versus the Nation: Changing Norms and the Rules of Sovereignty in International Relations." *International Organization* 48, no. 1 (Winter): 107–30.

Barnett, Michael. 1995. "The New United Nations Politics of Peace: From Juridical Sovereignty to Empirical Sovereignty." *Global Governance* 1, no. 1 (January–March): 79–97.

———. 1996. "Sovereignty, Nationalism, and Regional Order in the Arab States System." Pp. 148–89 in *State Sovereignty as Social Construct*, edited by Thomas Biersteker and Cynthia Weber. Cambridge: Cambridge University Press.

Bartelson, Jens. 1995. *A Genealogy of Sovereignty*. Cambridge: Cambridge University Press.

Batunsky, Mark. 1985. "Islam and Russian Medieval Culture." *Die Welt des Islams* 25: 1–27.

———. 1990. "Islam and Russian Culture in the First Half of the 19th Century." *Central Asian Survey* 9, no. 4 (December): 1–27.

———. 1994. "Russian Clerical Islamic studies in the Late 19th and early 20th Centuries." *Central Asian Survey* 13, no. 2 (June): 213–35.

Beissinger, Mark R. 1992. "Elites and Ethnic Identities in Soviet and post-Soviet Politics." Pp. 141–69 in *The Post-Soviet Nations: Perspectives on the Demise of the U.S.S.R.*, edited by Alexander J. Motyl. New York: Columbia University Press.

———. 1993. "Demise of an Empire-state: Identity, Legitimacy and the Deconstruction of Soviet Politics." Pp. 93–115 in *The Rising Tide of Cultural Pluralism: The Nation-state at Bay?* Edited by Crawford Young. Madison, WI: University of Wisconsin Press.

———. 1994. "The Relentless Pursuit of the National State: Reflections on Soviet and post-Soviet Experience." Paper presented at the conference on "Race and Ethnicity at the End of the 20th Century," Milwaukee, WI, September.

———. 1995. "The Persisting Ambiguity of Empire." *Post-Soviet Affairs* 11, no. 2 (April–June): 149–84.

———. 1996. "How Nationalisms Spread: Eastern Europe Adrift the Tides and Cycles of Nationalist Contention." *Social Research* 63, no. 1 (Spring): 1–11.

———. 2001. *Nationalist Mobilization and the Collapse of the Soviet Union.* Cambridge: Cambridge University Press.

———. 2006. "Soviet Empire as Family Resemblance." *Slavic Review* 65, no. 2 (Summer): 294–303.

Belin, Laura, and Robert W. Orttung. 1997. *The Russian Parliamentary Elections of 1995: The Battle for the Duma.* Armonk, NY: M. E. Sharpe.

Benningsen, Alexandre, and Chantal Lemercier-Quelquejay. 1967. *Islam in the Soviet Union.* London: Pall Mall Press.

Benningsen, Alexandre, and Enders Wimbush. 1980. *Muslim National Communism in the Soviet Union.* Chicago: University of Chicago Press.

Biersteker, Thomas, and Cynthia Weber, eds. 1996. *State Sovereignty as Social Construct.* Cambridge: Cambridge University Press.

Billig, Michael. 1995. *Banal Nationalism.* London: Sage.

Bilinsky, Yaroslav. 1968. "Education of the non-Russian Peoples of the Soviet Union 1917–1967: An Essay." *Slavic Review* 3 (Fall): 411–37.

Black, C. E. 1956. *Rewriting Russian History: Soviet Interpretations of Russia's Past.* New York: Praeger.

Blank, Stephen. 1983. "The Struggle for Soviet Bashkiria 1917–1923." *Nationalities Papers* 11, no. 1 (March): 1–26.

Blitstein, Peter. 2006. "Cultural Diversity and Interwar Conjuncture: Soviet Nationality Policy in its Comparative Context." *Slavic Review* 65, no. 2 (Summer): 273–93.

Brandenberger, David. 2002. *National Bolshevism: Stalinist Mass Culture and the Formation of Modern Russian National Identity, 1931–1965.* Cambridge, MA, and London: Harvard University Press.

Brass, Paul, ed. 1985. *Ethnic Groups and the State*. Towson, NY: Barnes and Noble Books.

Brassloff, Audrey. 1989. "Spain: the State of the Autonomies." Pp. 24–50, in *Nationalism and Federalism*, edited by Murray Forsyth. Leicester: Leicester University Press.

Brown-John, C., ed. 1988. *Centralizing and Decentralizing Trends in Federal States*. New York: University Press of America.

Broxup, Marie Benningsen. 1990. "Volga Tatars." Pp. 277–89 in *The Nationalities Question in the Soviet Union*, edited by Graham Smith. London and New York: Longman.

Brubaker, Rogers. 1994. "Nationhood and the National Question in the Soviet Union and post-Soviet Eurasia: An Institutionalist Account." *Theory and Society* 23, no. 1 (February): 47–78.

———. 1997. *Nationalism Reframed: Nationhood and the National Question in the New Europe*. Cambridge: Cambridge University Press.

Buchanan, Allen. 1991. *Secession: The Morality of Political Divorce from Ft. Sumter to Lithuania and Quebec*. Boulder, CO: Westview Press.

Bucheit, Lee. 1978. *Secession: The Legitimacy of Self-determination*. New Haven, CT: Yale University Press.

Bukharaev, Ravil. 1999. *The Model of Tatarstan under President Mintimer Shaimiyev*. New York: St. Martin's Press.

Burgess, Michael, and Alain Gagnon, eds. 1993. *Comparative Federalism and Federation*. Toronto: University of Toronto Press.

Cerny, Philip. 1993. "Plurilateralism: Structural Differentiation and Functional Conflict in the post-Cold War World Order." *Millennium* 22, no. 1: 27–51.

Chamber of Commerce of the Republic of Tatarstan. 1996. *Tatarstan: Path-breaker in Political and Economic Reform*. London: Flint River Press.

Collias, Karen A. 1990. "Making Soviet Citizens: Patriotic and Internationalist Education in the Formation of a Soviet State Identity." Pp. 73–93 on *Soviet Nationalities Policy*, edited by Henry Huttenbach. London: Mansell.

Connor, Walker. 1984. *The Nationality Question in Marxist-Leninist Theory and Strategy*. Princeton, NJ: Princeton University Press.

———. 1992. "Soviet Policies Toward the non-Russian Peoples in Theoretic and Historic Perspective." Pp. 30–49 in *The Post-Soviet Nations*, edited by Alexander J. Motyl. New York: Columbia University Press.

Conquest, Robert. 1991. *Stalin: Breaker of Nations*. New York: Viking.

Corrigan, Philip, and Derek Sayer. 1985. *The Great Arch: English State Formation as Cultural Revolution*. London: Basil Blackwell.

Daulet, Shafiga. 1989. "The First all-Muslim Congress of Russia." *Central Asian Survey* 8, no. 1 (March): 211–41.

DeBardeleben, Joan. 2003. "Fiscal federalism and How Russians Vote." *Europe-Asia Studies* 55, no. 3 (May): 339–63.

Deklaratsiya Verkhovnogo Soveta Respubliki Tatarstan O Vkhozhdenii Respubliki Tatarstan v Sodruzhestvo Nezavisimykh Gosudarstv. (Declaration of the Supreme Soviet of the Republic of Tatarstan on the Entering of the Republic of Tatarstan into the Commonwealth of Independent States). 1991. December 26. Pp. 8–12 in

Belaya Kniga Tatarstana: Put' k Suverenitetu 1990–1995 (White Book of Tatarstan: The Path to Sovereignty 1990–1995), edited by R. Khakimov. Special issue of the journal *Panorama-Forum* (1996), Vol. 5, no. 8.

d'Encausse, Helene Carrere. 1993. *The End of the Soviet Empire: The Triumph of the Nations*. New York: Basic Books.

De Villiers, B., ed. 1994. *Evaluating Federal Systems*. Boston: Martinus Nijhoff Publishers.

Dogovory Mezhdu Rossiskoi Federatsii i ee Regionami. (Agreements Between the Russian Federation and its Regions). 1997. Moscow.

Doty, Roxanne Lynn. 1996. "Sovereignty and the nation: Constructing the boundaries of national identity." Pp. 121–47 in *State Sovereignty as Social Construct*, edited by T. Biersteker and C. Weber. Cambridge: Cambridge University Press.

Drobizheva, L. M., A. R. Aklaev, V. V. Koroteeva, and G. U. Soldatova. 1996. *Demokratizatsiya i Obrazy Nationalizma v Rossiiskoi Federatsii 90-x Godov. (Democratization and the Forms of Nationalism in the Russian Federation in the 1990s)*. Moscow: Izdatelstvo Mysl'.

Dunlop, John. 1993. *The Rise of Russia and the Fall of the Soviet Empire*. Princeton, NJ: Princeton University Press.

———. 1998. *Russia Confronts Chechnya: Roots of a Separatist Conflict*. Cambridge: Cambridge University Press.

Duursma, Jorri. 1996. *Fragmentation and the International Relations of Micro-States*. Cambridge: Cambridge University Press.

Elazar, Daniel. 1998. *Constitutionalizing Globalization: The Post-modern Revival of Confederal Arrangements*. Oxford: Rowman and Littlefield.

Elazar, Daniel, ed. 1994. *Federal Systems of the World: A Handbook of Federal, Confederal, and Autonomy Arrangements*. New York: Longman.

Eley, Geoff, and Ronald Suny. 1996. "Introduction: From the Moment of Social History to the Work of Cultural Representation." Pp. 3–38 in *Becoming National*, edited by G. Eley and R. Suny. Oxford: Oxford University Press.

Emizet, Kisangani, and Vicki Hesli. 1995. "The Disposition to Secede: An Analysis of the Soviet Case." *Comparative Political Studies* 27, no. 4 (January): 493–536.

Evangelista, Matthew. 2002. *The Chechen Wars: Will Russia Go the Way of the Soviet Union?* Washington, DC: Brookings Institution.

———. 2003. *The Chechen Wars: Will Russia Go the Way of the Soviet Union?* Washington, DC: Brookings Institution Press.

Faller, Helen. 2006. "The Influence of Tatar Language Revival on the Development of Divergent Referential Worlds." Pp. 304–34 in *Rebounding Identities: The Politics of Identity in Russia and Ukraine*, edited by Dominique Arel and Blair A. Ruble. Washington, DC and Baltimore: Woodrow Wilson Center Press and Johns Hopkins University Press.

Farukshin, Midkhat. 1994. "Politicheskaya elita v Tatarstanye." (Political Elites in Tatarstan). *Politicheskiye Issledovaniya*. no. 5–6: 67–79.

Fisher, Alan. 1968. "Enlightened Despotism and Islam under Catherine II. *Slavic Review* 27, no. 4 (Winter): 542–63.

Forsyth, Murray, ed. 1989. *Nationalism and Federalism*. Leicester: Leicester University Press.

Fowler, Michael Ross, and Julie Marie Bunck, eds. 1995. *Law, Power and the Sovereign State: The Evolution and Application of the Concept of Sovereignty*. University Park, PA: Penn State Press.

Frank, Allen. 1994. *Islamic Regional Identity in Imperial Russia: Tatar and Bashkir historiography in the 18th and 19th centuries*. PhD dissertation in the Department of Central Eurasian Studies, Indiana University.

Frank, Allen, and Ronald Wixman. 1997. "The Middle Volga: Exploring the Limits of Sovereignty." Pp. 140–89 in *New States, New Politics: Building the Post-Soviet Nations*, edited by Ian Bremmer and Ray Taras. New York: Cambridge University Press.

Friedrich, Carl. 1968. *Trends of Federalism in Theory and Practice*. New York: Praeger.

Gagnon, Alain-G., and Charles Gibbs. 1999. "The Normative Basis of Asymmetrical Federation." Pp. 73–93 in *Accommodating Diversity: Asymmetry in Federal States*, edited by R. Agronoff. Baden-Baden, Germany: Nomos Verlagsgesellschaft.

Gagnon, Alain-G., and James Tully, eds. 2001. *Multinational Democracies*. Cambridge: Cambridge University Press.

Gagnon, Alain-G. 2001. "The Moral Foundations of Asymmetrical Federalism: A Normative Exploration of the Case of Quebec and Canada." Pp. 319–37 in *Multinational Democracies*, edited by Alain-G. Gagnon and James Tully. Cambridge: Cambridge University Press.

Gaifullin, Vasil' G. 1995. "Shkola Zavtrashnevo Dnya (Tomorrow's Schools)" *Tatarstan* no. 7/8: 14–17.

———. 1996. "Podkhody k Natsional'nomy obrazovaniyu." ("The Path to National Education.") *Informatsionno-Metodicheskii Byulleten' Apparat Presidenta Respubliki Tatarstan (Informational Bulletin of the Administration of the President of the Republic of Tatarstan)*. no. 8: 45–47.

Gammer, Moshe. 1994. *Muslim Resistance to the Tsar: Shamil and the Conquest of Chechnia and Daghestan*. London: Frank Cass.

Geertz, Clifford. 1973. *The Interpretation of Cultures*. New York: Basic Books, Inc.

———. 1980. *Negara: The Theatre State in Nineteenth-century Bali*. Princeton, NJ: Princeton University Press.

Gellner, Ernest. 1983. *Nations and Nationalism*. Oxford: Oxford University Press.

Geraci, Robert, and Michael Khodarkovsky. 2001. *Of Religion and Empire: Missions, Conversion and Tolerance in Tsarist Russia*. Ithaca, NY, and London: Cornell University Press.

Geraci, Robert. 1997. "Russian Orientalism at an Impasse: Tsarist Education Policy and the 1910 Conference on Islam." Pp. 138–62 in *Russia's Orient: Imperial Borderlands and Peoples, 1700–1917*, edited by Daniel Brower and Edward J. Lazzerini. Bloomington, IN: Indiana University Press.

Gerner, Kristian, and Stefan Hedlund. 1993. *The Baltic States and the End of the Soviet Empire*. London: Routledge.

Gibatitidinov, Marat. 2005. Specialist in National Education at the Tatar Institute of History at the Tatar Academy of Science. Interview with Author. Kazan. June 9.

Goble, Paul. 1990. "Readers, Writers, and Republics: The Structural Basis of Non-Russian Literary Politics." Pp. 131–47 in *The Nationalities Factor in Soviet Politics and Society*, edited by Mark R. Beissinger and Lubomyr Hajda. Boulder, CO: Westview Press.

———. 2006. "Window on Eurasia: Many Russians Feel Putin Not Authoritarian Enough." Article posted to Johnson's Russia List, March 13, 2006. www.cdi.org/russia/johnson /default.cfm

Golden, Peter. 1982. *An Introduction to the History of the Turkic Peoples*. Wiesbaden: Otto Harrassowitz.

Gorenburg, Dmitry. 1999. "Identity Change in Bashkortostan: Tatars into Bashkirs and Back." *Ethnic and Racial Studies* 22, no. 3 (May): 554–80.

———. 2003. *Minority Ethnic Mobilization in the Russian Federation*. Cambridge: Cambridge University Press.

———. 2006 . "Soviet Nationalities Policy and Assimilation." Pp. 273–303 in *Rebounding Identities: Multicultural Legacies in Russia and Ukraine*, edited by Blair Ruble and Dominique Arel. Washington, DC: Johns Hopkins University Press and Woodrow Wilson Center Press.

Gottlieb, Gidon. 1993. *Nation against State*. New York: Council on Foreign Relations Press.

Gow, James. 1997. "Shared Sovereignty, Enhanced Security: Lessons from the Yugoslav War." Pp. 151–80 in *State Sovereignty: Change and Persistence in International Relations*, edited by Sohail H. Hashmi. University Park, PA: Pennsylvania State University Press.

Graney, Katherine. 1998. "The Volga Tatars: Diasporas and the Politics of Federalism." Pp. 153–78 in *Nations Abroad: Diaspora Politics and International Relations in the Former Soviet Union*, edited by Charles King and Neil J. Melvin. Boulder, CO: Westview Press.

———. 1999a. "Projecting Sovereignty in Post-Soviet Russia: Education Reform in Tatarstan and Bashkortostan." *Europe-Asia Studies* 51, no. 4 (June): 611–32.

———. 1999b. *Projecting Sovereignty: Statehood and Nationness in Post-Soviet Russia*. PhD Dissertation, Department of Political Science, University of Wisconsin–Madison.

———. 2001a. "Sharing Sovereignty in Post-Soviet Russia: Tatarstan in the International Arena." Pp. 264–94 in *Minority Nationalism and the Changing International Order*, edited by Michael Keating and John McGarry. Oxford: Oxford University Press.

———. 2001b. "Ten Years of Sovereignty in Tatarstan: End of the Beginning or Beginning of the End?" *Problems of Post-Communism* 48, no. 5 (September/October): 32–41.

———. 2004. "The Gender of Sovereignty: Constructing Statehood, Nation and Gender Regimes in Post-Soviet Tatarstan," Pp. 44–64 in *Post-Soviet Women Encountering Transition: Nation Building, Economic Survival and Civic Activism*, edited by Kathleen Kuehnast and Carol Nechemias. Washington, DC, and Baltimore, MD: Woodrow Wilson Center Press and Johns Hopkins University Press.

———. 2006. "'Russian Islam' and the Politics of Religious Multiculturalism in Russia." Pp. 89–115 in *Rebounding Identities: The Politics of Identity in Russia and Ukraine*, edited by Dominique Arel and Blair A. Ruble. Washington, DC and Baltimore: Woodrow Wilson Center Press and Johns Hopkins University Press.

———. 2007. "Making Russia Multicultural: Kazan' at Its Millennium and Beyond." *Problems of Post-Communism* 54, no. 6 (November/December): 17–27.

Grigorenko, Galina. 1997. " Il'dus Sadykov." *Ploshchad' Svobody.* no. 16 (July): 11.

Gubadullin, Rustam M. 1995. *Tatarskoye National'noye Dvizheniye v Reshenii Problemy Gosudarstvennogo Vozrozhdeniya Tatarstana (The Tatar National Movement in the Resolution of the Rebirth of the State of Tatarstan)*. Candidate dissertation in the Department of History, Kazan State University, Kazan, Russia.

Guboglo, M. H., R.G. Kuzeev and R. Kh. Shakhazarov, eds. 1997. *Resursyi Mobilizovannoi Ethnichnosti* (Resources for the Moblization of Ethnicity). Moscow and Ufa: Gorbachev Fund.

Guiliano, Elise. 2000. "Who Determines the Self in the Politics of Self-determination? Identity and Preference Formation in Tatarstan's Nationalist Mobilization." *Comparative Politics* 32, no. 3 (April): 295–316.

Gurr, Ted Robert. 1993. *Minorities at Risk: A Global View of Ethnopolitical Conflicts*. Washington, DC: United States Institute of Peace Press.

Guttman, Amy, ed. 1992. *Multiculturalism and the "Politics of Recognition."* Princeton, NJ: Princeton University Press.

Habermas, Jurgen. 1996. "The European Nation-state—Its Achievements and its Limits." Pp. 281–94 in *Mapping the Nation*, edited by Gopal Balakrishnan. London: Verso.

———. 2001. *The Postnational Constellation*. Cambridge: MIT Press.

Hahn, Gordon M. 2003. "The Impact of Putin's Federative Reforms on Democratization in Russia." *Post-Soviet Affairs* 19, no. 2 (April–June): 114–53.

———. 2004. "Provoking Communalism in Putin's Russia." *Rfe/Rl Russian Political Weekly* 4, no. 1 (January 8).

Hale, Henry. 1998. "Regionalization of Autocracy in Russia." PONARS Memo #42. www.csis.org/ruseura/ponars/pm/

———. 2003. "Explaining Machine Politics in Russia's Regions: Economy, Ethnicity and Legacy." *Post-Soviet Affairs* 19, no. 3 (July–September): 228–63.

Hall, J. A. and Ikenberry, G. J. 1989. *The State*. Minneapolis: University of Minnesota Press.

Hall, Rodney Bruce. 1999. *National Collective Identity: Social Constructs and International Systems*. New York: Columbia University Press.

Halperin, Morton, and Daniel Scheffer. 1992. *Self-Determination in the New World Order*. Washington, DC: Carnegie Endowment for International Peace.

Hannum, Hurst. 1996. *Autonomy, Sovereignty, and Self-determination: The Accommodation of Conflicting Rights*. Philadelphia: University of Pennsylvania Press, Second Edition.

Harty, Siobhan, and Michael Murphy, eds. 2005. *In Defense of Multinational Citizenship*. Vancouver and Toronto: University of British Columbia Press.

Hashmi, Sohail H., ed. 1997. *State Sovereignty: Change and Persistence in International Relations*. University Park, PA: Pennsylvania State University.

Hauslohner, Peter. 1987. "Gorbachev's Social Contract." *Soviet Economy* 3, no. 1 (January–March): 54–89.

Hendley, Kathryn. 1997. "Legal Development in post-Soviet Russia." *Post-Soviet Affairs* 13, no. 3 (July–September): 228–51.

Herrera, Yoshiko M. 2002. "Attempts Under Putin to Create a Unified Economic Space in Russia. " PONARS Policy Memo # 231. www.csis.org/ruseura/ponars/pm/

———. 2005. *Imagined Economies: The Sources of Russian Regionalism*. Cambridge: Cambridge University Press.

Hirsch, Francine. 1997. "The Soviet Union as a Work-in-progress: Ethnographers and the Category Nationality in the 1926, 1937 and 1939 Censuses." *Slavic Review* 56, no. 2 (Summer): 251–78.

———. 2005. *Empire of Nations: Ethographic Knowledge and the Making of the Soviet Union*. Ithaca, NY, and London: Cornell University Press.

Hobsbawm, Eric, and Terence Ranger. 1983. *The Invention of Tradition*. Cambridge: Cambridge University Press.

Hocking, Brian, ed. 1993a. *Foreign Relations and Federal States*. London: Leicester University Press.

———. 1993b. *Localizing Foreign Policy*. New York: St. Martin's Press.

Holdsworth, Julia. 2004. "Change and Contesting Identities: the Creation and Negotiation of Landscape in Donetsk." *Anthropology Matters Journal* 6, no. 1: 8–22.

Holm, H. H., and Georg Sorenson, eds. 1995. *Whose World Order?* Boulder, CO: Westview Press.

Horowitz, Donald. 1985. *Ethnic Groups in Conflict*. Berkeley, CA: University of California Press.

———. 1997. "Self-determination: Politics, Philosophy and Law. Pp. 421–63 in *Ethnicity and Group Rights*, edited by Ian Shapiro and Will Kymlicka. New York: New York University Press.

Hough, Jerry. 1998. "The Political Geography of European Russia: Republics and Oblasts." *Post-Soviet Geography and Economics* 39, no. 2: 63–95.

Hroch, Miroslav. 1985. *Social Preconditions of National Revival in Europe*. Cambridge: Cambridge University Press.

Isaenko, Anatoly, and Peter Petschauer. 2000. "A Failure That Transformed Russia: The 1991–1994 Democratic State-building Experiment in Chechnya. *International Social Science Review* 73, no. 1/2: 1–32.

Iskhakov, Damir M. 1993a. "Sovremennoye Tatarskoye Natsional'noye Dvizheniye: Pod'yem i Krizis (The Contemporary Tatar National Movement: Rise and Crisis). *Tatarstan* 8 (August): 25–31.

———. 1993b. *Tatary: Popularnyi Ocherk Etnicheskoi Istorii i Demografii (Tatars: Sketch of Ethnic History and Demography)*. Naberezhnye Chelny: Gazetno-knizhnoye izdatel'stvo "KAMAZ."

———. 1995. "Nas Teper' Bol'she (Now We Are More), *Idel*, no. 11/ 12: 2–3.

———. 1996. Model' Tatarstana i Natsionalizm Tatar (The Tatarstan Model and Tatar Nationalism). Manuscript. Kazan.

Jackson, Robert, and Carl Rosberg. 1982. "Why Africa's Weak States Persist: The Empirical and the Juridical in Statehood. *World Politics* 35, no. 1 (October): 1–25.

Jackson, Robert. 1990. *Quasi-states: Sovereignty, International Relations, and the Third World*. Cambridge: Cambridge University Press.

———. 1995. "International Community Beyond the Cold War." Pp. 59–83 in *Beyond Westphalia? State Sovereignty and International Intervention*, edited by Gene Lyons and Michael Mastanduno. Baltimore, MD: Johns Hopkins University Press.

James, Alan. 1986. *Sovereign Statehood: The Basis of International Society*. London: Allen and Unwin.

Jewsiewicki, Bogumil, and V. Y. Mudimbe. 1995. "Meeting the Challenge of Legitimacy: Post-independence Black African and post-Soviet European states." *Daedalus* 124, no. 3 (Summer): 191–204.

Jones, Barry, and Michael Keating, eds. 1995. *The European Union and the Regions*. Oxford: Oxford University Press.

Kabinet Ministrov Respubliki Tatarstan. 1996. *Respublika Tatarstan: Vremya Bol'shik Peremen. (The Republic of Tatarstan: Time of Great Changes)*. Kazan': Tatarskogo gazetno-zhurnal'nogo izdatel'stvo.

Kahn, Jeffery. 2000. "The Parade of Sovereignties: Establishing the Vocabulary of the New Russian Federalism." *Post-Soviet Affairs* 16, no.1 (January–March): 58–89.

———. 2002. *Federalism, Democratization, and the Rule of Law in Russia*. Oxford: Oxford University Press.

Kaiser, Robert J. 1994. *The Geography of Nationalism in Russia and the U.S.S.R.* Princeton, NJ: Princeton University Press.

———. 1997. "Homeland-making in Russia's Republics." Paper presented at the AAASS Conference, Seattle, WA.

"Kak nam pisat' svoyu istoriyu? (How Should We Write Our History?)" 1996. *Idel*, no. 3/4: 40–45.

Kaplan, Cynthia. 1998. "Ethnicity and Sovereignty: Insights from Russian Negotiations with Estonia and Tatarstan." Pp. 251–274 in *The International Spread of Ethnic Conflict*, edited by David A. Lake and Donald Rothchild. Princeton, NJ: Princeton University Press.

Kappeler, Andreas. 1994. "Czarist Policy Towards the Muslims of the Russian Empire." Pp. 141–56 in *Muslim Communities Reemerge: Historical Perspectives on Nationalism, Politics and Opposition in the Former Soviet Union and Yugoslavia*, edited by Andreas Kappeler and Edward Allworth. Durham, NC: Duke University Press.

Karmis, Dimitrios, and Alain-G. Gagnon. 2001. "Federalism, Federation and Collective Identities in Canada and Belgium: Different Routes, Similar Fragmentation." Pp. 137–75 in *Multinational Democracies*, edited by Alain-G. Gagnon and James Tully. Cambridge: Cambridge University Press, 137–75.

Katzenstein, Peter, ed. 1997. *The Culture of National Security: Norms and Identity in World Politics*. New York: Columbia University Press.

Keating, Michael. 1996. *Nations Against the State: The New Politics of Nationalism in Quebec, Catalonia, and Scotland*. London: St. Martins Press.

———. 2001. *Plurinational Democracy: Stateless Nations in a Post-sovereignty World*. Oxford: Oxford University Press.

Keating, Michael, and John McGarry, eds. 2001. *Minority Nationalism and the Changing International Order*. Oxford: Oxford University Press.

Keohane, Robert. 1995. "Hobbes's Dilemma and Institutional Change in World Politics: Sovereignty in International Society." Pp. 165–86, in *Whose World Order: Uneven Globalization and the End of the Cold War*, edited by Hans-Henrik Holm and Georg Sorenson. Boulder, CO: Lynne Rienner.

Khakimov, Rafael'. 1993. *Sumerki Emperii*. (*Twilight of Empire*). Kazan': Tatarskoye Knizhnoye Izdatel'stvo.

———. 1995. *Belaya Kniga Tatarstana: Put' k Suverenitetu 1990–1995 (White book of Tatarstan: The Path to Sovereignty 1990–1995)*. Special issue of the journal *Panorama-Forum* 5, no. 8. Kazan'.

Khalid, Adeeb. 1997. "Representations of Russia in Central Asian Jadidist Discourse." Pp. 188–202 in *Russia's Orient: Imperial Borderlands and Peoples, 1700–1917*, edited by Daniel Brower and Edward J. Lazzerini. Bloomington, IN: Indiana University Press.

———. 1998. *The Politics of Muslim Cultural Reform: Jadidism in Tsarist Central Asia*. Berkeley, CA: University of California Press.

Khalitov, Niyaz K. 2005. Deputy directory for scientific research for the museum complex Kazan Kremlin. Author interview. Kazan. June 10.

Khaliullin, I. Kh. 1995. "Sredneye Povolzh'ye i Nizhneye Prikam'ye v XIIIv. (The Middle Volga and Lower Kama Region in the 13th c.)" Pp. 118–37 in *Materialy po Istorii Tatarskogo Naroda* (Material on the History of the Tatar People). Kazan': Institut Yazika, Literatury i Istorii im. G. Ibragimova Akademii Nauk Tatarstana.

Kharisov, Faris Fakhrazovich. 1997. Minister of Education of the Republic of Tatarstan. Interview by author. Kazan. August 12.

Khasanova, Gulnara. 2005. "Tysyachetletiye Kazan'i Kak Simbol Natsional'nogo Vozrozhdeniya" ("Kazan Millennium as a Symbol of National Rebirth"), special submission to the website of Radio Azatlik/Radio Svobodi (www.azatliq.org/), August 28, 2005. Author's personal copy.

King, Charles. 2000. "Post-Communism: Transition, Comparison, and the End of 'Eastern Europe.'" *World Politics* 53 (October): 143–72.

———. 2001. "The Benefits of Ethnic War: Understanding Eurasia's Unrecognized States." *World Politics* 53, no. 4 (July): 524–52.

King, Charles, and Neil Melvin, eds. 1998. *Nations Abroad: Diaspora Politics and International Relations in the Former Soviet Union*. Boulder, CO: Westview Press.

Kinossian, Nadir. 2005. "Urban Governance in a Transitional Economy: A Case Study of Kazan." MA Thesis in the Department of Political Science, University of Missouri-St. Louis.

Kirimli, Sirri Hakan. 1990. *Nationalist Movements and National Identity among the Crimean Tatars (1905–1916)*. PhD Dissertation in the Department of History, University of Wisconsin-Madison.

Knop, Karen, Sylvia Ostry, Richard Simeon, and Katherine Swinton, eds. 1995. *Rethinking Federalism: Citizens, Markets and Governments in a Changing World*. Vancouver: University of British Columbia Press.

Konitzer-Smirnov, Andrew. 2003. "Incumbent Electoral Fortunes and Regional Economic Performance During Russia's 2000–2001 Regional Executive Electoral Cycle." *Post-Soviet Affairs* 19, no. 1 (January–March): 46–79.

Krasner, Stephen 1999. *Sovereignty: Organized Hypocrisy*. Princeton, NJ: Princeton University Press.

———. 2001. *Problematic Sovereignty: Contested Rules and Political Possibilities*. New York: Columbia University Press.

———. 2005. "The Case for Shared Sovereignty." *Journal of Democracy* 16, no. 1 (January): 69–83.

Kusznir, Juia. 2007. "The New Russian-Tatar Treaty and Its Implications for Russian Federalism. " *Russian Analytical Digest* 16 (March 6): 2–6.

Kymlicka, Will. 1995. *Multicultural Citizenship: A Liberal Theory of Minority Rights*. Oxford: Clarendon Press.

———. 2001. "Western Political Theory and Ethnic Relations in Eastern Europe," Pp. 13–105 in *Can Liberal Pluralism be Exported? Western Political Theory and Ethnic Relations in Eastern Europe*, edited by W. Kymlicka and M. Opalski. Oxford: Oxford University Press.

Kymlicka, Will, and Wayne Norman, eds. 2000. *Citizenship in Diverse Societies*. Oxford: Oxford University Press.

Kymlicka, Will, and Magda Opalski, eds. 2001. *Can Liberal Pluralism be Exported? Western Political Theory and Ethnic Relations in Eastern Europe*. Oxford: Oxford University Press.

Lapidoth, Ruth. 1997. *Autonomy: Flexible Solutions to Ethnic Conflicts*. Washington, DC: United States Institute of Peace.

Lapidus, Gail. 1984. "Ethnonationalism and Political Stability." *World Politics* 36, no. 4 (July): 555–80.

———. 1998. "Contested Sovereignty: The Tragedy of Chechnya." *International Security* 23, no. 1 (Summer): 5–49.

Lazzerini, Edward J. 1981. "Tatarovedenie and the 'New Historiography' in the Soviet Union: Revising the Interpretation of the Tatar-Russian Relationship." *Slavic Review* 40, no. 4 (Winter): 625–35.

———. 1986. "The Revival of Islamic Culture in Pre-revolutionary Russia: Or, Why a Prosopography of the Tatar Ulema?," Pp. 367–72 in *Passe Turco-Tatar, Presente*

Sovietique: Studies Offered to Alexandre Benningsen, edited by Chantal Lemercier-Quelquejay and S. E. Wimbush. Paris: Etudes.

———. 1992. "Beyond Renewal: The Jadid Response to Pressure for Change in the Modern Age." Pp. 151–66 in *Muslims in Central Asia: Expressions of Identity and Change*, edited by Jo-Ann Gross. Durham, NC: Duke University Press.

———. 1994. "Defining the Orient: A 19th century Russo-Tatar Polemic over Identity and Cultural Representation." Pp. 33–45 in *Muslim Communities Reemerge: Historical Perspectives on Nationalism, Politics and Opposition in the former Soviet Union and Yugoslavia*, edited by Edward Allworth. Durham, NC: Duke University Press.

———. 1997. "Local Accommodation and Resistance to Colonialism in 19th Century Crimea." Pp. 169–87 in *Russia's Orient: Imperial Borderlands and Peoples, 1700–1917*, edited by Daniel Brower and Edward J. Lazzerini. Bloomington, IN: Indiana University Press.

Levy, Jacob. 1997. "Classifying Cultural Rights." Pp. 22–66 in *Ethnicity and Group Rights*, edited by Ian Shapiro and Will Kymlica. New York: New York University Press.

Liebowitz, Denise, and Tony Simon. 2000. "Capital Cities, Special Cities." *Canada Plan* 40, no. 3 (April–June): 38–39.

———. 2002. "Plans in Time." *American Planning Association Journal*. 68, no. 2 (Spring): 128–31

Lieven, Anatol. 1994. *The Baltic Revolution: Estonia, Latvia and Lithuania and the Path to Independence*. Second ed. New Haven, CT: Yale University Press.

———. 1998. *Chechnya: Tombstone of Russian Power*. New Haven, CT: Yale University Press.

Luchshikh Skhol Kazani. (*Best Schools of Kazan*). 1996. Kazan: Khoter.

Luckyj, George. 1975. "Socialist in Content and National in Form." Pp. 1–9 in *Discordant Voices: The Non-Russian Soviet Literatures 1953–1973*, edited by George Luckyj. Oakville, Ontario: Mosaic Press.

Lustick, Ian. 1993. *Unsettled States, Disputed Lands: Britain and Ireland, France and Algeria, Israel and the West Bank-Gaza*. Ithaca, NY: Cornell University Press.

Lyons, Gene, and Michael Mastanduno, eds. 1995. *Beyond Westphalia? State Sovereignty and International Intervention* Baltimore, MD: Johns Hopkins University Press.

Mann, Michael. 1993. "Nation-States in Europe and Other Continents: Diversifying, Developing, Not Dying." *Daedalus* 122, no. 3 (Summer): 115–40.

Martin, Janet. 1983. "Muscovite Relations with the Khanates of Kazan and Crimea. *Canadian-American Slavic Studies* 17, no. 4: 435–53.

Martin, Terry. 2001. *The Affirmative Action Empire: Nations and Nationalism in the Soviet Union, 1923–1939*. Ithaca, NY: Cornell University Press.

Materialy S'yezda Narodov Tatarstana. (*Material from the Congress of Peoples of Tatarstan*). 1993. Kazan: Tatarskoye Knizhnoye Izdatel'stvo.

McAuley, Mary. 1997. *Russia's Politics of Uncertainty*. Cambridge: Cambridge University Press.

McCarthy, Frank. 1973. "The Kazan' Missionary Congress." *Cahiers du Monde Russe et Sovietique* 14 (July): 308–32.

McNeely, Connie. 1995. *Constructing the Nation-state*. Westport, CT: Greenwood Press.

Meyer, John. 1995. "Foreword." Pp. ix–xiv in *Constructing the Nation-state*, by Connie McNeely. Westport, CT: Greenwood Press.

Michelmann, H., and P. Soldatos, eds. 1990. *Federalism and International Relations: The Role of Subnational Units*. Oxford: Claredon Press.

Miftakhov, B. M., and Islamov, F. F. 1994. *Istoriya i kul'tura rodnovo kraya*. (History and Culture of Our Religion). Kazan: Magarif.

Migdal, Joel. 1988. *Strong Societies and Weak States: State-Society Relations and State Capabilities in the Third World*. Princeton, NJ: Princeton University Press.

———. 1994. "Introduction: Developing a State-in-society Perspective." Pp. 7–36 in *State Power and Social Forces: Domination and Transformation in the Third World*, edited by Joel Migdal, Atul Kohli, and Vivian Shue. Cambridge: Cambridge University Press.

Migdal, Joel, Atul Kohli, and Vivian Shue, eds. 1994. *State Power and Social Forces: Domination and Transformation in the Third World*. Cambridge: Cambridge University Press.

Ministerstvo Obrazovaniya Respubliki Tatarstan (MORT). 1991a. "Kontseptsiya Razvitiya Tatarskovo Obrazovaniya (Conception of the Development of Tatar Education)" *Panorama* 8: 15–30.

———.1991b. "Uchebnye Plany Srednikh Obshcheobraovatel'nikh Shkol 1991–1992. (Study Plan for Middle Schools 1991–1992) *Magarif* 7: 21–25.

———.1994. Prikaz #270 (Order #270). October 24.

Minnulin, Robert Mugallimovich. 1997. Chair of the Committee on National and Cultural Questions, State Soviet of Tatarstan. Interview with author, Kazan, April 2.

Monclus, Francisco Javier. 2000. "Barcelona's Planning Strategies: From 'Paris of the South' to the 'Capital of the West Mediterranean.'" *GeoJournal* 51, no. 1–2: 57–63.

Motyl, Alexander. 1987. *Will the Non-Russians Rebel?* New York: Columbia University Press.

———. 1990. *Sovietology, Rationality and Nationality: Coming to Grips with Nationalism in the U.S.S.R.* New York: Columbia University Press.

Mnogonatsional'nyi Tatarstan (Multinational Tatarstan). 1993. Kazan: Apparat Prezidenta Respubliki Tatarstan, 1993.

Moses, Joel C. 2003. "Voting, Regional Legislatures and Electoral Reform in Russia." *Europe-Asia Studies* 55, no.7 (November): 1049–1075.

Muiznieks, Nils R. 1995. "The Influence of the Baltic Popular Movements on the Process of Soviet Disintegration." *Europe-Asia Studies* 47, no. 1 (January): 3–25.

Mukhametshin, Farid. 1995. *Respublika Tatarstan: Ot Referenduma do Dogovora.* *(The Republic of Tatarstan: From the Referendum to the Treaty).* Kazan': Tatarskoye knizhnoye izdatel'stvo.

———. 1996. "Tatarstan—Perspektivnyi Partnyer Dlya Mezhdunarodnogo Sotrudnichestva. (Tatarstan—Promising Partner for International Cooperation)." *Tatarstan* 2 (February): 3–11.

Mukhametshin, Rafik. 2000. *Islam v Obshchestvenno-Politicheskoi Zhizni Tatarstana v Kontsye XX veka* (Islam in the Socio-Political Life of Tatarstan at the End of the 20th c). Kazan': Izdatel'stvo "Iman".

Musgrove, Thomas D. 1997. *Self-determination and National Minorities.* Oxford: Clarendon Press.

Mustafin, M. R., and R. G. Khuzeev. 1994. *Vsye O Tatarstanye. (Everything About Tatarstan).* Kazan': Tatarskoye knizhnoye izdatel'stvo.

Mustafin, R. A., and A. Kh. Khasanov. 1995. *Pervyi Prezident Tatarstana: Mintimer Shaimiyev (First President of Tatarstan: Mintimer Shaimiyev).* Kazan': Tatarskoye Kniznoye Izdatel'stvo.

Nekrich, Alexander M. 1978. *The Punished Peoples.* New York: W. W. Norton.

Nudelman, Alexander. 2003. "The Presidential Envoys: Limited Success and a Limited Future." *RFE/RL Russian Political Weekly* 3: 7 (February 13).

Opalski, Magda. 2001. "Can Will Kymlicka Be Exported to Russia?" Pp. 298–319 in *Can Liberal Pluralism be Exported? Western Political Theory and Ethnic Relations in Eastern Europe,* edited by Will Kymlicka and Magda Opalski. Oxford: Oxford University Press.

Osterud, Oyvind. 1997. "The Narrow Gate: Entry to the Club of Sovereign States." *Review of International Studies* 23, no. 2 (April): 167–84.

Ostrowski, Donald G. 1998. *Muscovy and the Mongols: Cross-cultural Influences on the Steppe Frontier, 1304–1589.* Cambridge: Cambridge University Press.

Pelenski, Jaroslaw. 1974. *Russia and Kazan: Conquest and Imperial Ideology 1438–1560.* The Hague: Mouton.

Petrov, Nikolai. 2005. "From Managed Democracy to Sovereign Democracy: Putin's Regime Evolution in 2005." PONARS Policy Memo no.396 (December) Available on-line at: www.csis.org/ruseura/ponars/pm/.

Pipes, Richard. 1950. "The First Experiment in Soviet Nationalities Policy: The Soviet Bashkir Republic 1917–1920." *The Russian Review* 9, no. 4 (October): 303–19.

Plenipotentiary Representation of the Republic of Tatarstan in Moscow. 1997. *Suverennyi Tatarstan: Sovereign Tatarstan.* Moscow: INSAN Publishers.

Poslaniye Prezidenta Respubliki Tatarstan. (Address of the President of Tatarstan). 1996. Kazan': Apparat Prezidenta Respubliki Tatarstan.

Premdas, Ralph. 1990. "Secessionist Movements in Comparative Perspective." Pp. 12–31 in *Secessionist Movements in Comparative Perspective,* edited by Ralph Premdas, S. W. R. de A. Samarasinghe and Alan Anderson. New York: St. Martin's Press.

Presidium Verkhovnogo Soveta Republiki Tatarstan. 1992. *Zayavleniye Presiduma Verkhovnogo Soveta Republiki Tatarstan*. (*Announcement of the Presidium of the Supreme Soviet of the Republic of Tatarstan*). March 6. Reprinted in *Belaya kniga Tatarstana: Put' k suverenitetu 1990–1995* (*White Book of Tatarstan: The Path to Sovereignty 1990–1995*), edited by R. Khakimov. Special issue of the journal *Panorama-Forum* (1996) 5: 8: 14–15.

———. 1993. *Zayavleniye Presiduma Verkhovnogo Soveta Republiki Tatarstan*. (*Announcement of the Presidium of the Supreme Soviet of the Republic of Tatarstan*). June 24. Reprinted in *Belaya kniga Tatarstana: Put' k suverenitetu 1990–1995* (*White Book of Tatarstan: The Path to Sovereignty 1990–1995*), edited by R. Khakimov. Special issue of the journal *Panorama-Forum* (1996) 5: 8: 26–27.

Putin, Vladimir. 2004a. Speech at the enlarged meeting with the Government and Heads of Regions. September 13. www.kremlin.ru/eng/speeches

———. 2004b. Concluding remarks at the enlarged meeting with the Government and Heads of Regions. September 13. www.kremlin.ru/eng/speeches

———. 2004c. Speech at the meeting of the Presidential Council for Coordination with Religious Organizations. September 29. www.kremlin.ru/eng/speeches

Putnam, Robert D. 1988. "Diplomacy and Domestic Politics: The Logic of Two-level Games." *International Organization* 42, no. 3 (Summer) 427–60.

"Pyatiletnii aksakal (Five-year review)." 1996. *Vestnik:Informatsionyi byllenten' Ministerstvo Obrazovaniya Respubliki Tatarstan (MORT)* no. 1/2: 79–80.

Ramazanov, Marat Davidovich. 1997. Head of the Milli Mejlis of the Tatars of Bashkortostan. Interviews with author, Ufa, July 7 and July 29.

Reaume, Denise G. 2000. "Official Language Rights: Intrinsic Value and the Protection of Difference." Pp. 245–72 in *Citizenship in Diverse Societies*, edited by Will Kymlicka and Wayne Norman. Oxford: Oxford University Press.

Remington, Thomas F. 2003. "Majorities Without Mandates: The Russian Federation Council Since 2000." *Europe-Asia Studies* 55, no. 5 (July), 667–91.

Requejo, Ferran. 2001. "Political Liberalism in Multinational States: The Legitimacy of Plural and Asymmetrical Federalism." Pp. 110–32 in *Multinational Democracies*, edited by Alain-G. Gagnon and James Tully. Cambridge: Cambridge University Press.

Riker, William. 1964. *Federalism: Origin, Operation, Significance*. Boston: Little, Brown and Co.

Roeder, Philip. 1991. "Soviet Federalism and Ethnic Mobilization." *World Politics* 43, no. 2 (January): 196–232.

Rokkan, Stein, and Derek Unwin. 1983. *Economy, Territory, Identity: The Politics of West European Peripheries*. London: Sage Publications.

Rorlich, Azade-Ayse. 1986. *The Volga Tatars: A Profile in National Resilience*. Stanford, CA: Hoover Institution Press.

Rothchild, Donald, and Victor Olorunsola, eds. 1983. *State Versus Ethnic Claims*. Boulder, CO: Westview Press.

Rothschild, Joseph. 1981. *Ethnopolitics: A Conceptual Framework*. New York: Columbia University Press.

Sayer, Derek. 1994. "Everyday Forms of State Formation: Some Dissident Remarks on 'Hegemony'." Pp. 367–412 in *Everyday Forms of State Formation*, edited by Gilbert M. Joseph and Daniel Nugent. Durham, NC: Duke University Press.

Schafer, Daniel E. 1992. "The Construction of Nationality in the Russian Civil War: The Case of Bashkiria." Paper presented at the American Historical Society Annual Meeting.

———. 1993. "The Question of Muslim Autonomy in White-controlled Siberia 1918–1919." Paper presented at the Missouri Conference on History.

———. 1995. *Building Nations and Building States: The Tatar-Bashkir Question in Revolutionary Russia, 1917–1920*. PhD dissertation in the Department of History, University of Michigan.

Schamiloglu, Uli. 1990. "The Formation of a Tatar Historical Consciousness: Sihabaddin Marcani and the Image of the Golden Horde." *Central Asian Survey* 9, no. 2 (June): 39–50.

Seminar at the Institute of History of the Academy of Science of Tatarstan. 1997. Author's notes. Kazan. February 20.

Shageeva, Rosa. 2005. Assistant Director of the Museum of National Culture "Kazan." Author interview. Kazan. June 7.

Sharafutdinova, Gulnaz. 2000. "Chechnya Versus Tatarstan: Understanding Ethnopolitics in Post-communist Russia." *Problems of Post-Communism* 47: no. 2 (March–April): 13–22.

Sheehy, Ann. 1990. "Fact Sheet on Declarations of Sovereignty." *RFE/RL Report on the USSR* . (9 November): 23–25.

Shehadi, Kamal. 1997. "Clash of Principles: Self-determination, State Sovereignty, and Ethnic Conflict." Pp. 131–50, in *State Sovereignty: Change and Persistence in International Relations*, edited by Sohail H. Hashmi. University Park, PA: Pennsylvania State University.

Shnirelman, Victor A. 1995. *Who Gets the Past? Competition for Ancestors Among non-Russian Intellectuals in Russia*. Washington, DC: Woodrow Wilson Center Press.

Shteppa, Konstantin F. 1962. *Russian Historians and the Soviet State*. New Brunswick, NJ: Rutgers University Press.

Simpson, Gerry. 1996. "The Diffusion of Sovereignty: Self-determination in the post-Colonial age." *Stanford Journal of International Law* 32: 255–86.

Slezkine, Yuri. 1994. "USSR as Communal Apartment." *Slavic Review* 53, no. 2 (Summer): 414–52.

Smith, Anthony. 1986a. *The Ethnic Origins of Nations*. London: Basil Blackwell.

———. 1986b. "State-making and Nation-building." Reprinted on pp. 59–89 in *The State: Critical Concepts*, edited by John Hall. London: Routledge (1994).

Smith, Graham. 1998. "Russia, Multiculturalism and Federal Justice." *Europe-Asia Studies* 50, no. 8 (December): 1393–1408.

Sokolovsky, Sergei. 2002. "Census Categories Construction in the First All-Russian Census of 2002." Paper prepared for the Russian Census Workshop, Brown University Watson Institute, Providence, RI, March 2002.

Solnick, Steven. 1995. "Federal Bargaining in Russia." *East European Constitutional Review* 4, no. 4 (Fall): 52–58.

———. 1996. "The Breakdown of Hierarchies in the Soviet Union and China." *World Politics* 48, no. 2: (January): 209–238.

Sorenson, Georg. 1997. "An Analysis of Contemporary Statehood: Consequences for Conflict and Cooperation." *Review of International Studies* 23: 253–269.

Sovmestnoye Zayavleniye Presidiuma Verkhovnogo Soveta T.S.S.R., Sovet Ministrov T.S.S.R., Tatarskogo Reskoma K.P.S.S., Tatarskogo Ressovprofa Ob Uchasii Respubliki Tatarstan v Zaklyuchenii Soyuznogo Dogovora. (Joint Announcement of the Presidium of the Supreme Soviet of the Tatar S.S.R., Council of Ministers, Tatar Republic Committe of the Communist Party and Tatar Republican Council of Professors on the Participation of the Republic in the conclusion of the Union Treaty). 1991. March 8. Reprinted in *Belaya kniga Tatarstana: Put' k suverenitetu 1990–1995 (White Book of Tatarstan: The Path to Sovereignty 1990–1995),* edited by R. Khakimov. Special issue of the journal *Panorama-Forum* (1996) 5, no. 8: 9–11.

Sovremennye Mezhnational'nye Protsessy v T.S.S.R. (Contemporary Inter-ethnic Processes in the Tatar A.S.S.R.). 1991. Kazan': Academiya Nauk S.S.S.R.

Spinner, Jeff. 1994. *The Boundaries of Citizenship: Race, Ethnicity and Nationality in the Liberal State.* Baltimore, MD: Johns Hopkins University Press.

Stepan, Alfred. 2000. "Russian Federalism in Comparative Perspective." *Post-Soviet Affairs* 16, no. 2 (April–May): 133–76.

Stoner-Weiss, Kathryn. 1999. "Central Weakness and Provincial Autonomy: Observations on the Devolution Process in Russia." *Post-Soviet Affairs* 15, no. 1 (January–March): 87–106.

Strange, Susan. 1996. *The Retreat of the State: The Diffusion of Power in the World Economy* Cambridge: Cambridge University Press.

Sultanov, Farit Mirzaevich. 1997. Director of the Center for the History and Theory of National Education of the Institute of History of the ANRT. Interview by author. Kazan. March 19.

———. 1999. *Islam i Tatarskoye Natsional'noye Dvizheniye v Rossiiskom i Mirovom Musal'manskom Kontekstye: Istoriya i Sovremennost' (Islam and the Tatar National Movement in Russian and World Muslim Context: History and Contemporary Perspectives).* Kazan': Shkola.

Suny, Ronald. 1993. *The Revenge of the Past: Nationalism, Revolution and the Collapse of the Soviet Union.* Stanford, CA: Stanford University Press.

Surkov, Vladislav. 2005. "Suverenitet—Eto Politicheskii sSnonim Konkurentosposobsnosti. (Sovereignty—Political Synonym for Competitiveness)." Speech given to United Russia plenum on February 7, 2006. www.edinros.ru/news.html?id=111148.

Swayze, Harold. 1962. *The Political Control of Literature in the Soviet Union.* Cambridge, MA: Harvard University Press.

Tagirov, Engel'. 1996. *Tatarstan: National'no-gosudarstvennyye Interesy. (Tatarstan: National-state Interests).* Kazan': Izdatel'stvo Kazanskogo finansovo-ekonomicheskogo instituta.

———. 1997. *Tatarstanskaya Model': Mify i Real'nost'*. (*The Tatarstan Model: Myth and Reality*). Kazan': Izdatel'stvo Ekopolis.

Tagirov, Indus Rizakovich. 1993. *Tatary i Tatarstan*. (*Tatars and Tatarstan*). Kazan'.

Tamir, Yael. 1995. *Liberal Nationalism*. Princeton, NJ: Princeton University Press.

Tatar Public Centre. 1990. "Program of the T.P.C." *Central Asian Survey* 9, no. 2 (June): 155–65.

Tatary srednego povolzh'ya i priural'ya. (*Tatars of the Middle Volga and Ural regiona.*) 1967. Moscow: Izdatel'stvo Nauka.

Taylor, Charles. 1992. "The Politics of Recognition," Pp. 25–73 in *Multiculturalism and the Politics of Recognition*, edited by Amy Guttman. Princeton, NJ: Princeton University Press.

Teague, Elizabeth. 1994. "Russia and Tatarstan Sign Power-sharing Treaty." *Radio Free Europe/Radio Liberty Research Report*. 3, no. 14 (April 8): 19–27.

Thomson, Janice. 1995. "State Sovereignty in International Relations: Bridging the Gap Between Theory and Empirical Research." *International Studies Quarterly* 39, no. 2 (June): 213–33.

Tillet, Lowell. 1969. *The Great Friendship: Soviet Historians on the non-Russian Nationalities*. Chapel Hill, NC: University of North Carolina Press.

Tilly, Charles. 1996. "The State of Nationalism." *Critical Review* 10, no. 2 (Spring): 304–05.

Togan, Zaki Validi. 1997. *Vospominaniya*. (*Memoirs*). Moscow.

Triesman, Daniel. 1997. "Russia's Ethnic Revival: The Separatist Activism of Regional Leaders in a Postcommunist Order." *World Politics* 49, no. 2 (January): 212–49.

———. 1999. *After the Deluge: Regional Crises and Political Consolidation in Russia*. Ann Arbor, MI: University of Michigan Press.

Tully, James. 1995. *Strange Multiplicity: Constitutionalism in an Age of Diversity*. Cambridge: Cambridge University Press.

———. 2001. "Introduction." Pp. 1–33 in *Multinational Democracies*, edited by Alain G. Gagnon and James Tully. Cambridge: Cambridge University Press.

Turnerelli, Edward Tracy. 1854. *Russia on the Borders of Asia: Kazan, the Ancient Capital of the Tatar Khans*. Volumes I and II. London: Richard Bentley.

Tyunikov, Yu. S., and F. F. Kharisov, and G. F. Khasanova. 1994. *Natsional'noe Samosoznanie: Sushchnost' i Printsipy Formirovaniya*. (*National Self-Consciousness: Its Essence and Principles of Formation*). Kazan: MORT.

Tyunikov, Yu. S., F. F. Kharisov, G. F. Khasanova, and I. Ya. Kuramshin. 1995. *Strategiya i Zadachi Razvitiya Natsional'novo Gimnazicheskovo Obrazovaniya*. (*Strategies and Tasks of Developing National Gymnasium Education*). Kazan: MORT.

Ukaz Prezidenta Respubliki Tatarstan #183: O Sozdanii Departamenta Vneshnikh Svyazei Prezidenta Respubliki Tatarstan. (*Decree of the President of Tatarstan #183: On the Founding of the Department of Foreign Relations of the President of the Republic of Tatarstan*). 1995. Reprinted in *Vedomosti Verkhovnogo Soveta Tatarstana* (July–August): 31–34.

Valeev, Mudaris Kharisovich. 1995. Director of publishing house Magarif. Interview by author, Kazan, August 22.

Valeev, Rafael Mirkasimovich. 1996. Director of the Department of Monuments and Historical Legacies of the Ministry of Culture of Tatarstan. Interview by author, Kazan, October 18.

Valeeva-Suleymanova, Guzel' Fuadovna. 1993. "Natsional'naya Kul'tura Tatarstana: Puty Vosrozhdeniya. (The National Culture of Tatarstan: Path to Rebirth). *Tatarstan* 12 (December): 47–52.

———. 2002. "Kontseptsiya I Perspektivyi Natsional'nogo Muzeya (Conception and Perspectives on National Museums)." Pp. 109–20 in *Iskusstvo I Etnos: Novyie Paradigmyi (Art and Ethnos: New Paradigms)*, edited by G. F. Suleymanova. Kazan': Izdatelstvo Dom Pechati.

Verdery, Katherine. 1996. *What Was Socialism, and What Comes Next?* Princeton, NJ: Princeton University Press.

Verkhovnogo Soveta Respubliki Tatarstan. 1992a. *Postanovleniye Verkhovnogo Soveta Respubliki Tatarstan O Merakh po Realizatsii Gosudarstvennogo Suvereniteta Respubliki Tatarstan. (Announcement of the Supreme Soviet of the Republic of Tatarstan About Measures for the Realization of the State Sovereignty of the Republic of Tatarstan).* March 21. Reprinted in *Belaya kniga Tatarstana: Put' k suverenitetu 1990–1995 (White Book of Tatarstan: The Path to Sovereignty 1990–1995)*, edited by R. Khakimov. Special issue of the journal *Panorama-Forum* (1996) 5, no. 8: 16–17.

Verkhovnogo Soveta Respubliki Tatarstan. 1992b. *Postanovleniye Verkhovnogo Soveta Respubliki Tatarstan O Provedenii Referenduma Respubliki Tatarstan po Voprosu o Gosudarstsvennom Statusye Respubliki Tatarstan. (Announcement of the Supreme Soviet of the Republic of Tatarstan About Holding a Referendum on the Question of the State Status of the Republic of Tatarstan).* March 21. Reprinted in *Belaya kniga Tatarstana: Put' k suverenitetu 1990–1995 (White Book of Tatarstan: The Path to Sovereignty 1990–1995)*, edited by R. Khakimov. Special issue of the journal *Panorama-Forum* (1996), no. 8: 13.

Vsei Musei Kazani: Sparvochnik-Mutevotitel' (The Museums of Kazan: Brief Sketches and Guidebook). 2004. Zaman: Kazan.

Vujacic, Veljko, and Victor Zaslavsky. 1991. "The Causes of Disintegration in the U.S.S.R. and Yugoslavia." *Telos* 88, (Summer): 120–40.

Wagenaar, Michiel. 2000. "Townscapes of Power." *GeoJournal* 51, no. 1–2 (May): 3–13.

Walker, Edward. 2003. *Dissolution: Sovereignty and the Break-up of the U.S.S.R.* Lanham, MD: Rowman and Littlefield.

Weber, Cynthia. 1995. *Simulating Sovereignty: Intervention, the State and Symbolic Exchange.* Cambridge: Cambridge University Press.

Weber, Eugene. 1976. *Peasants into Frenchmen: The Modernization of Rural France 1870–1917.* Stanford, CA: Stanford University Press.

Wendt, Alexander. 1992. "Anarchy is What States Make of It." *International Organization.* 46, no. 2 (Spring): 416–17.

Werth, Paul. 2001. "Big Candles and 'Internal Conversion': The Mari Animist Reformation and Its Russian Appropriations." Pp. 144–72 in *Of Religion and Empire:*

Missions, Conversion, and Tolerance in Tsarist Russia edited by Robert P. Geraci and Michael Khodarkovsky. Ithaca, NY: Cornell University Press.

White, Stephen. 1992. *Gorbachev and After*. Cambridge: Cambridge University Press.

Wixman, Ronald. 1986. "Applied Soviet Nationalities Policy: A Suggested Rationale." Pp. 449–68 in *Turco-Tatar Past, Soviet Present: Studies Presented to Alexandre Benningsen*, edited by S. E. Wimbush, G. Vienstein and Ch. Lemercier-Quelquejay. Paris: Editions de l'ecole des hautes etudes en science sociales.

Woodward, Susan. 1995. *Balkan Tragedy: Chaos and Disillusion After the Cold War*. Washington, DC: Brookings Institution.

Yack, Bernard. 1996. "The Myth of the Civic Nation." *Critical Review* 10, no. 2 (Spring): 193–211.

Yavuz, Hakan. 1993. "Nationalism and Islam: Yusuf Akcura and Uc Tarz-i Siyaset." *Journal of Islamic Studies* 4, no. 2: 175–207.

Yin, Robert K. 1994. *Case Study Research: Design and Methods*. Thousand Oaks, CA: Sage Publishers.

Young, Crawford. 1994. *The African Colonial State in Comparative Perspective*. New Haven, CT: Yale University Press.

———. 1999. "Sultanistic Regimes." *Journal of Democracy* 10, no. 3 (July): 165–68.

Zakiev, M. Z. 1995. "Problemy Etnogeneza Tatarskogo Naroda. (Problems of the Ethnogenesis of the Tatar People)." Pp. 12–94 in *Materialy po Istorii Tatarskogo Naroda* (*Material on the History of the Tatar People*). Kazan': Institut Yazika, Literatury i Istorii im. G. Ibragimova Akademii Nauk Tatarstana.

Zakirov, Rinat Zinurovich. 1996. Director of the National Cultural Center Kazan (NKTs Kazan). Interview by author, Kazan, October 26.

Zakon o Yazikakh Narodov Respubliki Tatarstan i Programma Meropriyatii po Realizatsii Zakon o Yazikakh Narodov RT (*Law on the Languages of the Republic of Tatarstan and Programmatic Measures for Its Realization*). 1996. Kazan.

Zaripov, Radik Abdullovich. 1997. Head of the Department of National Education and Textbook Provision of the Ministry of Education of Tatarstan. Interview by author. Kazan. March 24.

———. 2005. Head of the Department of National Education and Textbook Provision of the Ministry of Education of Tatarstan. Interview by author. Kazan. June 8.

Zayavleniye Verkhovnogo Soveta Tatarskoi Sovetskoi Sotsialisticheskoi Respubliki. (Announcement of the Supreme Soviet of the Tatar S.S.R.). 1991. April 16. Reprinted in *Belaya kniga Tatarstana: Put' k suverenitetu 1990–1995* (*White Book of Tatarstan: The Path to Sovereignty 1990–1995*), edited by R. Khakimov. Special issue of the journal *Panorama-Forum* (1996) 5, no. 8: 7–8.

Zenkovsky, Serge. 1953. "A Century of Tatar Revival." *American Slavic and East European Review* 12, no. 3 (October): 303–18.

———. 1960. *Pan-Turkism and Islam in Russia*. Cambridge: Harvard University Press.

———. 1958. "The Tatar-Bashkir feud of 1917–1920." *Indiana Slavic Studies* 2: 37–52.

Index